NAVIGATING
NEW TERRAIN

NAVIGATING NEW TERRAIN

Work and Women's Spiritual Lives

CLAIRE E. WOLFTEICH

PAULIST PRESS
New York • Mahwah, N.J.

Scripture quotations are from the New Revised Standard Version Bible, copyright © 1989 by the Division of Christian Education of the National Council of the Churches of Christ in the U.S.A., and are used by permission.

"Rosie the Riveter" song lyrics used with permission of the Fred Ahlert Music Corporation.

Cover design by Trudi Gershenov
Book design by ediType

Library of Congress Cataloging-in-Publication Data

Wolfteich, Claire E.
    Navigating new terrain : work and women's spiritual lives / Claire E. Wolfteich.
        p.   cm.
    Includes bibliographical references and index.
    ISBN 0-8091-4148-5
    1. Catholic women – Religious life – United States – History – 20th century.
    2. Women employees – Religious life – United States – History – 20th century.
    3. Work – Religious aspects – Catholic Church – History of doctrines – 20th century.   I. Title.
    BX1407.W65 W65 2002
    261.8'3443 – dc21

                                                                    2002012056

Published by Paulist Press
997 Macarthur Boulevard
Mahwah, New Jersey 07430

www.paulistpress.com

Printed and bound in the
United States of America

*To the memory of Mildred Clegg
and to my mother,
upon whose work I build.
And to Emily and Kathryn,
as you walk your own paths*

Contents

Acknowledgments

I wish to acknowledge the support of the Cushwa Center for the Study of American Catholicism at the University of Notre Dame, which funded research for this book with a faculty fellowship. I am grateful to Cushwa colleagues who informed early stages of this work, including Sandra Yocum Mize, Mary J. Oates, Kathryn Kish Sklar, and R. Scott Appleby.

Boston University also provided important support in this research and writing venture. My colleagues who participated in the practical theology research colloquiums offered encouragement and critical commentary. This book owes much to the work of three research assistants. Sarah Dekoven's unfailing conscientiousness, insight, and energetic research helped bring this book to completion. Georgia Maheras brought a lively interest, interviewing skills, and detailed bibliographic work. Barbara Kszystyniak worked on the project in its earlier stages, doing expansive literature searches and working with me to bring focus to an enormous topic. I am grateful for the distinct contributions each of these women made to the book.

I have had the opportunity to present portions of this research in academic lectures, at workshops for church groups, and in my Boston University School of Theology graduate course "Work and Faith." Feedback on those occasions undoubtedly shaped and sharpened my thought. I thank my students in particular for their wisdom and energy around this topic.

I am deeply thankful to the women who opened up their lives to me in interviews for this book. I hope that the result will honor their work.

Introduction

When Mary Parella had her first child in the early 1970s, her father sent her a retirement card. They both expected that she, a teacher, was finished with work outside the home. She would stay home and raise her children. It did not work out that way. Parella ended up taking jobs during many of her child-rearing years, in a range of fields from insurance to retail to software. Her family remained central to her, but she had to maneuver constantly to mold her work around the needs of her family. And she found that her early identity as a teacher wove its way into the whole of her life. Parella was, in fact, in the middle of powerful social change that — over the past sixty years — has swept women into the paid work force, opened professional opportunities, exposed increasing numbers of women to the stresses of the workplace, and altered women's roles and identities.

In 1940, 28 percent of American women worked outside the home. In 1998 about 60 percent of women held paying jobs.[1] Mothers of small children have made a striking entry into the labor force. Twenty-three percent of married women with children younger than age six worked outside the home in 1950. That number jumped to nearly 65 percent by 1998.[2] Many poor, minority, and single women had worked for wages before World War II. However, the influx of middle-class, white, married, and older women over the past sixty years raised particularly complex questions for religious institutions. The shifts in women's work roles significantly altered the social order, the family, civil society, and women's self-understandings. And yet we know little about how women's sharply increased participation in the labor force affects religious beliefs, practices, and institutions. Nor have religious traditions brought their theological riches to bear on this new situation.

1

This situation demands attention. Much has been written about women's changing work roles, yet very few authors look at this as a religious issue. It is. This book sets out to explore two questions: What are the theological and spiritual issues raised by women's increasing work force participation, and what theological and spiritual resources do religious traditions hold to address those issues? I will show that women's decisions about work involve not only economic and social choices, but also deeply religious choices, questions, and hopes. Explorations of these questions will be most fruitful when they are grounded in specific study of particular faith communities and particular historical and cultural contexts. Spirituality is deeply contextual, influenced by religious tradition and a wide range of social forces. Thus, this book will look closely at one particular but diverse group — American Catholic women from 1940 to the present — and will respond with particular attention to the spiritual roots and theological frameworks within the Roman Catholic tradition.

Yet the book is intended for a wide audience concerned with the interrelationships between religion and socioeconomic change. I set the Catholic experience within the broader American cultural and religious context. And while Catholic women's reflections are important primary sources, I also weave them together with selected Protestant women's voices, often expressing parallel questions and insights. Readers from traditional religious backgrounds may resonate with Catholic debates over authority, with the importance of the tradition, with the emphasis on family. Readers from different backgrounds may find their own situations illuminated by entering into the struggles of this varied group of women. Engagement with others' stories can clarify one's own values, context, and worldviews.

Moreover, while I focus on the United States, the implications of this study extend well beyond the American situation. This book addresses critical questions about work, questions that grow more and more pressing around the world in our globalized economy. For example, the rapidly developing Irish economy (the "Celtic Tiger"), which has been fueled by large numbers of educated women in the work force, poses enormous religious and ethical questions for a society more accustomed to the problems of poverty, unemployment, and emigration. The Irish Catholic bishops ponder their new context and its effects on the traditionally Catholic spirituality of the people: "It is becoming more difficult to give practical expression to spiritual values — to show that a job, while paid, is primarily about the service of others, to protect the quality of time given to family and friends, to enjoy quiet and solitude, and to practise prayer and contemplation."[3] From Ireland to South Africa, South Korea to India, societies increasingly must address the impact of women's changing work roles. This study is intended to help diverse readers, then, to dig into the questions of meaning that arise with women's changing roles in their own particular religious and cultural contexts.

For, indeed, questions about who we are, what we should be doing, and who we hope to become are universal.[4] There is a hunger today across faith traditions to connect work with meaning, values, and spirituality. The thriving "spirituality-and-business" movement, for example, has received national publicity in major business magazines and national newspapers. A *Business Week* cover story reported: "Today, a spiritual revival is sweeping across Corporate America as executives of all stripes are mixing mysticism into their management, importing into office corridors the lessons usually doled out in churches, temples, and mosques."[5] Corporations host yoga sessions, prayer breakfasts, and Talmud studies. They hire workplace chaplains and spiritual consultants. Several hundred people gather each year in Boston for an international symposium on spirituality and work. The movement crosses religious lines; seekers buy *The Tao at Work* as well as *Jesus, CEO*.[6] New Age spirituality also appears prominently. Judi Neal, for example, directs the Connecticut-based Center for Spirit at Work, whose newsletter presents work-related inspiration from wide-ranging sources including the Tao, Swami Chetananda, Native American practices, and the Body Centered Transformation teachings of the Hendricks Institute.[7]

As women increasingly move into the work force — and into high-level professional positions — questions about spirituality and work take on particularly complex dimensions. How do women navigate the culture of the paid work force — including the expectations, relationships, and definitions of success implicit there? How does wage work influence women's sense of identity and purpose? How does it shape their attitudes about the importance of family and religion, spheres traditionally dependent on women? Women are being formed by their work — in the home, in the church, and in secular jobs. Work gives an experience of community and friendship, or an experience of isolation and competition. Work shapes definitions of success and fulfillment. Work presents spiritual and ethical challenges. Women form habits through their work — habits of integrity or cutting corners, habits of balance or dissipation, habits of believing they are worth something or not.

Yet religious groups have not looked in depth at how changing work roles shape women or how women creatively respond to their new situations.[8] They have not responded adequately to the new theological and social questions that women's changing work roles pose. They risk losing women and creating a great gap between institutional religion and women's everyday realities and frameworks of meaning. Women too have difficulty articulating the spiritual meaning of their work. They risk compartmentalizing their faith from their work, in effect maintaining a private piety that cannot touch important spheres of their lives. Or they may unduly elevate secular values, expectations, and definitions of success.

In my view, the silence on this issue has at least two related sources: a deep ambivalence about the religious value of women's work outside the home and a lack of religious language adequate to women's new social and economic roles. These difficulties can be traced to powerful nineteenth- and twentieth-century ideals of womanhood that linked women's holiness and virtue with domesticity, that indeed saw women's private roles as critical to church, state, and American culture. Women's increasing employment in the twentieth century seemed to threaten a whole host of cherished institutions and values. Women carried, then, a heavy spiritual responsibility as they took work outside the home. The intricate tensions and confusions about women's spirituality have yet to be untangled. This book seeks to begin to untangle them, with sensitivity to the institutions that sought protection in the midst of social change, and with deep respect for the women who navigated their way into meaning in the midst of complex cultural debates.

The Cult of True Womanhood and Catholic Teaching

As industrialization progressed in the nineteenth century, American cultural forces drew boundaries around women's nature and sphere. Ideals of womanhood, most typically described as the cult of True Womanhood or the cult of domesticity, solidified a split between the private and the public. These ideals defined the home as women's separate sphere, a private realm separated from the male, public sphere of work and politics. Promoted by women's magazines and religious tracts, the cult of True Womanhood defined desirable female qualities (or what historian Barbara Welter calls the "four cardinal virtues"): purity, submissiveness, piety, and domesticity.[9] These ideals did give women power, but it was a power that simultaneously restricted them to the private sphere. Women exercised influence through their domesticity, in their virtuous influence on children and men, the rougher sex.

The cult of True Womanhood was a middle-class ideal that did not represent all women's experience. Immigrant women and African American women, for example, could not afford the luxury of "true womanhood."[10] Moreover, middle-class Protestant women pushed on the boundaries of true womanhood through their leadership in charitable causes, abolition, and women's rights; Elizabeth Cady Stanton and the Grimké sisters are two prominent examples. However, such women faced strong cultural resistance. Women's magazines, for example, harshly criticized educated, activist women: "They are only semi-women, mental hermaphrodites."[11] The message was clear: public activity could undermine true womanhood. "Let the men take care of politics, we will take care of the children!" declared one woman's magazine.[12]

For middle-class women, the ideal of domesticity exerted a powerful privatizing influence. Nancy Cott describes the life of New England women in the 1830s: "Women's public life generally was so minimal that if one addressed a mixed audience she was greeted with shock and hostility."[13] Toward the end of the century (1884), Friedrich Engels in London wrote this sharp critique of the effects of the patriarchal, isolated family and the privatization of the woman's role:

> The administration of the household lost its public character. It was no longer the concern of society. It became a *private service*. The wife became the first domestic servant, pushed out of participation in social production. Only modern large-scale industry again threw open to her — and only to the proletarian woman at that — that avenue to social production; but in such a way that, when she fulfils her duties in the private service of her family, she remains excluded from public production and cannot earn anything; and when she wishes to take part in public industry and earn her living independently, she is not in a position to fulfil her family duties.[14]

Church work was seen as acceptable, for it developed purity, domesticity, and submissiveness, all traits valued in true women. In reality, church activity did more than socialize women into culturally acceptable qualities; it also cultivated women's leadership. As social historian Hugh McLeod notes about the European context, church provided one acceptable sphere of public activity for women, and one area of independence from husbands.[15] In the United States, middle-class Catholic laywomen found volunteer opportunities in the growing network of schools and social service agencies, such as the Society of Saint Vincent de Paul. As economic historian Mary J. Oates points out, such volunteer work made the public-private boundary more permeable for middle-class women by mid-century.[16]

Still, the strong cultural ideal of womanhood closely linked religion with women's domestic vocation. By equating religion with domesticity and submission, the cult of True Womanhood undermined the public power of religion and its role as social critic. In effect, then, this cultural construct worked to keep both women and religion private. The result was both a curtailment of women's public power and a weakening of the church's relevance to economic and political issues.

Protestant and Catholic churches reinforced the bourgeois ideal of womanhood. They tended to emphasize personal devotion and individual morality, topics that appealed particularly to middle-class women embedded in private life. This emphasis exacerbated the breach between male and female religious activity, as McLeod describes:

> If the stress of the clergy on issues of individual morality brought them in touch with the basic concerns of women, and the solutions that they offered often seemed practical, the church had much less to say to a world focussed on economic conflict, in which one party was guided by a faith in the market that found its ultimate expression in Social Darwinism, and the other party was increasingly learning to think in terms of the inevitable war between classes. If some of those involved in industry continued to connect their religion and their work — for instance paternalistic employees and some craftsmen — the logic of economic development was against them in the nineteenth century, as ever-larger firms took on an impersonal, bureaucratic character and human values got lost in the violence of the war between capital and labour.[17]

The privatization of religion, then, contributed to working-class alienation from the church. In my view, this privatized understanding of faith also would make it more difficult for women to leave the domestic sphere to take paid employment, as they would appear to be lessening a commitment not only to the home but also to the faith.

By the late nineteenth century, the papacy took an important step to counter the privatization of religion and working-class alienation. In his 1891 encyclical *Rerum Novarum* ("On Capital and Labor"), Pope Leo XIII addressed the problems of industrialization and class conflict that had so profoundly changed the social order. It was a statement that many describe as the founding of Catholic social teaching. *Rerum Novarum* aimed for a middle ground between unfettered capitalism and the socialist alternative. It rejected the idea of class warfare and defended private property. Yet it affirmed the rights of labor unions and endorsed state initiatives to protect workers. The statement also clearly endorsed the ideal of domesticity. *Rerum Novarum* emphasized the economic rights of the man as the head of the family with a sacred duty to provide for his dependents. Only with a fair wage and the right to pass along private property through inheritance could that duty be fulfilled: "It is a most sacred law of nature that a father should provide food and all necessaries for those whom he has begotten.... A family, no less than a State, is, as We have said, a true society, governed by an authority peculiar to itself, that is to say, by the authority of the father." Nature dictated too that women work best in the home: "Women, again, are not suited for certain occupations; a woman is by nature fitted for home-work, and it is that which is best adapted at once to preserve her modesty, and to promote the good bringing up of children and the well-being of the family."[18] With this encyclical, the church countered the privatization of religion that had coincided with the cult of domesticity, but it also reinforced the privatization of women. The church asserted its public role in the resolution of social conflict and the teaching of justice. At the same time, women were not seen as agents of this public religion. The pope declared that *women's* piety should be expressed through her domesticity, to which her nature suits her.

Church leaders continued to assert this privatized vision of women's vocation into the twentieth century. Catholic teaching consistently linked women's spirituality with domestic well-being. Pope Pius XI's 1930 encyclical *Casti Connubi* ("On Christian Marriage"), for example, articulated a strong vision of the holiness of marriage at the same time that it denounced women's public work. The spiritual vocation of the family depended on the mother's presence in the home. The encyclical condemned the "emancipation" of women, the idea that "the wife being freed from the care of children and family, should, to the neglect of these, be able to follow her own bent and devote herself to business and even public affairs."[19] To mark the fortieth anniversary of *Rerum Novarum,* Pius XI published the encyclical *Quadragesimo Anno* ("On Reconstruction of the Social Order," 1931), which also asserted women's domestic vocation: "Mothers should especially devote their energies to the home and the things connected with it."[20] These strong papal assertions of women's place in the home coincided with massive male unemployment during the Great Depression, a situation that propelled some American women into the work force to replace lost family wages.[21]

To Catholic leaders, the necessity of women's employment contradicted the natural order of things. To support women's domestic vocation, they lobbied for the "living" or "family" wage. Men should earn enough to enable their wives to stay in the home. Pius XI declared: "Most unfortunate, and to be remedied energetically, is the abuse whereby mothers of families, because of the insufficiency of the father's salary, are forced to engage in gainful occupations outside the domestic walls to the neglect of their own proper cares and duties, particularly the education of their children."[22] American labor advocates such as Fr. John A. Ryan, who directed the Social Action Department of the National Catholic Welfare Conference from 1919 to 1944, pressed hard for the family wage.

The religiously sanctioned, domestic ideal of womanhood, then, persisted into the twentieth century, creating alarm, conflict, confusion, and guilt as women (particularly, married women) moved increasingly into paid labor after 1940. Women were the bedrock of the family, the church, and all that was human in a dehumanizing time. What would happen when they "deserted" their posts? Religious and cultural leaders expressed alarm about women's new roles in the work force. In part they feared the effects of employment on women's own piety and virtue. Yet they also were concerned about the future of religion and protected private space in the new economic and social order. This book, then, is a story about the relationship between religion and economic change, about cultural definitions of place and a shifting social order, as well as individual searches for meaning. The nineteenth-century ideal of women's domesticity, reinforced by religious teachings, clashed in the twentieth century with economic changes and ideals of women's "liberation" that drew women increasingly into the paid work force. How women negotiate these changes, how religious institutions negotiate them, and how each perceive the social and spiritual stakes, will be important concerns of this book.

The Current Urgency

The Roman Catholic Church is now at a critical juncture. It has depended on women's labor to teach the faith in parochial schools, to staff church offices, to maintain social service agencies, to keep hospitals running, to decorate the altars, and to clean the churches. It has relied on women's unpaid labor in the home to educate, nurture, socialize, and pass the faith along to the next generation. It must make major adjustments as women increasingly take paid employment.

In the last twenty years, the American bishops have begun to examine women's work within church structures, but they have barely addressed women's changing work roles in secular spheres. This is very surprising in light of the fact that the church has powerfully framed work as a religious question. In his encyclical *Laborem Exercens* ("On Human Work"), Pope John Paul II states that human beings are "called to work" from their very creation by God. Indeed, human work "is a participation in God's activity." It is an imitation of God the creator, even a form of cocreation: "By their labor they are unfolding the Creator's work." Work is an essential part of human dignity: "Man's life is built up every day from work, from work it derives its specific dignity, but at the same time work contains the unceasing measure of human toil and suffering."[23] The American bishops' 1986 pastoral letter *Economic Justice for All* upheld work as a "vocation," a contribution to the public good, and a sharing in God's creative activity.[24] Given the centrality of work as a human vocation, given the power of work as a humanizing or dehumanizing force, why would the church not attend more closely to women's changing work roles? Since *Rerum Novarum* (1891), the church has addressed such critical social questions as class and work. Why the scant attention to gender, work, and social change?

The church's response is made more critical by its own current crisis of leadership, seen most recently in the sexual abuse scandals that have surfaced deep questions about the structures and culture of church leadership. The bishops acknowledge that while the church has relied on women's labor, it has denied countless women the opportunity to use their gifts in leadership positions within the church.[25] In my view, the impediments to female leadership create a dangerous gap between women's growing opportunities in the secular world and their roles within the church. Women's leadership in the church must be reexamined in light of their own changing situations and the wider ecclesial context; herein lies a challenging task but also a great opportunity.

The Need for Scholarship

This book seeks to contribute information and analysis at a critical moment. There is little scholarship to guide religious institutions at the present time. The study of women, work, and religion is a neglected topic across the disciplines. Theological literature, for example, gives inadequate attention to the relationship between work and women's religious lives. While a literature on theology and work does exist, rarely do scholars consider the particularities of women's work experiences and the enormous social and economic changes of the twentieth century. Pope John Paul II recognizes that women work outside the home, and he does affirm women's "equal dignity" and their "right to perform various public functions."[26] Yet he does not consider women's own varied understandings of work and its meaning when he insists on the priority of women's domestic role. Rather, he reiterates a theological position based on a certain view of women's nature; women have an "irreplaceable role" in the family and thus should be able to work "in accordance with their own nature." Employment must not interfere with "the primary goals of the mission of a mother."[27] Jesuit John Haughey has written several books about work and spirituality, but he does not reflect on women's changing economic roles.[28] Even feminist liberationist theologian Dorothee Sölle's book *To Work and to Love* does not look specifically at women's experience of work and social change.[29]

While the theological literature on women and work is inadequate, several projects contribute helpful resources.[30] Bonnie Miller-McLemore reflects theologically on women, work, and family in *Also a Mother: Work and Family as Theological Dilemma.*

Yet Miller-McLemore directs her attention predominantly to women's mothering work, whereas this book seeks to explore more fully work outside the home. She also approaches her topic from a Protestant theological perspective, while I aim to elucidate the specific influences of Catholicism.[31] Mary Stewart Van Leeuwen offers a neo-Calvinist exploration of gender in her book *Gender and Grace: Love, Work, and Parenting in a Changing World;* the book includes a helpful chapter on gender, work, and Christian vocation.[32] I have not found any broad scholarly work that has studied Catholic women and work from a theological perspective, or that addresses the general issue of women and work from a Catholic theological perspective. A few studies look at theologies of work in specific lay movements, such as the Grail.[33] Overall, however, theological scholarship has barely touched the surface of this topic.

Historians and social scientists long have debated the question of how modernization relates to secularization.[34] This is a critical issue in most societies today, particularly in countries experiencing rapid economic development. In his famous thesis about capitalism and the Protestant work ethic, sociologist Max Weber argued in effect that modernization and religion went hand in hand in post-Reformation Europe. Ascetic Puritan values inadvertently fueled the rise of capitalism. Yet ironically, noted Weber at the beginning of the twentieth-century, the capitalist no longer depends on religious foundations.[35] If anything, Europe became more secularized as it developed into a modern capitalist economy. Based on the European experience, social scientists commonly assumed a correlation between urbanization, industrialization, geographic and social mobility, and the decline of religious institutions.[36] However, this correlation does not appear in modernizing regions outside of Europe (e.g., the United States, Brazil, South Korea, and Indonesia), a fact that has led prominent social scientists to recant their earlier assumptions.[37] Modernization, with its accompanying pluralism, may in fact create disruptions and questions of meaning that propel people closer to religion. A study of women's increased work force participation informs this ongoing debate about the effects of the modern economy on religiosity. As women take a more central role in the processes of modernization, do they drift from religion or do they seek meaning and continuity in religion?

And yet few historians or social scientists have taken up this question. Prominent historians such as Carl Degler, Alice Kessler-Harris, and Thomas Dublin, for example, pay little attention to religion as they tell the story of women's changing work patterns.[38] Neither have historians of American Catholicism investigated women's increasing work force participation, despite the fact that this was a significant factor shaping the church and women's lives in the twentieth century.[39] Mary J. Oates and Leslie Tentler have made two important contributions to understanding of women and work before 1950: Oates with a chapter on Roman Catholic laywomen in the labor force, 1850–1950, and Tentler with a book on wage-earning women from 1900 to 1930.[40] Still, this research must be extended into the period after 1950. Oates herself points to the dire need for such historical scholarship: "It is difficult to exaggerate the paucity of data on Catholic working women."[41]

Social scientific literature tends to either omit mention of religion or simplistically assume that religion keeps women in traditional roles. Economist Barbara Bergmann, for example, writes: "People holding to religious traditions of female subservience preach against the emergence of women into the marketplace and the weakening of the husband-wife family it has caused. They sympathize not at all with the constricted life of the obligatory housewife."[42] Too many social scientists neglect the diversity among and within religious traditions, including the subtle ways that women even with conservative traditions negotiate changing roles.

One economist laments the dearth of social science research about the relationships among religion, work, and family: "Very little is known... about the impact of religion on women's decisions regarding the allocation of time between home and market."[43] A number of studies have attempted to address that question, but further work needs to be done.[44] Several social scientists have underscored the critical nature of this topic. Sociologist Bradley Hertel concludes: "By far the most significant challenge to organized religion lies in the work-related declines in membership and attendance attributable to full-time employment of married women."[45] Nancy Ammerman and Wade Clark Roof argue: "No single factor has been more responsible for shifts in the relationships among work, family, and religion than the massive entry of women into the workforce."[46] Clearly, further research on the relationship between women's changing work force participation and religion is strongly needed.

To my knowledge, moreover, there is no study that moves across disciplines to consider social change, theological dilemmas, and the ecclesial stakes in one integrated study. This is what I attempt to do in this book. I believe that such an interdisciplinary, integrated approach is vital. For while historians document social change, they usually do not constructively engage the questions of meaning and self-understanding so important to the people and institutions they study. That wrestling with meaning is more the province of theologians and philosophers. Nor do historians usually bring the past into dialogue with the present and the future. And yet the changes in women's lives over the past century must be considered as they relate to the future shape of spiritual life and the vitality of religious institutions. Theologians are concerned with the spiritual life and the church, but too often they do their reflection in a vacuum, apart from social analysis and historical understanding.

Thus, an interdisciplinary study is needed in order to adequately explore the importance of women's changing work roles, with an eye toward practical response. This book is primarily a work in practical theology, but it is informed by attention to historical context and social scientific data. Description is an important part of practical theology. This is particularly true in the case of women, work, and religion, as very little analysis has been done about this complicated relationship. However, description is but one step or "moment" in a larger process of theological reflection.[47] I do not aim for a comprehensive historical or sociological overview but rather a contextually sensitive exploration of the spiritual dimensions of women's changing experiences at work.

This is, to be sure, an ambitious project. Any interdisciplinary work is limited; the author cannot explore each field in as much depth as would an expert in that field. For example, I will not be able to address historical change in as much detail as would a purely historical work. Yet an interdisciplinary approach enables a more integrated, comprehensive understanding of a critical religious issue. Because women, work, and religion is quite a large topic, I can present only a case study and exploratory analysis. I do so through an examination of Roman Catholic women in the United States from 1940 to the present. Yet I am convinced that this particular study will shed light on larger questions that cut across religious and national boundaries. The book aims to deepen understanding, to stimulate theological reflection, and to guide religious institutions seeking to respond to significant social and economic transformation.

The Argument

Work influences women's religious lives in many ways. First, employment decisions propel women to consider and often to redefine their role in the family; one might even say that employment provokes questions about women's vocation (although, as we will see, many women would not use this word). Changes in the family obviously impact all aspects of society, which has counted on women's unpaid labor in the home. The impact of religion on the meaning women attach to home and to employment needs serious study. I show that increasing employment demands a reappraisal of both Catholic and Protestant notions of vocation and women's purposes in the world. Second, increased employment compresses time. Women — traditionally the backbone of local parishes and civic organizations — must make decisions about how they spend time. The result means big questions about the future vitality of religious institutions and how labor is compensated in the church. It also means that women struggle with a powerful sense of fragmentation. At the same time, I argue, religious traditions hold resources to address these spiritual issues. Third, work subtly shapes women's devotional lives — how and for what they pray, the models of holiness they embrace. Many women face a spiritual vacuum; their faith bears little relevance

to their daily economic and social lives. Placed in highly professional positions, for example, they find few saints who resemble
them. Some women creatively adapt traditional piety; others reject
or compartmentalize their faith. This is a terribly important situation for the church to understand. I argue for a re-envisioning
of models and indeed a reconsideration of dominant notions of
spirituality.

This study indicates that religion does not necessarily hold
women back in the workplace, nor does women's growing work
force participation generally lead to religious alienation. Work
does, however, subtly change women's theological assumptions
and devotional lives. Religious institutions have not understood
these changes or responded to them pastorally, nor do most
women expect that. The lack of pastoral guidance gives women
a kind of spiritual autonomy to work out the religious meaning
of their changing social and economic roles. Yet it also leaves a
great gap between everyday life and religious institutions, a gap
that ultimately endangers the vitality of the church and tests its
boundaries.

The Structure of the Book

The first two chapters of the book trace women's changing work
patterns from 1940 to the present, giving particular attention to
Roman Catholic women in the United States. These chapters do
not attempt a comprehensive historical overview. Rather, they provide a reflective descriptive analysis that establishes the context
for the theological chapters to follow. The reader will find snapshots of events and individuals that raise from different angles
theological questions that must be pursued. Several interrelated
themes emerge strongly from these historical materials on Roman
Catholic women, work, and the church: questions about vocation, identity, and discernment pushed by debates about women's
role in the family; the meaning and value of time; and holiness
and devotion in the face of social change. These themes will be
central to the book. To be sure, there are other theological and
spiritual issues imbedded in this rich story, themes that should be

explored in other works. This book, however, will look closely at this selected cluster of issues that, in my view, emerges strongly from the historical materials and remains vital to contemporary spirituality.

Chapter 1 focuses on the time period 1940–62, a period that includes the wartime era of Rosie the Riveter, postwar domesticity, the rise of lay Catholic movements, rapid suburbanization, consumerism, and the Cold War. Readers will gain a glimpse into the religious dimension of debates about women's changing roles, as clergy and lay leaders warned about the effects on women's purity, children's welfare, marriage, and the American way of life. Here religious voices, women's magazines, psychological "experts," and Cold War rhetoric all reinforced privatized, domestic ideals of womanhood — though not without ambiguity. Meanwhile, women's employment rates rose steadily, and many women wove their work lives together with traditional piety in surprising ways. Chapter 2 picks up the story in 1963, with the publication of Betty Friedan's *The Feminine Mystique,* the newly available birth control pill, the Second Vatican Council, and strides in civil rights legislation. Women's employment rates continued to rise too with the increasing shift toward a service economy, and by the 1970s a new ideal woman emerged: the career woman. The chapter situates women's changing work roles within debates about women's place and ideals of womanhood. These debates continued into the 1980s and beyond with the pontificate of John Paul II and American culture wars over the family.

The historical materials show important changes, developments, insights, and struggles that are highly relevant as women and the church look toward the future. Over the past sixty years, women have wrestled with the meaning of their changing roles. They have assessed and reassessed the value of their work. They have negotiated changing cultural and religious ideals of womanhood. They have carved out creative ways to pray, challenged blind spots of the tradition, suffered from injustice and ecclesial inattention, and lived with dissonance and confusion. They also have earnestly sought connections to their religious traditions, and many have found dignity in faith communities that they could not find on the job. Practical theologians must take account of their stories, must gain a richly contoured understanding of how the present situation came to be, in order to most adequately articulate theological visions and identify spiritual practices formative for the present and the future.

Rooted in the contextual realities, then, subsequent chapters offer a more sustained theological reflection on topics surfaced in the first section. I continue to introduce women's own experiences, theological questions, and insights as I constructively engage these topics. Chapter 3 looks at vocation as a theological framework for addressing debates about women's role in family and employment. I bring women's vocational questions into dialogue with Protestant and Catholic teachings on vocation. I argue for a careful retrieval of the notion of vocation, one that takes into account key issues of identity and that avoids uncritical acceptance of unjust work, a distorted emphasis on productivity, or a singular focus on domestic vocations. Chapter 4 picks up the theme of time from a theological perspective, analyzing women's experience of conflict and fragmentation. I look particularly to the liturgy as a framework of meaning, a means of sanctifying time. I argue for a seasonal perspective on vocation, a retrieval of the practice of Sabbath, and a eucharistic spirituality that finds grace in fragmentation. Chapter 5 argues that traditional models of holiness promote a sanctity far removed from the everyday lives of working women. In light of women's own creative adaptations of piety, I explore potential directions for re-envisioning models of holiness. The final chapter concludes with an exploration of pastoral approaches, a guide to religious institutions setting out to respond to this tremendous social and economic transformation.

Defining *Spirituality*

Underlying much of this book is the fundamental question: How to define *spirituality?* This is a central question for all who seek meaning and holiness in the complexities of everyday life. Women's changing social and economic roles raise important questions about our very definitions of holiness and goodness. If we do not ask these questions and begin to reflect on them, many women will flounder without spiritual models and religion will lose its power to speak to public issues. In addition, the church will lose the wisdom that many women can offer as they negotiate changing roles and seek to articulate the meaning of their lives.

Many people today distinguish between *religion* and *spirituality*. That is not a distinction I want to promote, but at the moment it captures an important reality. Some perceive religion as an oppressive institution, stifling the spirit. Keeping spirituality alive outside of religion allows those who have been alienated by religious institutions, or who seek truth from many places, to identify and nurture this quest. In my view, however, religion can be an integral part of spirituality when religion is understood not only as institution but also as community and prayerful ritual. The church is a community of disciples that struggles to impart wisdom and to worship God in deed and word. Rituals pattern us into that wisdom and worship, giving us words when we do not have any, building rare moments of silence into our schedules. In this book, I will not focus primarily on people whose spiritual search takes them outside of institutional religion, but rather on women who struggle within religious traditions as they seek meaning and self-transcendence in their own lives.[48]

The women I study are Christians, and most live within Christianity's particular embodiment in Roman Catholicism. To be more specific, then, I will be discussing Christian spirituality, by which I mean the human desire for God, an orientation of one's life toward the sacred, intimacy with Christ (John 15:4–7), life in the Spirit (Rom 8:5–11; 1 Cor 12:4–12), and discipleship that bears fruit (John 15:8). However, particular people in specific contexts understand and live out these ideas in different ways. I aim to show that the very question of how one defines spirituality is an important part of this story.

Ultimately, I hope that *spirituality* would be understood more in its traditional roots, almost synonymous with *theology*. That is, *spirituality* is the life of faith seeking understanding, an understanding that has power to transform. *Spirituality* is not just about subjective experience; rather, it is the dynamic process of seeing one's experience through the lens of truth and meaning. Christians trust the lens they have been given in Jesus Christ. Although their sight may be quite dim, they persist in the hope that Christ illumines the path and the Spirit sustains them as they walk. The spiritual search is most full when experience dialogues with scripture, tradition, and reason. Ultimately, spirituality is both transforming search and trustful waiting. It is hope kept real through disciplines and practices that keep us close to the sources of grace and to community. At its best, religion is a guide on that path providing the wisdom of fellow travelers, a community to walk with, powerful symbols, and tangible sources of grace. It is my contention that spirituality should not be divorced from theology. Every understanding of spirituality — indeed, every spiritual practice — implicitly makes theological claims. As I examine women's spiritual lives, I will explore what is at stake theologically. I also will strive to articulate understandings of *spirituality* that do justice to women's lives while recovering powerful wisdom from the tradition.

Conversations with Tradition

Any effort to understand and to guide contemporary persons in the spiritual life must involve rigorous exploration of the situation. Yet such exploration is enhanced by conversation with traditional spiritual teachings. People inevitably are shaped by tradition even if they strain against it. Moreover, thinkers and seekers and spiritual guides of the past may bring insight to contemporary struggles. This conversation — a point and counterpoint — reveals wisdom, inadequacies, and untruths in both traditional texts and in current assumptions. As Jesuit theologian Karl Rahner writes:

> The spirituality of the future will always be lovingly and familiarly immersed in the documents of the history of the piety of past times, since this is its own history. It will never leave aside as of no interest to itself the history of the saints, of the liturgy, of mysticism. . . . This first statement of course does not exclude but includes the possibility that many individual forms and shapes of the piety of the past in

their concreteness are no more than what has been and the Church must have the sober courage forthrightly to abandon them.[49]

The hermeneutic interplay or conversation between tradition and contemporary experience leads to a new understanding of the world in its relationship to God. When critically reflected upon, this new understanding will be faithful to the best and truest wisdom of the tradition while also resonant with a new historical context. This is a living tradition — open to critique, available as resource and formative guide.

Looking at Context

Spirituality should not be studied out of context. While people across religious traditions share a desire for self-transcendence, the particulars of one's historical, cultural, and religious situation influence one's spiritual life. Economic status, education, political assumptions, gender, and language, for example, all shape how people perceive themselves, others, and the transcendent. These do not predetermine a certain path, but they give it contour. As mysticism scholar Bernard McGinn writes, spirituality is "an experience rooted in a particular community's history."[50] To best understand work and spirituality, then, one must look closely at a particular group of workers coming out of a particular religious and cultural heritage. A study of spirituality is most meaningful if it focuses on a specific group's experience, and only then suggests broader implications. Hence, this study focuses primarily on Roman Catholic women in the United States, although they will be seen in relation to Protestant women and the larger American social context. Catholic women provide a particularly interesting angle of vision into the issue of women and work, for they carry with them a complex religious and social heritage that simultaneously affirms the religious import of work and emphasizes women's domestic vocation.

The time period on which I focus, 1940 to the present, is a period of notably sharp change in women's economic roles, and hence, greatly important to this study. This historical period, however, is but one in a larger story of women's changing economic roles. American women have always worked in various capacities. They have long faced questions about their role in the family, how to define themselves, how to understand their calling as women. The women's movement of the 1960s profoundly influenced attitudes toward work and family. Yet feminism is not new to the twentieth century; the woman's movement of the mid-nineteenth century raised up voices such as Sarah Grimké, Lucy Stone, and Lucretia Mott. Women labor leaders such as United Farm Workers cofounder Dolores Huerta fought for just working conditions in the mid- to late twentieth century. Before her, the Irish immigrant Mother Jones (1830–1930) and the striking Lawrence textile workers in 1912 fought their own fights. It is not that the past sixty years represent a radical break from the past, but that the particularities of this time period do bring us to a different place that warrants special attention. The particularities of this time period are critical. They include, for example, the centrality of wage labor in the American economy, the almost complete separation of work from the home, rapid suburbanization, the fear of Communism, changing patterns of immigration, the rise of a service economy, the emergence of the civil rights and the feminist movements, the Second Vatican Council, the pontificate of John Paul II, American culture wars, and shifts toward a more technological economy. As I will show, contextual particularities shape the contours of religious life.

Most of the women discussed in the book identify themselves as Catholics, at least at some point in their lives. I found them through their letters and articles in Catholic magazines and in the archival notes of religious organizations. I gleaned part of their stories through references in secondary works of historical scholarship. I listened to their voices speaking in oral histories and personal interviews conducted for this book. The women interviewed come mostly (although not exclusively) from the Boston area. Some are members of a predominantly white parish, St. Ignatius of Loyola, located near Boston College in a suburb called Chestnut Hill. Others belong to predominantly African

American and Latino parishes in the Roxbury neighborhood of Boston — St. Mary of the Angels, St. John–St. Hugh, and St. Patrick's. The complexity and variety of their spiritual journeys emerge through their first-person accounts. Some women requested that their names not be used; I refer to them by their initials only. The youngest woman interviewed was thirty-four years old. The oldest was ninety.

Class is a particularly thorny issue in women's studies. Some historians have seen gender as the primary category of analysis, more central than class, race, or ethnicity. As historian Nancy Hewitt notes, scholarship about nineteenth-century women by Barbara Welter, Nancy Cott, and others emphasized the influence of the cult of True Womanhood, the correlation of ideology with separate spheres of activity for men and for women, and the bonds of sisterhood among women. Such scholarship drew largely on white, middle- and upper-middle-class experience and did not adequately address class differences among women. Attention to black and white working-class women's experience shows that industrialization resulted in class stratification and conflict, and that class often proved a more cohesive bond than did gender.[51] While this book focuses on women as a group, the class differences among women are critical, particularly on the subject of work. Roman Catholic women are quite diverse socioeconomically, ethnically, and regionally. I begin to address such differences as I examine the varied experiences of white, black, and Latina Catholics. Still, there are class, racial, and ethnic differences that cannot be fully addressed in a study such as this. A more developed class analysis of women, work, and religion will add to my own foundational study.

Moving into the Story

We move now into the story of spirituality and women's changing roles in the workplace. This book cannot tell the whole story, but it explores important angles. This is a story about negotiating meaning amid competing cultural and religious ideals. It is a story of how people try to make sense of their lives, retaining important sources of identity but also carving out new self-understandings and worldviews. It is a story about prayer and adaptation. It also is a story about the relationship between religion and social change, a struggle about the meanings of private and public worlds. This book aims to further that search for meaning, that prayer, and, ultimately, the work of the church in a time of great social change.

Chapter One

Rosie the Riveter
and Ideals of Womanhood

*Women, Work, and the Church
from 1940 to 1962*

Rosie the Riveter was a strong symbol of the new woman at work, a symbol that pushed the boundaries of the domestic ideal. Wartime propaganda posters featured Rosie, that muscled, proud woman who leapt into the void during World War II, building planes and whacking steel in her overalls. Norman Rockwell's portrayal of Rosie splashed across the cover the *Saturday Evening Post* (May 29, 1943). Sporting denim and goggles, dirt smeared across her cheek and bulging biceps, Rosie holds a rivet gun across her lap. A giant American flag drapes behind her. Rosie was the patriotic team player, the single woman or housewife cheerfully jolted into the workplace for the sake of the American way, and cheerfully returning to domesticity when the men returned. The popular song "Rosie the Riveter" (1942) gave her the traditionally male role of protector, but hinted that her unconventional work would serve a later domestic aim:

> All the day long,
> Whether rain or shine,
> She's part of the assembly line.
> She's making history,
> Working for victory,
> Rosie the Riveter.
> Keeps a sharp lookout for sabotage,
> Sitting up there on the fuselage.
> That little girl will do more than a male will do.
> Rosie's got a boyfriend, Charlie.

> Charlie, he's a Marine.
> Rosie is protecting Charlie,
> Working overtime on the riveting machine.
> When they gave her a production "E,"
> She was as proud as she could be.
> There's something true about,
> Red, white, and blue about,
> Rosie the Riveter.[1]

In reality, there were many different kinds of "Rosies." Women like Helen Studer fit the image of the woman who temporarily — and only out of necessity — jumped into a wartime job. Studer, a forty-four-year-old mother of a serviceman, went to work at Douglas Aircraft in 1942. She was happy to leave the work force after the war.[2] But Rosie was also a woman like Marie Baker, a typical housewife until she decided to leave her husband and take a job at North American Aircraft "because I was going to be very independent. I wasn't going to ask for any alimony or anything. I was just going to take care of myself."[3] Wartime work attracted independent women like Baker; it also transformed some workers into independent women half-amazed at their newfound skills, economic power, and social networks. Mexican American Beatrice Morales Clifton, for example, recalled her experience at Lockheed Aircraft:

> Later, as I got going, I learned to rivet and buck. I got to the point where I was very good. . . . I had a lot of friends there. . . . I was just a mother of four kids, that's all. But I felt proud of myself and felt good being that I had never done anything like that. . . . I went from 65 cents to $1.05. That was top pay. It felt good and, besides, it was my own money.[4]

African American women like Fanny Christina Hill seized the chance to move out of low-paying domestic work. Hill got work at North American Aircraft, while her sister took a job at Douglas Aviation. Even though Hill reported that blacks got the worst of the wartime jobs, her defense job still improved her standard of living:

> When North American called me back, was I a happy soul! I dropped that job and went back. That was a dollar an hour. . . . That

wasn't traveling fast, but it was better than anything else because you had hours to work by and you had benefits and you come home at night with your family....

Well, my sister always said "...Hitler was the one that got us out of the white folks' kitchen."[5]

World War II opened the door to what became a major transformation of women's economic and social roles. While many single and minority women had always worked for wages, the new group of female laborers drawn in by World War II included large numbers of white, married, older, and middle-class women. For while women's work roles had expanded after the First World War, women wage earners had remained primarily unmarried and young. Women had faced intense pressure to leave paid employment upon marriage. According to historian Leslie Tentler, female employment rates rose during the period 1900–1930 but the working-class white woman's labor force experience did not challenge economic structures or cultural norms. Women worked for low wages in circumscribed, segregated employment sectors. Tentler argues that white working-class women's employment experience reinforced traditional gender roles and socialized women into domesticity and dependency.[6]

The telephone industry provides an excellent example. Companies such as AT&T hired large numbers of single women in highly sex-segregated fields that reinforced the values of obedience and discipline. O'Farrell and Kornbluh state:

> By 1920 the company employed 190,000 telephone operators, mostly women, and 192,000 male electricians. From Boston to San Francisco AT&T hired many young Catholic women, often referred by other family members, who were single, well educated, bright, dependable, and, as in parochial school, very good at following the many company rules.[7]

Although the number of married women in the work force did rise during the Great Depression, as women took jobs to replace wages of unemployed husbands, women workers encountered intense hostility and outright discrimination. Women workers were portrayed as stealing jobs from men, as "thieving parasites." In a 1937 survey, 82 percent of the public disapproved of working wives.[8]

Thus, the influx of older, married women into the work force during World War II, performing jobs that pushed the accepted norms of women's work, put pressure on religious and cultural norms. Married women and women over the age of thirty-five significantly expanded the female labor force, which increased 57 percent between 1941 and 1945.[9] Housewives comprised 75 percent of the new group of female workers.[10] These changes challenged the domestic ideal and its accompanying feminine virtues of obedience, purity, and piety.

Family Concerns and the Propaganda Campaign

The wartime transformation unsettled norms of women's domestic, private nature and elevated concerns about the family. Social commentators used stark language to describe the perilous situation of the American family, which they saw as besieged by evil forces. In 1944, for example, the Methodist Church sounded this warning:

> The home is the foundation of society and vital to the stability of both church and state. Though ordained of God and the source of so much that is dear to us, the home is suffering from open attack by evil forces, competition with business, and sheer neglect. We are faced with an alarming increase in divorce, juvenile delinquency, broken lives, and disregard of life's sanctities that the very existence of civilization is threatened.[11]

Those who had to promote women's new roles faced a delicate job. They sought to affirm the centrality of women's private roles while encouraging women to assume decidedly "unfeminine" public labors. In the wartime propaganda campaign, the family was used to justify the war effort, and hence, to give women's new "manly" public roles a private validity. As historian Robert Westbrook writes:

> Such obligations — to families, to children, to parents, to friends, and generally, to an "American Way of Life" defined as a rich (and richly commodified) private realm of experience — were tirelessly invoked in the campaign to mobilize Americans for World War II and formed the centerpiece of the propaganda produced by the

state and its allies in Hollywood, the War Advertising Council, and elsewhere.[12]

Thus, women were asked to join the war effort while still upholding the ideal of domesticity and the private-public dichotomy. Wartime work would be a temporary intervention necessary to protect men's lives in battle and ultimately to keep the cherished family and private world secure. The culture remained ambivalent about mothers in the wartime work force. The government provided little childcare, for example, thus maintaining the ideal that women would care for their own children even while stepping into the labor force.

Despite the reality that married women were being solicited for wartime work, cultural messages still implied that women's wartime production roles would not supplant their primary roles as homemakers and consumers. Rather, employment was a temporary venture, serving to protect cherished private roles. This was, of course, a very fine line to tread, and not a few religious voices responded with anxiety.

Religious Warnings

The American Catholic bishops, for example, were quite wary of women's industrial work. They feared damage to children's welfare, mothers' health, and women's moral purity. They also warned about government interference in the family (recall the Catholic tradition of subsidiarity, according to which higher order institutions, such as government, should support but not take over the functions of smaller institutions, such as the family).[13] In 1942, the bishops issued this cautious statement, gingerly balancing patriotism with a concern to get women out of the work force:

> Every effort must be made to limit, as far as necessity permits, the employment of mothers in industry, particularly young mothers. Due provision in harmony with American traditions should be made for the day care of the children of working mothers. The health and moral welfare of mothers employed in industry should be thoroughly safeguarded. With a full realization of the role which women must play in winning the war and of the extreme measures

that our government must take, we ask that all try to realize the dangers involved, especially the moral dangers.[14]

In the bishops' view, employment threatened women's purity and piety. Indeed, the church, the family, and in fact the whole social order depended on women's domesticity. The following year, the bishops more strongly warned against American shortsightedness: "Nor will the prudent, wise, political authority, for any seeming temporary advantage, fail to recognize the function and dignity of woman in society and to warn her against the false economy of our times, which turns her mind and heart away from the home, thereby depriving the family, State, and Church of her proper contribution to the common welfare."[15]

The National Council of Catholic Women, a large federation of parish-based and diocesan women's groups, repeatedly cautioned against the further employment of wives and mothers in wartime industry.[16] Catholic social scientists also saw great danger. At an American Catholic Sociological Society meeting in Cleveland, for example, the Rev. Bernard Mulvaney of the Catholic University of America stated: "The widespread substitution of women for men in all fields of employment is an important reason for a great drop in birth rates during and after the war. . . . It will require nothing short of a religious revolution to bring about a change."[17]

Moreover, Catholic magazines and newspapers sounded their concern. Writing in the *Catholic World,* Jesuit Joseph Schuyler linked the American way of life with God's domestic plan for women, arguing that the American home was in a process of "dissolution" approaching "chaos." Women's wartime work was at best a "necessary evil," but if not stopped it would destroy the American way of life. Schuyler's argument appealed to women's created nature: "Let us realize that God made women to be mothers, not to work a factory machine or to spend their lives in a sweat-shop."[18] Industrial work contravened women's nature.

The more liberal *Commonweal* approved of some strategic use of women workers during the war crisis, but insisted that "the core of the feminine group is and must remain the women on the home front."[19] More sharply, the Brooklyn *Tablet* cautioned that the Women's Army Auxiliary Corps was "no more than an opening wedge, intended to break down the traditional American and Christian opposition to removing women from the home and to degrade her by bringing back the pagan female goddess of de-sexed, lustful sterility."[20] According to this odd attack, wartime work stripped women of their mothering nature. Subtly, the *Tablet* contrasted the unlusting but fecund mother Mary with the pagan, lascivious, but sterile goddess. Good Catholic women, of course, would aspire to the former model.

Pushing the Boundaries

How would the muscled, determined Rosie melt back into a quiet, demure homemaker (which, if not the reality, was at least a cherished, pious image)? Women's new experiences in the work force and their new public importance pushed the boundaries of their identities, their sense of place. Although large numbers of women left the work force immediately after the war, many women did not want to permanently relinquish their newly found skills, independence, or earning power. While more than 2 million women voluntarily left the work force in 1946, and 1 million were laid off, 2.75 million women entered the labor force in the same year.[21] Women's labor force participation rose throughout the postwar decade.[22]

Some women who had worked before the war found surprising new career opportunities in its wake. AB, for example, was born into an Irish Catholic family in 1910 and grew up in Malden, a working-class city outside of Boston. At a time when Boston College was not yet accepting women, she took a bold step and enrolled at the largely Methodist Boston University. After graduating in 1932, the German major was offered a scholarship to study in Germany. However, with Hitler coming to power, she turned it down. Instead, she took a high school teaching position in New Jersey, moving away from family and friends. In New Jersey she met her husband; they married in 1935. AB continued to teach business until 1943, when she and her husband moved back to

Boston. She worked the rest of the war years as a secretary at Submarine Signal Company. Her domestic life worsened, eventually resulting in divorce from her abusive husband, with no children. At the same time, her professional life blossomed as a result of the postwar baby boom, which sparked the building of homes and schools. In 1946, she went to work for a group of army engineers who had returned from the war and started a business in construction equipment. AB managed the office for the burgeoning business for five years. She then moved to Park Construction Company, first as office manager and then as treasurer of the company.[23]

Following World War II, the African American magazine *Ebony* proclaimed the end of the era of the black domestic servant. A 1947 editorial looked forward to women's new opportunities to work in their *own* homes, due to wartime advances:

> And so today in thousands of Negro homes, the Negro mother has come home — come home perhaps for the first time since 1619 when the first Negro families landed at Jamestown, Virginia.... It finally took modern industrial life to inter Mammy. But in her place came the domestic, forced out of her home to supplement the low wages, if any, of her husband.... Then World War II caused a kitchen revolution. It took Negro mothers out of white kitchens, put them in factories and shipyards. When it was all over, they went back to kitchens — but this time their own.... As Negro men dropped their brooms and mops to move out of menial occupations into industry, their wives were able to stay at home and become housewives.... Even if she is forced back into white kitchens, the Negro mother — once having tasted freedom and independence in her own home — will not stay.[24]

Ebony editors emphasized women's choice and agency: "Not that a woman's place is in the kitchen necessarily. Nobody wants to tie a woman to her hearthstone with hackneyed phrases and ideas about where her place is. But... every woman should be able to choose whether she wants to devote her days to her children and her home or to a career girl's job."[25]

African American Ruth Grant (b. 1923) was able to claim that choice. Grant married in 1945 and chose to step out of the work force for five years after her son was born the following year. "For the first five years I didn't work because I was with my son. I never wanted anyone to take care of my son. I only started working when my son became school-aged." After taking courses, she began working full-time as a legal secretary when her son started school in 1951. Her husband worked at a shop in the neighborhood, and he cared for their son until she returned from work. Grant took great pride in breaking through racial and gender boundaries to become a legal secretary in New York, and she enjoyed her work: "I loved life and I loved work. I've always tried to make a difference some way. I've never been afraid to try things. . . . I was very successful as a legal secretary. I really think I was one of the few, probably first, African American women that worked around Broadway who really had the opportunity to work as a legal secretary."[26]

World War II brought women greater job mobility, a taste of their earning power, and a measure of independence. Following the war, shifts from a manufacturing to a service economy continued to draw women into the work force. White-collar jobs outnumbered blue-collar jobs by the mid-1950s.[27] Women took jobs as retail clerks, secretaries, government workers, office assistants, and bank tellers. Yet while women increasingly entered the labor force, gains in job mobility and pay equity did not keep pace. Women gained access to a fairly limited range of jobs:

> Unlike women workers during World War II, those in the postwar workforce were confined to a female job ghetto. Ninety-five percent of all women worked in just four job categories: light manufacturing (i.e., home appliances and clothing); retail trade; clerical work; and health and education. And within these categories, high-status work was usually male, low-status work female. . . . Job segregation helped keep women's work low-paid and dead-end.[28]

And despite optimism about African American women's expanding work opportunities during the war, school records from the 1950s, for example, show that the large majority of parents of Catholic African American schoolchildren were working class. Mothers held jobs as domestic servants and office workers.[29]

Women workers faced pay inequity, justified by the needs of male heads of households. AB, the divorced office manager for a construction company in the 1950s, for example, encountered discrimination when it came to salaries and benefits. Her boss did not establish a pension fund for the office staff. AB recalls: "I just never was paid as much as I was worth. . . . I'd say something to my boss about how I should get more, at least as much as Jack, and he'd say, 'He's married and he's got eight kids.' He was a great guy, but he was a real male chauvinist. But he'd say, 'You know how much you mean to the company.' "[30]

Still, for middle-class white women, the war broke through an ideal of womanhood that elevated the private and linked domesticity to piety and virtue. During the war, the virtuous woman leapt into the public world — at least temporarily — in order to save the country and the home. Religious critics swiftly attacked this shift in the ideal of womanhood, and American culture in the postwar years quickly would elevate domesticity, but the wartime experience left an unsettling and creative tension in women's roles.

Women's Magazines, June Cleaver, and the "Experts"

Women in the 1950s continued to move into the work force, even as the dominant cultural ideal at this time emphasized domesticity and the happy homemaker. This was the "baby boom" period. Women's fertility rates soared in the late 1940s, as men returned from the war, and climbed throughout the 1950s.[31] The baby boom went hand in hand with a powerful ideal of the domestic woman. This was the era of *Father Knows Best* (1954–63) and *Leave It to Beaver* (1957–63). June Cleaver, the television housewife, donned dresses and heels and pearls. Looking good, she kept the house spotless, despite the antics of sons Wally and Beaver. As the character Eddie Haskell remarked to June: "Your kitchen always looks so clean. It looks as though you never do any work in here."[32] In reality, women were working hard in an out of the kitchen. Even as women had more children, the proportion of married and older women in the work force expanded in the 1950s. Thus, cultural ideals of the good domestic woman coexisted with — or resisted — social change.

As married women increasingly entered the work force, popular American women's magazines glamorized the housewife and mother. In 1951 *Ladies' Home Journal* editor Margaret Hickey, for example, urged women to remain at home rather than going to work. She warned that child neglect and juvenile delinquency had resulted from women's wartime work.[33] To bolster her claims, she cited a church spokesman who called for "stronger efforts to keep mothers in the home rearing their babies and young children" and educators and childcare "experts" who "agree that the dangers of separation from natural home environment may have lasting effects upon the development of the child under six years of age."[34] Psychological "experts" cited in these magazines reinforced the ideal of motherhood. Dr. Benjamin Spock, for example, wrote an article in the *Ladies' Home Journal* praising the value and satisfaction of motherhood when compared to other professions women might hold. Noting that "the spiritual qualities that good parents develop in their children are as immortal as great works of art," Spock concluded: "Occupation housewife and mother? . . . Probably the only occupation which, if well done, is guaranteed to give a feeling of full satisfaction for one's entire life."[35] Indeed, as women's employment rates climbed in the 1950s, a kind of civil religion supported by "experts" and popular culture jumped in to exalt the ideal of domesticity upon which religious institutions relied.

For the most part, middle-class women at this time structured their employment around their most demanding years of childcare, quitting work when their first child was born and staying out of the labor force until the last entered school. (This pattern would change by the 1970s.) Thus, there was not in actuality as direct a conflict between work and home as the cultural debate implied, nor as would emerge in later decades. Still, women had to have felt the dissonance between the hyperdomestic ideals of womanhood and their growing presence in the work force.

The Perceived Clash:
Domesticity and Higher Education

The dissonance played itself out, for example, in debates about women, higher education, and careers. Catholics were gaining access to higher education as they entered the middle class. Yet higher education for women challenged norms of womanhood and the primacy of the domestic vocation. The postwar years were no heydey for women's higher education. Large numbers of veterans enrolled in college after World War II (1945) and after the Korean War (1953), due to the incentive of the G.I. Bill: "The huge influx of veterans restricted the number of women who could be accommodated, and men dominated the campus from the late 1940s through the 1950s.... The pattern of early marriage and child-bearing that characterized the 1950s kept many qualified young women out of college."[36] Indeed, women in the 1950s actually lost ground gained by women in the early twentieth century. As historian Mary P. Ryan reports, between 1940 and 1966, the percentage of women in professions decreased from 45 to 38 percent, and those were highly concentrated in "traditional" female fields such as nursing, teaching, and social work. Numbers of female college graduates fell to only one in four in 1950, down from about 40 percent in 1940. Only one of four female college students considered a career, and large numbers dropped out of college to marry.[37]

Higher education and career ambitions clashed with the virtues required in private life. Education gave women a sense of their own abilities. It made them more critical thinkers, more independent. Professional work and earning power formed women according to the values of the male "public" world. How to reconcile these transformations with the fairly dependent and submissive housewife exalted in women's magazines and religious teachings?

An anonymous letter in the lay Catholic magazine *Integrity* in the mid-1950s poignantly captured this tension. A wife and mother argued that cultural pressures toward independence threaten women's true nature and happiness. Education was one of those pressures, deluding women into thinking that they should have their own voice (sadly, the woman chose to keep her own voice unidentified). Women found themselves in a painful conflict between the qualities that lead to success in public life (autonomy, financial acumen, outspokenness) and the qualities that bring success in private life (submission, dependence): "The pattern of life today creates a strange conflict in woman's life. She is taught to be above all self-sufficient, economically independent, politically vociferous, etc. But in order to decide to marry someone, she must make an act of surrender that is decidedly opposed to everything that makes up woman's independence. I believe that many possibly good marriages never come to be because the girl can't accept this very complete and actually very humiliating circumstance."[38]

The author did not reject the "humiliating" circumstance, for women's faith and purity depended on marriage in her view. The solution she proposed, rather, was to deemphasize intellectual education for girls and emphasize instead social development and marriage:

> Perhaps future mishaps could be avoided by education. Less stress on the intellectual in our colleges and high schools (for girls), more emphasis on the natural state which is marriage as well as its supernatural aspects, more careful planning of social development for our young girls with — let's face it — marriage in view.... For those not born to the religious life, the hazards to faith and purity can only with difficulty be offset without marriage (a personal opinion).[39]

The anonymous woman thus saw a tension between the intellectual (suited to men) and the natural (suited to women). Women's faith and purity depended on the "natural" state of marriage (with its supernatural, sacramental aspects), a state that demanded submission, dependence, and even humiliation. This perceived dichotomy between faith, purity, and marriage, on the one hand, and economic independence, intellect, and voice, on the other hand, would explode into spiritual revolt and confusion in the 1960s.

Going Against the Grain:
Single Woman Pursues Law Degree, Profession

At a time when American culture and religious groups so emphasized motherhood and domesticity, Catholic single woman Janet Mary Riley (b. 1915) was going against the grain. She earned a law degree from Loyola University in New Orleans in 1952 and garnered a spot as a law professor there by 1956, one of the first female law professors in the country. Riley's accomplishment was particularly significant when one considers the context: "Because professional schools discouraged female enrollment and because World War II veterans monopolized so many student slots, there were actually fewer women doctors and lawyers in the 1950s than two decades before."[40]

Riley grew up in New Orleans, attended parochial school and public high school, and then graduated from Loyola University (after attending the women's branch, Ursuline College) in 1936. A college teacher — a nun — encouraged her to be a lawyer. At that point, Riley had considered only teaching, nursing, and social work. The nun planted a seed that later came to fruition. Riley first taught and then went to library school. She worked as an army librarian during World War II and then as a law librarian at Loyola University. While working, she began to take law school classes and eventually got her degree in 1952, when she was thirty-seven years old. She never married.[41]

Few law firms interviewed women at that time, said Riley. She was fortunate to receive two offers, but decided to stay and teach at Loyola when her dean asked her to apply for a newly authorized faculty position. She recalls: "I had been teaching Legal Bibliography one hour a week while I was Law Librarian, but when I started teaching substantive law courses, this predominantly male student body — at the beginning it was almost totally male — were really shocked. They did not come to law school expecting to be taught by a woman."[42] In fact, Riley says that many people were "skeptical" because she was a single woman. They wondered, "What's wrong with her?" Her single status also led to lower salaries and difficulty in gaining promotions, she said. The school justified paying men because they had to support families. Even single men were paid more, because some day they might get married and need to support families. Riley recalls the injustice: "I did have dependents, just not children." Riley helped to support a niece and, later, her two grandnephews.[43]

Riley went on to earn an LL.M. degree from the University of Virginia in 1960. She also became a member of a secular institute for working women, the Society of Our Lady of the Way, "hoping by our lives to penetrate women's occupational fields." She took the vows of poverty, chastity, and obedience (one-year vows beginning in 1966, perpetual vows in 1973). Riley thus ruled out marriage and wholly embraced her career as her vocation. The Society "adopts our careers as its apostolate."[44] As Riley remarked: "We do encourage people to perfect their expertise in whatever their career is. The theory is that we are penetrating, infiltrating.... I'm trying to think of a word that does not sound sneaky, we are in the world but not of the world."[45] Riley in fact remained quiet about her religious mission: "Though I worked in a Catholic university, I never told my dean or colleagues. I thought that my work for the Louisiana State Law Institute, drafting and testifying for changes favoring women in Louisiana law, would be less effective if it were known that I had vows."[46]

Riley was a devout Catholic who believed that women could have a vocation either in or outside of the home. As a lawyer, she worked to modify community property laws to give women the right to share in the management of finances within a marriage, whether they were homemakers or wage earners:

> Our theory was that whichever path she chooses, working outside or inside, she is contributing to society's good and to the family in a monetary, economic way and should have equality. Her work in the home should be recognized. So when people tell me, "Oh, you're a feminist, you work to get women out of the home," I say, "No, I work for them to get equal protection whether in the home or out of the home." But it was a hard thing to get across. They kept on coming back saying, "Oh, you're working to ruin the household, the family." ... Women's rights as human beings were not being recognized.[47]

Riley also used her legal work to advance civil rights. In the early 1950s, she helped draft a legal memorandum in support of black students who had staged a sit-in at McCrory's. While she received no pay for her efforts, the case eventually made it to the Supreme Court and triumphed in *Lombard vs. Louisiana* (1963). She could not afford to go to the Supreme Court when the case was argued.[48]

Sisters Mobilize for Professional Training

During this "domestic interlude"[49] of the 1950s, marriage and children, on the one hand, and career, on the other, often appeared as two different paths, vocations that rarely intersected. Debates about womanly ideals and higher education also touched women on another vocational path — vowed religious life. Religious orders made important moves in the 1950s to improve the education and professional training of young sisters. Religious organizations depended on the inexpensive labor of Catholic sisters. Nuns were particularly important as Catholic educators; they staffed the rising numbers of parochial schools. Yet many of the young recruits were inadequately trained for these jobs. New sisters often began teaching directly after graduating high school, receiving higher education only through summer school courses over a period of twenty years. Several important events propelled sisters toward higher education and professional training. Sister Mary Emil Penet, I.H.M., headed up a committee of the National Catholic Education Association to address the problem in the early 1950s. Pope Pius XII at the same time instructed religious orders to improve sisters' education, raising their level of professional training to that of lay teachers.[50] In 1954, the NCEA formally established the Sister Formation Conference, dedicated to "the advancement of the religious, cultural, and professional formation of Sisters."[51] The Conference sought to invigorate the spiritual formation, personal development, and professional training of sisters.

On the ground, this was difficult. Pressured to staff the expanding schools during this "baby boom" era, bishops and parish pastors often resisted the release of sisters from teaching duties for full-time education. The Conference, however, proved itself a strong force. Sisters increasingly attained college and graduate degrees and emerged with a stronger sense of leadership and creative vision. During the 1950s, sisters found educational and leadership opportunities in religious life that would have been nearly impossible in secular life at that time. They also encouraged countless Catholic women to pursue an education and increasingly provided models of educated, professional leadership for the growing numbers of middle-class Catholic women. At the same time, higher education and professionalization led to conflicts with more submissive ideals of religious women, in an interesting parallel with the conflicts increasingly facing laywomen: "Finding themselves bound by rules and a vision of what 'good sisters' were: docile, obedient, and submissive, they had to forge a new image wherein they could exercise decision-making, leadership, and effectiveness in a male-oriented Church. This transformation did not come easily."[52]

Lay Movements and Working Women

Lay Catholic movements in the postwar years — movements such as the Grail, *Integrity* magazine, Cana Conference, and the Christian Family Movement (CFM) — highlighted the family as a central religious issue and powerful means of social transformation in the postwar American context. In diverse ways, they reinforced the ideal of domesticity current in American culture. This is a complex story, however, for movements such as Young Christian Workers (YCW) and the Grail trained single women for apostolic mission, even as they taught them the virtues of feminine piety and domesticity. Moreover, while lay movements underscored the importance of family, women (even married women) took important leadership roles within the movements: Patty Crowley cofounded the CFM, Carol Jackson edited *Integrity* under a pseudonym, and Janet Kalven set out a vision for Grail women.

Young Christian Workers was a specialized form of Catholic Action that began in the United States in the late 1930s and took hold in about thirty-five cities by 1947.[53] Dominated by women in the postwar years, YCW gave single women an important role in the church's battle against Communism. The movement trained "Mary O'Hara," for example, who left office work in order to fight Communism in the factories of a Midwestern city:

> Mary is a Catholic, working for the recognition of the non-Communist union. And she received her training in a form of Catholic Action known as the Young Christian Workers.... If the

mass of American workers are ever going to be converted to Christianity, they will hear of Christ and come to love Him through people like Mary, who share their problems and their pleasures, who are interested in them and make sacrifices for them. As Mary puts it: "No one else is doing anything except the Commies."[54]

Yet YCW also encouraged its young women toward a traditional ideal of domesticity — to marry, stay at home, and appreciate their motherly roles (as the booklet "A Challenge to Girls in the YCW," which exalted the "beauty of homemaking," demonstrated).

Like Young Christian Workers, the Grail sought to develop young single women as bold Christianizing forces in the world. At the same time, the Grail emphasized women's specific call to domestic life and linked women's spirituality closely to the private sphere. Brought to the United States in 1940 and headquartered in Loveland, Ohio, the Grail gathered young women together for summer retreats — training by immersion in the Christian apostolate. American leader Janet Kalven told the young women that they were "apostles," "co-offerers of the Holy Sacrifice of the Mass," and "lay priests [sharing] in Christ's mission as prophet and teacher."[55] And yet, said Kalven, women's "real career" was as wife and mother; business and other professional work should be temporary at best. Feminism was destroying the differences between the sexes and hence impeding the needed reconstruction of the social order. It was misguided "to think as women that we must be in the forefront of public affairs, politics, or business to influence the course of the world." Rather, as wife and mother, women could pass on cultural and religious traditions and inspire men through their love.[56]

Grail leaders recognized that women's roles in the workplace were changing, and they tried to channel that shift in ways that would preserve women's distinctive (complementary) nature. For example, the Grail Council on Service Careers, established in the 1950s, sought to draw single women into careers such as teaching, social work, and nursing, where they could be "exercising an influence as women."[57] Such service jobs extended women's nurturing qualities and protected feminine spirituality. Thus, while the Grail inspired young women to witness boldly to their faith, the movement in this preconciliar era channeled that witness into domestic work and traditionally feminine types of labor.

The Christian Family Movement, which also flourished in the postwar concern about the family, developed women's leadership even as it relied heavily on middle- and upper-class married women who did not work outside the home. The Christian Family Movement emerged in the Midwest around 1947, became an international movement, and claimed about fifty thousand American members by its peak in the early 1960s.[58] It aimed to strengthen families by attending to the wider social context. Women such as Patty Crowley, Regina Weissert, and Helene Bauer played important roles in the development of the movement.[59] With their husbands, countless women ran local CFM chapters. And yet for the most part the movement depended on women who did not work outside of the home. As Burns writes:

> Since the first national meeting, CFM has been plagued by the fact of its upper-middle-class, white, professional membership. Repeated efforts had been made to attract working-class and minority members. One basic problem that tended to bar working-class involvement was lack of leisure time. The backbone of CFM was the wives, most of whom did not have to work outside the home.... The working class did not have this luxury — most wives worked. Add to that irregular hours and shift work, and the barriers to participation were high.[60]

Religious organizations did depend particularly on those middle- and upper-middle-class women, who had more leisure time. As middle-class women increasingly joined the labor force, then, religious groups found themselves in a challenging situation. Who would supply the church's free labor? Would the domestic ideal of womanhood collapse?

Susie and *Glamour* Magazine: The Charges of Materialism

Debates about women's proper sphere erupted into charges of "materialism." As women increasingly took paid work, critics accused them of putting material goods — especially luxury items — above their husbands and children. As a blanket charge, of course, this was unfair. Women worked for many reasons, including economic need, a desire to "get out of the house,"[61] and enjoyment. Yet the 1950s was an affluent era of consumption and rapid suburbanization, and women's wages did help to support rising standards of living. America enjoyed a decade of prosperity following World War II; by one account, real income rose 25 percent between 1946 and 1959.[62] With mass production of the automobile, the construction of highways, increased home construction, and generous federal mortgage programs, Americans streamed out of the cities and into the suburbs in the postwar decade. This move accelerated a process of suburbanization that had begun in the 1920s.

By 1950, Catholics too were moving out of the working classes and into the suburbs, lessening the class differences that had separated them from Protestants. Declining rates of immigration meant that the percentage of Catholics in the middle class grew more quickly. Catholic immigration slowed considerably after the Johnson-Reed Act, passed in 1924, went into effect in 1929. The act limited immigration from southern and eastern Europe. The decline in Catholic immigrants profoundly affected the American Catholic community, leading to an increasingly assimilated and wealthier population: "It meant that within the next generation, by about the mid-1950s, Catholicism would become a church of the middle class."[63]

At the same time, a new leisure industry developed in the postwar boom years, accompanied by a culture of consumerism. Women took jobs in part to supplement their family income for leisure goods. In effect, some middle-class women became producers outside the home in order to become more powerful consumers within it. Diner's Club issued the first American credit card in 1950; credit cards gave Americans greater purchasing power. By the end of the 1950s, 90 percent of American families had a television. "Time-saving" household appliances such as dishwashers, washing machines, electric mixers, and "Hoovers" hit the market, with advertising campaigns targeted at women.

Observers imagined that women's time had expanded dramatically. The priest-sociologist Andrew Greeley wrote: "Even
those [women] who have chosen marriage for their careers are
surrounded by so many labor-saving gadgets that they are free
forever from the drudgery of housework."[64] Technology seemed
to hold the key to a leisurely future. In reality, though, technology did not necessarily decrease women's household work hours.
According to economist Juliet Schor, the hours put in by full-time
homemakers remained roughly the same from the 1910s to the
1970s: "with all these labor-saving innovations, no labor has been
saved. Instead, housework expanded to fill the available time.
Norms of cleanliness rose. Standards of mothering grew more
rigorous."[65]

Women's rising work force participation prompted sharp critiques of "materialism," that is, excessive consumption and attachment to luxury goods. In the Methodist magazine *Together,* a
female author in 1959 told women: "Rubbish! You can go home
again — when you accept the fact that the need of your presence
is considerably greater than any need for a new garment or a
new car."[66] In this Cold War context, "materialism" also carried
Marxist overtones. Women's domesticity served as a defense of
the American way of life against Communist infiltration. Hence,
the same female author warned that mothers' work outside the
home would weaken the family, drawing a parallel to Communist communes: "If the absentee mother is unimportant, what is
our objection to the communes of China, the frank purpose of
which is to destroy the family and its influences? Perhaps the Com-
munists know that a mother can be a prime source of richness
for her children, a creator of attitudes."[67] The implication was
clear: women's work outside the home bolstered materialism and
weakened American resistance to Communism.

Catholics, fierce critics of Communism in the 1950s, saw a
particularly dangerous slippery slope. Materialism and notions of
female independence drove married women's employment, which
led to contraception, child neglect, social disruption, and even
divorce, according to some. It was not only the hierarchy who critiqued women workers. Editors of the lay magazine *Integrity,* for

example, argued that popular American culture threatened Catholic values, encouraging women's employment and materialism:

> Similarly accented by those who mold mass mentality is a materialistic attitude toward marriage. The superficiality of "Glamour's" concern over the condition of the family is evident when contrasted with the rest of its contents. "Luxuries are necessities" is the keynote...it is assumed that Susie will work after marriage. ...Susie decides she won't have children for the first couple of years....She leaves a back door open — divorce.[68]

A Young Christian Workers booklet ("A Challenge to the Girls of YCW") similarly accused women of undervaluing their domestic roles and selfishly taking time from family life for material gain: "Perhaps she doesn't see the beauty of homemaking because her mother constantly complained of being an unappreciated slave, or because her mother was so taken up with a career and the accumulation of material goods that the house was only a sleep-and-eat stop between jobs."[69] To critics, women's employment threatened a whole range of fundamental Catholic values (thereby opening the door both to Protestant individualism and to Communist values).

The Catholic Marriage Manual by Rev. George Kelly, published in 1958 with the *imprimatur* and the introduction of New York archbishop Cardinal Francis Spellman, warned married women not to work outside the home except in cases of great economic necessity. Kelly attributed the rise of working women to families' growing desire for luxuries. In his view, wives' employment undermined women's subservience in marriage, encouraged materialism, threatened women's moral purity, and endangered children. Women's employment injured male pride and disturbed marriages: "Friction may easily develop over the question of who is head of the household." Moreover: "Work outside the home may also foster traits undesirable in a wife. She may become economically independent, and be less willing to make sacrifices and emotional adjustments to keep relations with her husband on a happy basis. She is often flattered by other men, with the possibility of flirtations and serious romantic entanglements." Employment and its accompanying materialism represented a clear and present *danger;* the manual repeated this word several times. Wage work weakened women's virtue: "She faces the danger that she will overemphasize the importance of dress and adornment, and that there will be a lessening of her womanly qualities and refinement." Most seriously, women's materialism risked children's safety: "The greatest danger of all, of course, is that in her pursuit of material benefits, the upbringing of her children will be seriously neglected. Social workers uniformly attest to the fact that delinquency rates are greatest among those children without mothers at home to supervise their activities." *The Catholic Marriage Manual* warned: "An added danger of a materialistic philosophy is that it makes couples 'contraception-minded.' "[70]

Such writings must be seen within the context of postwar Catholic concern for the family. As historian Debra Campbell writes: "The Catholic Church in America had long considered itself the defender of the family against the threats of free love, divorce, contraception, and mixed marriages, and its concern for the family intensified noticeably in the postwar era."[71] The weight of these charges of materialism also can be traced back to the ideal of domesticity and the privatization of religion dating from the nineteenth century. As a divide grew between private and public worlds, women were linked with spirituality. Piety was a "cardinal virtue."[72] Men, on the other hand, were linked with the material. They earned the wages; they got their hands dirty. In this ideal world, women had the daunting vocation to save men from materialism. When women moved into that material world for more than a temporary excursus (during single years or extreme economic necessity), they endangered their very spiritual nature — not to mention the social good and the future of religious institutions. That ideal persisted into the twentieth century and became entangled in anti-Communist rhetoric. Women's domesticity was a guard against materialism in rapidly industrializing society threatened by Communism: "Let man exercise his grubby wit as he elects, on inventions, and even in literature and art. As long as we have women who by love can transform them, materialism will never conquer the world. Wise men build houses only that women can make them homes."[73] The sentiment expressed in this wartime comment in the *Catholic Mind* emerged in the 1950s, the

Cold War decade of domesticity, as a sharp critique of married women's employment.

While critics of women's employment accused women of materialism and child neglect, women themselves tended to see employment as a necessary or beneficial dimension of their domestic roles. Women's work could improve the family's standard of living, without undermining the man's primary role as breadwinner: "Many working women came to see themselves as 'temporary' workers whose income was directed toward a specific goal: school clothes for the kids, a new refrigerator, or a larger house."[74] Working-class white women, Latinas, and African Americans had even stronger arguments for the domestic importance of their work roles. In the mid-1950s, the Diocesan Labor Institute of Connecticut held small group meetings with Catholic trade unionists. The director of one Institute chapter reported: "The moral law would be kept better if more women stayed home. The men at the meetings felt the same way, but the women smiled and thought they still had more reasons for working than not working — chiefly to support the home."[75] In her study of twenty-four Chicana women who started working in the Santa Clara Valley cannery industry in the postwar years, Patricia Zavella shows that Chicana women made choices that they thought would best accommodate their primary role in the home: "Virtually all of the women originally sought work for economic reasons." One woman named Lupe stated: "I did it for my family. We needed the money. Why else?"[76] Many women took part-time or seasonal employment in order to accommodate family, even though their transitory work marginalized them in the economy and reinforced their position of dependence at home.[77] Chicano families did adapt to the wife's employment, but women's work did not fundamentally challenge ideals of domesticity or roles within the family and culture.[78]

Employment long had been an essential component of family responsibility for African American women. Historian Jacqueline Jones writes: "Black women had incorporated both traditional (homemaking) and nontraditional (paid employment) roles into their personal ideologies of work, without needing to identify themselves exclusively in terms of either one role or the other the way white wives often did."[79] Magazines such as *Ebony* gave black women positive feedback for their multiple roles. A 1953 editorial, for example, praised the African American woman's influential role as homemaker, her faith and strong church attendance, and her superior educational and economic power.[80] An article about Los Angeles "lady cops" Selma Raines and Joan Pierson described the women as "comely," the "gentler, prettier arm of law." Underneath a photo of the policewomen firing a .38 special in target practice, the caption noted that Joan Pierson is married and has two young children.[81] *Ebony* also featured accomplished professional African American women who combined career and family, women such as doctors Jane and Barbara Wright of Harlem. These sisters, daughters of a surgeon, managed to pursue successful careers without neglecting their "wifely chores."[82] Both were married to lawyers from good Methodist families. According to the article, the Wright husbands enjoyed their wives' professional accomplishments and intellectual interests; they "see nothing wrong with having career wives."[83] African American women's experiences undoubtedly diverged from those of white middle-class women, who faced a sharper cultural dichotomy between employment and home. Yet across class and race, women often saw their work and family lives as complementary spheres, despite cultural criticism.

Devotion

Because women tended to see employment as a complement to domestic responsibilities, some were able to become bold prayers, petitioning heaven for just salaries, for work that they could fit around their family's needs, even for help to break into traditionally male fields. For most Catholics the decades before 1960 were the era of "pray, pay, and obey" Catholicism. Catholic women located their spirituality in the traditional practices of Mass, confession, and devotions to Mary and the saints. As Boston Catholic MK (b. 1920) put it:

> I am what you might call an old-time Catholic who grew up with
> rules and regulations. As far as being spiritual and the fact that I

really thought too much about it, let's face it: I didn't. We went to Mass . . . we probably went to Confession every two weeks. . . . We did what we were supposed to do. I can't talk for everybody. You lived a decent life, and you never really thought about it. You did what you were supposed to do; you didn't stop and analyze why you were doing it.[84]

MK worked for Bell Atlantic in Boston from 1941 to 1982. Occasionally her variable work schedule made it difficult to attend Sunday Mass. In her view, the conflict put her in a state of mortal sin and required Confession: "It was difficult. They did not have a Saturday Mass. They had quite a few Masses in the morning, but if you had to work at 7 A.M. . . . Maybe I did miss it once or twice. You'd go to Confession and tell him; he'd give you absolution. But it wasn't something you just took for granted, like, oh well, I missed Mass. If you missed Mass, it was a mortal sin as far as we were concerned."[85] Prescribed religious practices were central to devotional life.

Women could rely on these practices as their work roles changed. While some women simply saw their jobs as a necessary part of life, irrelevant to their faith, others wove traditional devotion together with their economic situations. Devotional magazines are one important source of information about women's spiritual lives in the pre–Vatican II era. Novenas to Mary and prayers to St. Jude, the patron saint of hopeless causes, particularly reveal ordinary women's life situations, hopes, and theological beliefs.[86] Part of these devotions includes publishing a letter of thanksgiving for favors granted; these letters provide valuable written records. They show that as women moved increasingly into the work force in the 1940s and 1950s, there was not a devotional rupture but rather a blending of traditional devotions and changing social roles. In fact, professional advancement led some women to a deeper commitment to traditional prayer practices, such as the offering of novenas, to which they attributed their success.

Women's letters show their family commitments; they resorted to devotional practices to help blend family and employment. In 1953, for example, a woman from Los Angeles related her gratitude to St. Jude:

This is to acknowledge a favor I am certain St. Jude helped me receive from Our Lord. I had been looking for work to do at home as I have two young boys and no one to care for them. I had been praying to St. Jude for a long time. Work actually came to my door at a time when I needed it more than ever. Work came from a person I didn't even know was in the manufacturing business. My hopes of getting work at home were practically gone when St. Jude came to my help. I am indeed humbly grateful.[87]

The novena to Our Sorrowful Mother gained great popularity in the late 1930s and early 1940s. A Servite priest introduced the devotion in 1937 in Chicago; it quickly became "a mass movement promoted by a religious magazine, a radio program, and a national publicity campaign."[88] As historian Jay Dolan notes, it was not unusual for working-class Catholics to pray the novena for jobs and financial success.

Women as well as men looked to Mary for help in finding jobs or advancing in their careers. Indeed, women even saw Our Sorrowful Mother as an advocate as they attempted to break into traditionally male fields. Women continued in the devotion, moreover, years after the novena declined in popularity in the mid-1940s.[89] In 1945, Janet Ivancak from Chicago expressed thanks to Mary for help in finding a better job with a salary increase: "I was unhappy in my old position so I asked Mary for a new job which she granted at the second Friday of my second Novena. Shortly afterwards, I received a raise. This better position enables me to carry on with my education. I asked Our Holy Mother's assistance with that also, and she is always by my side."[90] *Novena Notes* published Ivancak's letter, followed by the traditional intercessory prayer: "Mother most chaste, Pray for us."

That same year, single woman Patricia Dikin, also of Chicago, gave Mary credit for a raise received:

I had placed my petition to Our Sorrowful Mother in the petition box two weeks ago asking her aid in receiving an increase in salary. Hardly a week later my employer inquired how many months had passed since my last increase. (Every previous one had been asked for and I naturally dreaded the ordeal.) Well, this time my increase became effective automatically and I am sure my petition is the answer as our company has never applied this policy before.[91]

Older women increasingly sought paid work in the postwar years. In 1955, Our Sorrowful Mother intervened on behalf of an older woman from Massachusetts seeking clerical work: "I want to publicly thank Our Sorrowful Mother for finding me a position. At my age it was not easy to find a clerical position. On Good Friday, I finished the Novena, and on the following Wednesday I went back to work. I will continue to make Our Sorrowful Mother Novena as long as I am able to attend."[92]

Perhaps the most striking letter came from Anne Mary Benak of Waterloo, Iowa, in 1955. Benak, a woman in her early thirties, not only merged her Catholic piety with her working life; she relied on traditional devotional practices to help her break through nearly impermeable gender boundaries in the workplace. Benak wanted to become a licensed barber, and she believed that Mary Our Sorrowful Mother helped her to do just that. Benak wrote:

> Off and on I have made the Sorrowful Mother Novena since high school days, 1941, and have read and distributed many copies [of *Novena Notes*]....I want to publicly thank the Sorrowful Mother for granting me a seemingly impossible request. For many years I wanted to be a licensed barber. But since lady barbers are rather few, my friends and family would always discourage me. Finally I decided to ask the Mother of Sorrows for guidance. Needless to say, after attending The Novena it happened. The opposition was terrific, but with the Sorrowful Mother's help I took the step. I passed the exam with flying colors and obtained the best job of all my classmates. I then passed my apprenticeship exam and have a fine job.[93]

Some scholars see evidence of declining Marian devotion in the 1950s, well before the Second Vatican Council and the feminist movement of the 1960s and 1970s. One study found that participation in weekly novenas to Our Lady of Perpetual Help declined by 60 percent in Pittsburgh in the 1950s, at the same time that the city's women increasingly moved into the labor force: "The devotion to Our Lady of Perpetual Help's decline in popularity...must stem in some measure from a rejection of the belief that power derives from passivity. That rejection likely resulted when women saw an achievable alternative to the discourse that the devotion so firmly embraced, and that alternate path probably derived from women's increasing work outside of the home."[94] Yet women's own prayer notes indicate that it was not impossible to blend traditional devotions with work outside the home, even in the face of church opposition. In the 1950s, some women were able to live in that dissonance.

Even in 1960, working women showed a reliance on traditional devotion. Reflecting the fact that older women increasingly were entering the work force, letters of thanks appeared for Mary's special advocacy for these economically vulnerable women. Californian Mrs. Mary Egan, for example, wrote: "I am a retiree and the past 18 months I have prayed for a part time job to supplement my Social Security Pension. Yesterday I got a job.... Everyplace I went, I was too old. I am so grateful to OSM [Our Sorrowful Mother]."[95]

Most significant, however, is the fact that as married women gained *professional* opportunities and sought careers, they too could see Mary as an advocate. In 1960 a headline in *Novena Notes* announced: "Study, Prayer Win Professional Status for Novenite." Married woman Ruby Lewis of Downey, Illinois, wrote: "I promised the Sorrowful Mother that I would give public thanks if she would help me become a registered medical technologist. After much study, prayer, and one week after I had finished the novena, I received a letter saying that I had passed the examination and am now a registered medical technologist. I have made several novenas and have been blessed and helped by each one."[96]

In the very same month that Lewis's letter appeared in *Novena Notes,* the *Voice of St. Jude* published an article sharply critical of working mothers: "One glance at the bank balance or the price tag on a new Buick and some mothers go dashing down to the employment office to seek work outside the home.... They cannot devote adequate time to their children.... A realistic evaluation of necessities and luxuries and the establishment of Christian priorities may show no real need for seeking these questionable solutions."[97] Thus, in the same devotional magazines where married women thanked the saints for helping them find work and succeed professionally, one sees the recurrent charge of materialism and child neglect. Perhaps women subscribers dismissed these charges or did not think they applied to them.

By the mid-1960s, however, traditional devotions such as the rosary, novenas, and petitions to St. Jude clearly had lost their foothold. *Novena Notes* ceased publication in 1966 and the *Voice of St. Jude* became first *Jubilee* and then *U.S. Catholic* around the same time. In the transition to *U.S. Catholic,* the "letters of favors granted" disappeared. While Mrs. Lewis saw no conflict between her Marian devotion and her professional aspirations, many other women encountered far more spiritual strain as the decade progressed. For women's employment would more and more directly challenge the ideals of womanhood and women's spirituality upon which religious institutions depended.

Chapter Two

Debating Women's Place

Careers, Controversies, and the Time Crunch, 1963 to the Present

The year 1963 marked an important turning point in this story of women, work, and religion. It was in this year that feminist author Betty Friedan published *The Feminine Mystique,* a book that sharply challenged the domestic ideal of womanhood and its religious supporters. At the same time, the Presidential Commission on the Status of Women, established by John F. Kennedy two years earlier, documented sex discrimination in the workplace and recommended changes in hiring practices, childcare policies, and federal legislation. In 1963, as the Second Vatican Council opened the windows of the church to the modern world, Pope John XXIII issued *Pacem in Terris* ("Peace on Earth"). The encyclical urged laity to take an active role in public life and affirmed the rights of women. That same year, the prominent Belgian Cardinal Leo Suenens described women's rising employment outside the home as liberation from bondage. And, in 1963, Pope John XXIII established the Papal Birth Control Commission to study the question of artificial birth control. This year marked the start of a tumultuous period of change that challenged longstanding ideals of femininity, piety, and women's work.

Rates of female employment continued to rise in the 1960s, powered by the expanding service economy, civil rights legislation, the feminist movement, greater educational and professional opportunities, increased life expectancies, and decreased fertility rates. Rates of employment for married women increased across racial and ethnic lines, although the employment rates of married

Mexican American women continued to lag behind the rates of married white women and married black women. Still, Chicana rates of employment rose significantly in the 1960s.[1]

A Controversial Development:
The Birth Control Pill

Declining fertility correlated with married women's rising employment rates. After peaking around 1960, fertility rates dropped steadily until the late 1960s, when they rose briefly before dipping sharply in the early 1970s.[2] Through most of the 1970s, American women were giving birth on average to less than two children in their lifetime. Fertility rates increased somewhat in the late 1980s and early 1990s, but rates still hovered at 2.0 or less, far less than the 3.5 rates common in the late 1950s.

The development of the birth control pill factored significantly into the drop in fertility. The Food and Drug Administration approved the pill for contraceptive use in 1960. The pill gave women greater ability to plan pregnancies, and hence to make choices about motherhood, the number and spacing of children, and employment. The emergence of relatively reliable contraception was a critical change impacting women's work and their relationship to the Catholic Church. Educational and professional opportunities were expanding for women. The feminist movement portrayed work as the source of fulfillment and freedom for women. The Second Vatican Council opened the windows of the church to the modern world. Many American Catholic women assumed that the church would accept the new birth control pill. Catholic doctors often prescribed the pill for "regularity," if for no other reason. In 1963, Pope John XXIII established a commission of theologians, scientists, pastors, and several married couples to study artificial birth control. The Papal Birth Control Commission met over a period of four years, and eventually recommended the acceptance of artificial birth control within marriage. The commission's report was leaked to the liberal American Catholic newspaper the *National Catholic Reporter*, prompting further speculation that it was a done deal. A year later, however, in 1968, Pope Paul VI promulgated *Humanae Vitae,* which condemned artificial birth control.

Some American Catholic women — such as union organizer Dolores Huerta, who would raise eleven children — supported the pope's position. Many others were stunned. Patty Crowley, cofounder of the Christian Family Movement, had served with her husband, Pat, on the Papal Birth Control Commission. She had assembled numerous letters from lay married couples imploring the church to change its position. When the pope published *Humanae Vitae,* contradicting the recommendations of the commission, she recalls: "We were stunned. Pat just said, 'I don't believe it,' and hung up. We asked ourselves why we had ever gone to Rome in the first place."[3]

JM was a college student at Wellesley from 1966 to 1970. At that time, she said, Betty Friedan had "been around for a while"; feminism was developing and gaining influence. During this tumultuous period, Catholic women like JM had one foot in a religious world that opposed birth control, abortion, and women's ordination, and the other foot in a feminist movement that endorsed women's leadership, birth control, and abortion. Not surprisingly, many women could not straddle both worlds. JM recalls: "It was an exciting time and it [feminism] was something that I was pretty involved in, pretty interested in. . . . I wrote a paper in a course on birth control and abortion approaches . . . so I suppose it was a period of questioning all the givens. And the church could be pretty heavy-handed about their givens. There was an absolutism that really felt wrong to me."[4] Raised in an Irish Catholic neighborhood in Providence, Rhode Island, JM had attended parochial schools and a public high school before entering Wellesley. She grew apart from the church while in college, and then left it for nearly fifteen years. The feminist movement was alive, she said; the church was not. In the midst of so much social questioning, the church seemed strangely sure in its certainties.

Women such as Mercedes Espinoza steered a delicate course, maintaining their sense of religious identity even as they rejected aspects of church teaching. A Mexican American migrant worker in Texas and the Midwest, Espinoza explained in an interview in the mid-1970s:

> I want to give all my children the education that I didn't have, to provide all their necessities. . . . One thing I am going to do different is start by not having as many kids as my mother. You can't provide as much for them as you can if you have only four or five. That may seem like too many, but it's ten less than my mother had. I shouldn't criticize her, though. Before, with most Mexican women, people would say, "Oh, she got blessed with fifteen kids." Yeah, but who got blessed with feeding them? I think that there's a reason for the pope to say whatever he feels like saying, but there's also a reason to try to stop having children, because it's more of a sin to have twelve kids and not be able to feed them. . . . So I think that the pill, even if it's against the pope, I'm going to take it. I don't want my kids to have to leave home to find work, and when you have fewer kids, they wouldn't have to leave home to help.[5]

The church's condemnation of the pill — coming at a time when American women's work opportunities were expanding dramatically and feminism was emphasizing choice — created a tension that carried profound implications for the church, clerical authority, and women's religious identities.

Federal Initiatives Fight Gender Discrimination

The development of reliable contraception in the 1960s coincided with federal initiatives to reduce barriers against women at work. President John F. Kennedy established the Commission on the Status of Women, chaired by Eleanor Roosevelt, in 1961. The commission presented its report in 1963. At that time, roughly 60 percent of the women who worked were married, as compared to less than 40 percent in 1940. According to the commission, the great majority of women worked to earn money, although for some women "self-fulfillment" was an additional or even the primary motive. The commission documented sex discrimination in the workplace and recommended changes in hiring and promotion practices, childcare policies, and federal legislation. Specifically, it argued for an executive order to promote equal opportunity for women in private employment.[6]

In the same year that the President's Commission released its report, Congress passed the Equal Pay Act, making it illegal to pay women lower wages than men for an equivalent job. At that time, women working full-time earned on average fifty-nine cents for every dollar men earned. The following year, Title VII of the Civil Rights Act of 1964 outlawed employment practices, including hiring and compensation, that discriminated on the basis of sex, race, religion, or national origin. The Equal Employment Opportunity Commission was created to investigate charges of discrimination and reach settlements with employers. In its first year, it received 8,852 charges of discrimination, four times the number expected.[7] Although it did not have the power to bring lawsuits, the EEOC did require employers to submit annual reports detailing the numbers of women and minorities in various jobs. The commission also created guidelines for employers.

Such federal initiatives placed women's workplace situations within the framework of civil rights, giving teeth to claims that women had a right to work without discrimination based on sex or beliefs about women's role in the home. In practical terms, federal legislation helped to open educational and occupational doors for women by the late 1960s and early 1970s. However, the wage gap remained at around fifty-nine cents to the dollar into the 1980s.[8]

Betty Friedan and the Feminist Movement

The women's movement of the 1960s and 1970s (better described as the second wave movement, following on efforts by nineteenth-century feminists), profoundly affected women's understandings of themselves, spirituality, family, sexuality, and the value of wage work. Betty Friedan's 1963 bombshell *The Feminine Mystique,* for example, raised profound questions about women's identity and domestic calling. Friedan challenged the nineteenth-century ideal of womanhood, which was heavily promoted in the 1950s (of course, women's actual experiences in the 1950s did not necessarily mirror the cultural portrayals of women). She rejected the privatization and domestication of women that she believed religious teachings reinforced. According to Friedan, the "happy housewife" was bored, stunted, and anxious. After all: "The baked potato is not as big as the world, and vacuuming the living room floor — with or without makeup — is not work that takes enough thought or energy to challenge any woman's full capacity."[9]

Friedan sharply critiqued the domestic ideal that she saw supported by religion and women's magazines. The feminine mystique had been wrongly elevated to a spiritual ideal: "by the publishers of *McCall's* in 1954, the concept 'togetherness' was seized upon avidly as a movement of spiritual significance by advertisers, ministers, newspaper editors. For a time, it was elevated into virtually a national purpose."[10] Friedan quoted a former *McCall's* editor who said: "Suddenly, everybody was looking for this spiritual significance in togetherness, expecting us to make some mysterious religious movement out of the life everyone had been leading for the last five years — crawling into the home, turning their backs on the world — but we never could find a way of showing it that wasn't a monstrosity of dullness."[11] Friedan argued that women's realization and identity and self-transcendence — one might even say "spirituality" — depended on work outside the home.[12]

Friedan's writing raised, I argue, deep vocational questions. As the feminist movement developed and educational and employment opportunities widened, women found the meaning of their family roles called into question. They were, in effect, caught between competing ideals of womanhood. Free-lance writer Mary Freeman commented in the Catholic magazine *Commonweal* in 1962: "Home is no longer a warm spot in a cold world. The wind whistles all the way through. Nor are wives and mothers any longer sheltered vestals tending the sacred fire. None of the haloed roles are fully theirs today."[13] Women's struggles in the in-between spaces between feminist and Catholic ideals of womanhood bring to the fore questions of meaning and place central to women's spirituality.

Rising feminist consciousness brought devotional disruption and theological adaptation for some Catholics. Women such as Mary Gordon found themselves at odds, for example, with the dominant Catholic model of the good woman: the Virgin Mary. Gordon, a future novelist, was born in 1949 and raised on Long

Island, New York. She described her own rejection of Mary as she came into adulthood in the late 1960s and 1970s:

> In my day, Mary was a stick to beat smart girls with. Her example was held up constantly: an example of silence, of subordination, of the pleasure of taking the back seat. . . .
>
> For women like me, it was necessary to reject that image of Mary in order to hold onto the fragile hope of intellectual achievement, independence of identity, sexual fulfillment. . . .
>
> Women who were independent and intelligent rejected the Virgin Mary in favor of her son in the way that some feminists, particularly in the beginning of the movement, felt it necessary to radically reject those things that were associated exclusively with the female: dresses, make-up, domestic work, relations with men, children.[14]

Indeed, feminists sought to hold up models for women quite different from the meek Mary or the demure "happy housewife." For example, several prominent feminists created alternatives to the more domestically oriented women's magazines. In 1965, Helen Gurley Brown took the helm at *Cosmopolitan* and quickly shaped it into a daring magazine aimed at young, single, liberated, professional women. Brown promoted an image of womanhood: sexy, seductive, powerful, conniving, successful in career. Gloria Steinem founded the feminist *Ms.* magazine in 1972. Hard-hitting and political, *Ms.* gave voice to numerous feminist authors and advocated the Equal Rights Amendment and legal abortion.

Women also founded political organizations to bring about social change. Betty Friedan helped to found the National Organization for Women in 1966. NOW fought against sex discrimination in the workplace, winning a landmark case in 1969 against Southern Bell (*Weeks vs. Southern Bell*). The organization also promoted the Equal Rights Amendment and lobbied hard for abortion rights, which were given federal backing in the 1973 Supreme Court decision *Roe v. Wade*. The gap between American feminism and the Catholic hierarchy widened significantly due to their polar opposite positions on abortion. Abortion legislation gave women even greater control over reproduction, and hence, over their work lives. Yet Catholics (including substantial numbers of the laity) objected that the moral cost was intolerable.

Even as the feminist movement gained influence and political organization, it failed to reflect the reality of working-class women and women of color. Women protested that the feminist movement took a romantic view of work outside the home, undervalued motherhood, and reflected only middle-class white women's experience. As one African American woman remarked: "We've had the opportunity as black women to be forever liberated — to go out and work like dogs!"[15] Farm worker organizer Dolores Huerta considered herself "a feminist," but critiqued the movement for failing to reflect the reality of poor women's work: "But among poor people, there's not any question about women being strong — even stronger than men — they work in the fields right along with the men. When your survival is at stake, you don't have these questions about yourself like middle-class women do."[16] A fierce opponent of birth control and abortion, Huerta also criticized white feminists for undervaluing motherhood, which Mexican Catholicism so strongly affirmed: "And in our culture, raising kids is the most important thing you can do, not like among whites."[17] The feminist movement gave Huerta some tools to reconcile her private and public worlds, but it could not adequately absorb Huerta's Catholic and Mexican American identities.

African American Women and Critiques of "Matriarchy"

Questions about women's place were not limited to white middle-class groups. For example, while African American women long had worked for wages, combining employment with family responsibilities, they too found themselves in the midst of a debate in the 1960s. By 1960, black women remained heavily concentrated in low-paying service jobs. Fifty percent of the domestic workers in the United States in 1960 were African American women.[18] Still, black families depended on women's earnings, and black women were making gains relative to black men. The 1965 Moynihan report, sponsored by the United States Department of Labor, provoked a firestorm of controversy when it denounced female-headed households and criticized the "matriarchy" of the

African American family. These criticisms paralleled other denunciations of white suburban matriarchs, such as that by Catholic priest-sociologist Andrew Greeley, who in 1959 saw signs of a "new matriarchy" in the suburbs.[19] The 1960 White House Conference on Children and Youth sounded similar concerns.[20]

The Moynihan report stated that women were principal earners in many black families, even when the husband was present, and that women gained disproportionately from education and equal opportunity initiatives:

> More importantly, it is clear that Negro females have established a strong position for themselves in white collar and professional employment, precisely the areas of the economy which are growing most rapidly and to which the highest prestige is accorded.... Special efforts have been made recently to insure equal employment opportunity for Negroes.... However, it may well be that these efforts have redounded mostly to the benefit of Negro women, and may even have accentuated the comparative disadvantage of Negro men.[21]

Moynihan in effect suggested that black women were "out of place." They were at odds with the dominant cultural ideal of female domesticity and submissiveness: "Ours is a society which presumes male leadership in private and public affairs. The arrangements of society facilitate such leadership and reward it. A subculture, such as that of the Negro American, in which this is not the pattern, is placed at a distinct disadvantage."[22]

Of course, many objected to the report's criticisms of black women, who out of necessity had assumed the responsibility of supporting their families.[23] Moreover, Willie Cors argued in *Commonweal* that when women work outside the home and gain economic independence, they actually strengthen marriage and draw it closer to the spiritual ideal. Cors wrote:

> Economic dependence, such as that often endured by the Negro male, and still more often by the female of most ethnic groups, produces economic and familial inferiority.... It is my contention that marriage as an institution cannot survive if its foundation is the economic dependence of the female. Rather, the marriage of the future (and of the present, in enlightened circles) is a union of two free, equal, and economically self-sufficient persons who for

emotional, psychological, and spiritual reasons decide to unite their lives. The dominant feature of their alliance is the Christ-love they bear for one another.[24]

This Christ-bearing marriage of equals is quite different from the dependent, surrendering image of marriage painted a decade earlier by the anonymous *Integrity* author.

When put in the position of matriarch, not a few African American women gained strength from their faith. When Chicagoan Almedia Hunt found herself the "man of the house" with two small children, she "said a little prayer. I told God there's nobody but you and me and I know you can help." Almedia was able to support her family with a job at Spiegal, Inc.[25] *Ebony* helped to give credence to independent women, to wives and mothers who also made a living, even in traditionally "male" fields. A 1964 issue described police sergeant Vivian Strange as "no 'powder puff' cop" and noted that Strange carefully scheduled her demanding job responsibilities so that they didn't interfere with her role as housewife. "After all," says Sgt. Strange, "no matter how challenging and rewarding my police work is, I still have to keep the home fires burning."[26] Jones sees *Ebony* promoting the "superwoman" decades before white popular culture would promote that image. While the "superwoman" model glossed over working women's reality, argues Jones, it presented a powerful image to bolster the African American community in the midst of the civil rights struggle.[27]

A Door Opens: Hints of Church Affirmation

While feminism, birth control, civil rights legislation, and the controversy over the Moynihan report raised questions about women's place and the domestic ideal, the Catholic Church itself was undergoing massive change during the Second Vatican Council (1962–65). In the years of *aggiornamento,* the church began to revisit its stance toward women's roles (a fact ignored by Friedan). In 1963, the same year that Friedan published *The Feminine Mystique,* Pope John XXIII's *Pacem in Terris* reminded the laity that they had a duty to take an active part in public life. The encyclical affirmed women's increasing roles in the public sphere and their human rights both in the home and outside it: "The part that women are now playing in political life is everywhere evident.... Women are gaining an increasing awareness of their natural dignity. Far from being content with a purely passive role or allowing themselves to be regarded as a kind of instrument, they are demanding both in domestic and in public life the rights and duties which belong to them as human persons."[28] Interestingly, John XXIII asserted here that women's *nature,* her *human* nature and natural dignity, impel her to seek justice in public life. This argument shifted the prior emphasis on women's domesticity, derived from women's distinct feminine nature. Moreover, said the pope, men and women have "equal rights and duties" within the family.[29] *Pacem in Terris* represented a development in the thought of John XXIII, who earlier had expressed far more concern about changes to women's traditional roles. In a 1960 address, for example, the pope had cautioned women to protect their "open and delicate spirit," which could be damaged by activities outside the domestic realm.[30]

In 1963, the prominent Belgian cardinal Leo Suenens depicted women's growing employment outside the home as liberation; woman was "freed from her former shackles." Far from being unnatural, women's extra-domestic opportunities allow her "to make use of her natural gifts."[31] Women bring their feminine nature directly (rather than through her indirect domestic influence) into public life: "She takes part in her own characteristic manner in the social, economic and literary life of the world. She no longer acts through man by her influence on him, but in her own right and under her own colours.... They [women] are wanted, accepted and effective."[32] While Suenens seemed to accept women's subordination in the home, he affirmed women's equality in public work.[33]

The Second Vatican Council (1962–65) showed cautious openness to women's growing public roles, even while it emphasized the spiritual meaning of marriage and family. The family took on great ecclesiological significance; the "domestic church" lit the fire of faith in children.[34] Yet the spirituality of the family did not necessarily depend on traditional gender roles. The Council seemed even to invite an increasing leadership role for women in public spheres and in the work of the church: "Since in our days women are taking an increasingly active share in the whole life of society, it is very important that their participation in the various sectors of the Church's apostolate should likewise develop."[35]

Sisters Advocate Expanded Professional Roles

While the Council and leaders such as Pope John XXIII and Cardinal Suenens set a relatively positive tone for women in public roles, ecclesial life on the ground moved more slowly. As laywomen in the 1960s faced sharp questions about their vocation and fulfillment outside of the home, so too sisters encountered similar questions about their place outside of their traditional teaching and social service roles. Could sisters discern vocations outside of those circumscribed by church hierarchy? Major disputes followed the movement of some sisters outside of their traditional habits of work. A well-publicized example was the 1967 uproar over the Los Angeles sisters of the Immaculate Heart of Mary. The sisters infuriated the local church hierarchy when they abandoned their habits and announced a decision to expand beyond their traditional teaching roles (the community already included, for example, the famous artist Corita Kent). The Reverend Mother Caspary declared, in an announcement reprinted in the *Los Angeles Times:*

> we won't abandon our traditional works...but we also say that diversity in works is not to be discouraged, but encouraged. Thus we may assume social service, or work with economic opportunity projects, or such specialized tasks as with the mentally retarded, or with young people. If one of our sisters has a special talent or interest, we will encourage her to pursue it. She might be a commercial artist, or a newspaper woman, or a musician, or almost anything else.[36]

The archdiocese did not concur — not when it depended on the nuns to staff its parochial schools. The dispute between the IHM community and the archdiocese escalated all the way to the

Vatican, which ruled against the nuns, and prompted widespread debate in the United States. As reported by the *New York Times,* 315 of the 400 sisters of the Immaculate Heart of Mary left their vows to form a lay secular community open to married women and without formal ties to the church.[37] A laicized Anita Caspary headed up the community.[38]

The dispute illustrates a vocational tension for religious women in the 1960s and 1970s that paralleled the situation of women outside the orders. Sisters were continuing to develop and diversify professionally. The resulting expanded sense of women's "place" challenged longstanding notions of vocation — and threatened institutions on which the church depended. Nuns could comfortably take leadership in service fields such as education and nursing. Yet to move into more "secular" work threatened Catholic schools and hospitals — and the distinctiveness of religious orders. Similarly, middle-class women increasingly combined paid employment with their domestic roles, a move that challenged nineteenth-century ideals of womanhood and posed a threat (or at least a perceived threat) to the home and to the local parishes that depended on women's unpaid labor. Indeed, women in "secular" life increasingly were gaining professional roles that women previously had found most commonly in religious life. This would mark a major reversal and pose sharp new questions for the church.

The Time Crunch

Women were critical to religious and community organizations, which depended on their inexpensive or volunteer labor. Yet as women increasingly moved into the work force, their time constricted. Sociologist Arlie Hochschild reviewed studies on time allocation done in the 1960s and 1970s. She concluded that between wage work, housekeeping, and childcare, women worked on average fifteen hours longer per week than did men. Women spent far more time doing domestic chores and caring for children than did their husbands in dual-earner couples. Hochschild wrote: "Just as there is a wage gap between men and women in the workplace, there is a 'leisure-gap' between them at home. Most women work one shift at the office or factory and a 'second shift' at home."[39] What implications would the time crunch hold for religious institutions and women's spirituality?

Women such as Margaret Fortes, a black Catholic from Boston, played vital roles in their communities. Fortes had her first child in 1957 and promptly quit her job: "I wanted to stay home.... They wouldn't always be small. There would be time later."[40] She remained at home until the early 1970s, when the youngest of her five children began school. Her husband's military income supported the family, albeit on a tight budget. Fortes sewed, found inexpensive ways to feed the children, and kept the house running. She responded with disbelief to Friedan's comments about the bored housewife: "Bored? With five kids, what are you kidding? There was so much to do.... We didn't have material things, but we had a lot of fun."[41] (Note the implied link here between material acquisition and women's employment.) Her husband's Coast Guard job frequently took him away from home, and Fortes took primary responsibility for the home and the children's care: "At that time, I didn't even realize how much it all fell on me."[42] She also devoted large amounts of time to improving education in her community, a poor section of Boston. Fortes helped to start an alternative school and then a voluntary integration program (METCO) when one of her sons encountered enormous difficulties in the public schools. "The parents got together and we started METCO, and before that, Exodus, when we tried to do something in the Boston Public Schools. We were going to get a good education for our kids. And did I pray? Oh, yes, I prayed that we could do something with the schools."[43]

Mary Baker (b. 1921), an active union organizer and Catholic in the South, also served as a pillar of her church and community. She became particularly involved in union causes after the death of her husband in 1961. Interviewed in the 1970s, she described her extensive work for her local parish, the Democratic Party, and various community projects: "I'm church secretary, I take care of all the financial areas.... So somehow or another, it falls in line. I'm on the Election Commission of Aiken County.... Also secretary of the Democratic Party.... And then I was president of the

Women's Club Altar Society. Let's see what else I was involved in then...."[44]

What would happen to the schools, to the churches, to the community groups as women — even mothers of small children — increasingly added full-time jobs to their schedules? By the 1970s, women faced time pressures and conflicts between work and family as mothers — including mothers of preschool children — increasingly held down full-time employment. Widening educational and employment opportunities drew women into the work force, as did changing perceptions of women's fulfillment. Economic factors also played a role; many asserted that two incomes had become necessary to support a family, particularly given the high rate of inflation in the 1970s. Rising rates of divorce in the 1970s also heightened women's economic vulnerability. The costs of staying out of the paid work force rose accordingly. Women's income dropped dramatically after divorce: "In an effort to recoup some of their income loss, many divorced and separated mothers enter the work force for the first time or increase their working hours.[45]

Studies indicate that "whereas in the 1950's, women predictably participated in a succession of life roles, women in the 1970's were inclined to participate in these roles simultaneously."[46] The pattern of women's work across the life span from 1940 to 1970 followed an "m" curve, with women's highest rates of employment in their early twenties and in the late forties. However, "this curve flattened out in the 1970s as mothers of young children greatly increased their rates of participation."[47] In the 1970s and thereafter, then, employment more directly conflicted with the ideal of domesticity. Surges in employment by mothers of preschool children challenged cherished notions of women's place.

Rising labor force participation also squeezed time from one acceptable, virtuous, even pious, activity of women: volunteer work. (It should be noted, though, that trends in volunteering relate not only to women's changing roles but also to the professionalization of volunteer jobs in the church and community.[48]) Southern Catholic woman Caroline Hodges (b. 1927) saw a decline in volunteering, which she attributed to the women's movement and women's increased employment. She lamented that women's ideas about fulfillment were changing:

> Before the women's movement, we all felt that volunteer work was very fulfilling. You didn't need to be paid for something that you did well and was a needed service. But the women's movement emphasized that if what you did was worthy, then you should be paid for it.... The Junior League is quite different now because forty-five percent of the members in the local league work. They can only do placement at night or on weekends, and if you're a full-time professional person and mother, you don't really have the enthusiasm or the time or the incentive to give the creativity to projects.... The women's movement has really hurt volunteerism.[49]

Women did see that the culture valued paid work, and many demanded a part in this valued public arena. Writing in *Commonweal* in 1963, Jean Holzhauer asserted that women wanted a chance to put their training and abilities to work, not in volunteer work but in paid, professional work: "Volunteer work — civic committees, the P.T.A., the League, the Alumnae Association — is for the youngest mothers, who can do such things part-time, and often from home. The work women want, and desperately need, is, in our society, professional work: something to do that is important enough for someone to pay for, gladly."[50]

At the same time that American culture and women such as Friedan and Holzhauer equated paid work with value, however, religious groups and American culture still equated women's unpaid work with virtue. Persistent ideals of self-sacrifice and domesticity elevated women's private, uncompensated labor. This nettled women who chose to or had to spend their time earning a living. AC married in 1960 and had four children by 1968. With three children under the age of six, she went back to school at night for a graduate degree, then began part-time work. She remarked: "And why did the Church frown on those of us who balanced family and work, but praised women who gave hours of volunteer time outside their families to the Church?"[51] The church's appreciation for women's volunteer work seemed to some hypocritical and self-serving.

A New Ideal: The Career Woman

Meanwhile, in popular culture a new ideal woman emerged — the woman who could "bring home the bacon... fry it up in a pan... and never ever let you forget you're a man, 'cause I'm a woman," as the Enjoli perfume television commercial hymned in the late 1970s. The commercial featured a businesswoman strutting down the street in a suit and high heels, briefcase swinging jauntily; she was sexy, competent, and in control. She could work all day, bring home a paycheck, and, panning to the next scene, whip up dinner with ease, still in high heels. She was professional and competent in a man's world, but could as easily keep the home fires burning. And, this woman was *feminine* — a model for a perfume advertisement. The commercial tried to blend two ideals, the career woman and the domestic woman. It celebrated professional women — as long as they continued to keep home and family together. What the image ignored were the strains on women who tried to "do it all."

The rising numbers of career women and their sleek images in television commercials obscured another reality: the "feminization of poverty."[52] The numbers of female-headed households increased significantly in the 1960s and 1970s. Mother-only families grew between 35 and 40 percent during each of these decades in both white and black populations.[53] According to Census data, whereas in 1960 one of twelve children lived in a female-headed household, by 1983 more than one out of five children lived in such households.[54] Female-headed households accounted for a rising proportion of the poor, despite women's increased work force participation. Social scientist Diana Pearce wrote: "More and more women maintaining households alone are employed, but have not left poverty: they are the new working poor."[55] Debates raged about the causes of the feminization of poverty. Some attributed disparities to systematic discrimination in the workplace, for example, wage inequity and job segregation. Changing family structures, particularly rising rates of divorce, also accounted for increasing rates of female poverty. Some pointed to inadequate welfare systems. While the roots of the feminization of poverty were complex and multifaceted, the trend clearly indicated heightened strains on working women balancing employment with demanding family responsibilities.[56]

At the same time, as the Enjoli commercial implied, women in the 1970s increasingly were pursuing careers. *Working Woman* magazine began its run in 1976. Three years later, *Working Mother* was launched. Both magazines targeted female business professionals. Professionalization brought a marked shift in the meaning of women's work. Some women found community and identity in work that they did not find in domestic life. AB, whose marriage to an alcoholic husband had dissolved in the 1950s, thrived at work until her retirement in 1973. Work and professional leadership took on great significance for her during these years:

> I thought of it as a very important part of my life. It took the place of husband and children, of which I had none. The office family was important to me. And the other people I met, we started a chapter of Women in Construction, and that is something that is all over the country. I was a charter member of the Boston chapter, and later I was president of that. And the Business and Professional Women's club in Boston, I was an officer in that. They were all just wonderful adjuncts or parts of being a businesswoman.[57]

JM (b. 1948) also pursued a professional career. Her father was a doctor, so "medicine was the model of a profession in my family." After graduating from Wellesley in 1970, JM immediately went to study social work and psychology at the University of Michigan, earning a social work degree. After marrying and having two sons, she completed a doctorate in counseling psychology at the University of Texas in the mid-1980s. JM works as a psychologist, specializing in treating severely troubled patients. One of her sisters is a doctor.[58]

Catholicism, Motherhood, and Culture Wars

Women's expanding social and economic roles stood in contrast to women's more limited leadership opportunities in many churches. Some women broke from their religious heritage, frustrated with institutions slow to change. Others, however, sought new leadership within their religious groups and new constructions of their faith. Roman Catholic women established the Women's Ordination Conference in 1975. Led by laywomen and sisters such as Ruth Fitzpatrick and Theresa Kane, WOC protested the exclusion of women from priestly ministry and lobbied — without success — for a change in church teaching. Reform Judaism ordained its first woman rabbi, Sally Preisand, in 1972. Protestant denominations that had long struggled with women's ordination, such as the Episcopalians and the Evangelical Lutheran Church in America, finally allowed women's ordination in the 1970s. Women within denominations that already had accepted ordination also increasingly sought ordination and other paid religious positions (despite complaints of a "stained-glass ceiling"). Between 1972 and 1980, women's enrollment in seminaries increased by 223 percent; men's rate rose by only 31 percent during this time. The proportion of "religious workers" who were female increased at rates higher than in any other field, except for law.[59]

The election of John Paul II to the pontificate in 1978 sealed a sharp contrast between feminist notions of vocation and sexuality and the official teachings of the church, which steadfastly opposed women's ordination, promoted conservative sexual teachings, and encouraged women to embrace a domestic vocation. In 1981, for example, the pope's encyclical on work stated that "the true advancement of women requires that clear recognition be given to the value of their maternal and family role, by comparison with all other public roles and all other professions."[60] The 1988 apostolic letter *Mulieris Dignitatem* ("On the Dignity and Vocation of Women") contained an extended hymn to motherhood and to virginity, two vocations for women, "two particular dimensions of the fulfillment of the female personality."[61]

The American bishops lightened the emphasis on motherhood somewhat. In their 1986 pastoral letter *Economic Justice for All,* the bishops recognized women's roles in the workplace and spoke more uniformly of the responsibilities of and pressures on working *parents* (rather than simply the problem of working *mothers*). Reasserting papal teachings, they did argue that the economy should be structured so that women of young children do not need to take paid employment. Yet in the same paragraph, they spoke of the value of "the work of parents in the home" and called for policies that supported "parents' decisions to care for their own children." The bishops also denounced wage discrimination as "immoral" and supported full and equal employment for women and minorities.[62]

As the New Religious Right grew powerful in the 1980s with the presidency of Ronald Reagan and the rise of groups such as Concerned Women for America (founded in 1979 by Beverly LaHaye), debate about women's roles, family, and religious values became a prominent part of the American culture wars as well.[63] Conservatives and liberals or, as sociologist James Davison Hunter puts it, "orthodox" and "progressives," across religious denominations forged alliances in an effort to define the family and "family values." Conservative Catholics found allies in evangelical Protestants; together they defended the "traditional" family. While women's work roles were not central to this debate (issues such as abortion, homosexuality, and family forms took center stage), the value of domesticity and nineteenth-century ideals of womanhood were contested. Hunter writes: "What is in fact at stake is a certain *idealized* form of the nineteenth-century middle-class family: a male-dominated nuclear family that both sentimentalized childhood and motherhood and, at the same time, celebrated domestic life as a utopian retreat from the harsh realities of industrial society."[64] Hence, as mothers' rates of employment rose, women found themselves in the midst of vociferous public religious debate about the value of the bourgeois family and the more privatized, domestic ideals of womanhood.

By the late 1980s and 1990s, the pope was careful to affirm working women even as he reaffirmed the longstanding Catholic teaching about the complementarity of women's roles and nature. After long descriptions of women's maternal vocation, the 1988 apostolic letter *Mulieris Dignitatem* closed with a brief note of thanks to working women: "Therefore the Church gives thanks for each and every woman ... for women who watch over the human persons in the family ... for women who work professionally, and who at times are burdened by a great social responsibility."[65] In a 1995 letter to women issued in preparation for the United Nations Beijing Conference, Pope John Paul II applauded the humanizing and sensitizing effects of women in the workplace:

> Thank you, women who work! You are present and active in every area of life — social, economic, cultural, artistic and political. In this way you make an indispensable contribution to the growth of a culture which unites reason and feeling, to a model of life ever open to the sense of "mystery," to the establishment of economic and political structures ever more worthy of humanity.[66]

He also identified service as women's most fundamental calling: "in giving themselves to others each day, women fulfill their deepest vocation."[67] *Mulieris Dignitatem* did make the point that every person — man or woman — has a vocation to give of self. Yet it also asserted women's special vocation to service: "The moral and spiritual strength of a woman is joined to her awareness that *God entrusts the human being to her in a special way....* This entrusting concerns women in a special way — precisely by reason of their femininity — and this in a particular way determines their vocation" (italics in original).[68] Thus, church teachings struggled to acknowledge and affirm women's gifts in public work without relinquishing the particular and irreplaceable feminine vocation to motherhood.

Women's growing experience in the work force also continued to raise questions about their leadership — or lack thereof — within the church. The American bishops recognized the need to address such questions, noting in their 1998 statement *From Words to Deeds:* "Growing numbers of educated, talented, and experienced women are changing the face of the Church and society.... We emphasize the need to appoint women to positions that entail substantive responsibility and influence, so that the Church may reap the full benefit of their talents."[69] While the prohibition on women's ordination remained, American Catholic women did attain professional positions on parish and diocesan staff. By the late 1990s, for example, women held approximately one-fourth of top diocesan positions (e.g., chief of staff or chief

financial officer) and 40–50 percent of middle management positions (e.g., director of evangelization or director of religious
education). The percentages of women working in diocesan offices
(46 percent) roughly equaled the percentage of women in the
American labor force as a whole during this same time period.[70]
However, many highly educated women continued to face a gap
between their secular work and the leadership opportunities open
to them within the church. This is a marked change from the pre-
1960s period, when women received educational and professional
opportunities through religious life that were impossible to achieve
along secular paths.

Vocation and the Tradition

While women struggled with the church as they discerned their
own vocations, many nevertheless sought to anchor themselves
in the tradition, to critique it, to contribute to it, and to pass
it on. What follows are glimpses of two women's faith journeys, interwoven with their varied work identities, highlighting
the importance of connections, community, and a living tradition.

Passing on the Faith

Mary Parella singles out the birth of her children as an incredible
spiritual moment, "realizing the amazement and the awesomeness
of the birth of a child, just blowing you away." Born in 1945,
this Catholic woman from a Boston suburb was raised in the pre–
Vatican II era, graduated from Boston College shortly after the
close of the Council, and then went on to marry and have four
children. She taught until her first child was born in 1972, left
the work force for three years, then worked part-time in retail and
insurance until her youngest was in school, at which time she went
full-time as a supervisor for a software company. Parella had not
expected to return to the work force after her children were born.
"My father sent me a retirement card. I had no desire to work,"
says Parella. "I would have loved to stay home." She says that
she decided to take part-time employment to gain extra income
for the family, and that she and her husband (a teacher) always

worked opposite shifts so that they did not need to leave their children with a babysitter. She blended, then, a clear commitment to the domestic vocation with a nontraditional sharing of child-care. Parella made work decisions based on her family needs. Yet so too did her husband, she says. At one point, he took a different job, then went back to teaching in order to be more available to the family. "It was less money... but we chose to take him with a lower paying job and me supplementing it with an income to keep the family life moving together."

Parella's training as a teacher was quite formative. As she notes, although most of her work years carried her into other fields: "I taught in every job I had." The identity of teacher also carried over into her sense of her vocation in the family and her own devotional life. Raised in a strict Catholic environment, Parella continued to feel a strong responsibility to attend Mass and to bring her children to church: "A tremendous amount of spirituality was passed down from my parents. I always felt it's my role as a parent to carry on the tradition of faith-bearing to my children."[71] To be a mother, then, was to be a teacher of faith. Although her husband did not attend church with her, she made a great effort to pass on the faith to her own children and to those in the CCD classes she taught. She recounts her struggle to deal with her teenage children's lack of enthusiasm for religion. "I know for a while I did a number on myself, saying 'I didn't pass it on. It stopped.' But then I realize, I tried to pass it on, and it didn't work. Maybe at some point something comes up in a spiritual nature for these kids at a later point that brings them to religion. But my goal was to give them a basis of a belief." She prays constantly for her children's safety and for the "generations before me, because they were the ones who gave me my faith and that is why my role was to pass it on to the next generation."[72] Parella received the faith from the generations before, and she holds it like a gift, an inheritance, hoping to hand it down.

Seeking Connection to a Legacy

JM, the psychologist who drifted from the church in the late 1960s, returned to the church in the early 1980s after the birth of her sons.

"I never felt antagonistic. It just wasn't there for me. I always sort of felt that it was something I would come back to." She still struggles with aspects of the tradition, particularly as a therapist working with females on issues of sexuality, shame, and self-worth. Her work has given her another lens on the scriptures and tradition. For example, she feels a deep empathy with the woman that Jesus encountered at the well. She imagines this woman who has been married five times — a young girl married off, passed from one man to another, even abused. She is moved by a painting by Italian artist Masaccio depicting Adam and Eve being cast out of Paradise, for it "captures something moving and true about shame and loss." As she works with young girls who cannot eat, she wrestles with the mortification of the body emphasized in some Catholic spiritual writings.

Having returned to the church after more than a decade away, she is committed to the community and a reflective connection to the tradition. Yet she continues to work through what it means to be part of the community when there are many things she does not accept. "Sometimes I feel conflicted about that, and embarrassed. What makes it feel like home to me? And where are the points where you find a place within an institution when there are many things you don't accept?" Connections are extremely important to her, perhaps one reason why she is drawn by the importance of community in the Catholic tradition. The Spirit, she says, is all about connections. "I need a connection," she ways, "to this incredible legacy!"[73]

Summary

By the end of the twentieth century, women had gained access to educational and professional opportunities that previously were quite rare. The "career woman" had become an important cultural ideal — not fully embraced by church teachings but nevertheless pursued by many Catholic women. This new ideal virtually reversed the nineteenth-century ideal of domesticity — raising renewed concern about the family. Women in the late twentieth century were caught in the midst of these cultural debates, cherishing their families but simultaneously seeking money, fulfillment, and identity in their jobs. Women sought to integrate family and work and looked for meaning within the tension between two ideals of womanhood. The debates about women's place and self-realization pushed to the fore questions that are appropriately framed as *vocational* questions. Moreover, increasing time constraints raised issues about how time is valued, about choices and balance and fragmentation. And through it all, women needed ways to pray, models to follow, images of holiness that related to their everyday lives. Imbedded in seemingly secular social and economic developments, then, were deeply spiritual and religious issues.

As one looks back over the last six decades of the twentieth century, one can see the dramatic changes in women's work roles. In 1940, women accounted for about one-quarter of the total U.S. work force. By 1998 women accounted for roughly 46 percent of the total 131.5 million employed persons.[74] Sharply rising numbers of married women and mothers of small children entered the work force. In 1940, about one in four mothers of young children held employment. By the end of the twentieth century, about two-thirds of married women with preschool children worked outside the home.[75] These changes carry profound implications for women's spiritual lives and religious institutions. They call for careful theological reflection and response. In the spirit of those who, like JM, seek a connection to the "incredible legacy" of faith communities, I turn now more fully to this task. I will focus on a select cluster of important theological issues raised by women's changing roles: vocation, identity, and discernment; time; and models of holiness. This is an invitation, really, to begin a theological conversation that must continue beyond this book.

Chapter Three

Friedan and the Fiat

Theological Reflections on Vocation,
Identity, and Discernment

Growing up in New York Catholic schools in the 1950s, the future novelist Mary Gordon knew exactly what a "vocation" was. The nuns in their habits had a vocation. The priest in the parish had a vocation. A vocation was something distinct, something you either had or not, or perhaps lost somewhere along the way. Gordon dreamed of being a nun, until she hit seventh grade and fell in love with Joseph Montalbano. To the young girl all was clear: "I had lost my vocation." That sense of vocation stuck with Gordon into her adult years: "Nowadays when friends ask me what 'vocation' means, I sometimes look at them strangely, as if they'd just asked me to define the word 'bicycle.' 'Vocation' means a call to the religious life."[1]

Gordon is fairly typical of Catholics, who long have associated the word *vocation* with clergy and religious. MK, for example, began working as an information operator at Bell Atlantic in 1941, at the age of twenty-one. Her father had died, and her income was needed to support herself, her mother, and her two younger sisters. This Boston Irish Catholic would remain at the telephone company until her retirement some forty years later. She says that she never thought about her work as a vocation: "It was a job that I enjoyed, but I would never have put the word 'vocation' on it. To me vocation would be priesthood or sisterhood, but I never really thought about vocation in connection with my working life."[2] Most Catholics formed before the Second Vatican Council grew up with this understanding of vocation, but the connotation also lingers for younger Catholics.

On the other hand, one finds beautiful examples of women's vocational claims. Eileen Farrell (b. 1916), raised in the pre–Vatican II era, did not think of her work as a ministry and did not explicitly connect her work with spirituality. Still, she describes a taken-for-granted sense of vocation: "I knew I would be a nurse at five years old.... To me this was my vocation in life, to take care of sick people. I'm quite sure that God meant me to be a nurse. I haven't agonized over it. It was just something that one did."[3] Marian Burkhart, an English teacher and book reviewer, offers a compelling definition of vocation when she describes "that place I am to fill in his [God's] eternal plan that would without me be forever empty." That sense of her own place and God-given identity enables her "to flesh out my feeble praying by offering him what I do well — reading, thinking, conversing, cooking — even bed-making, if we are really considering the quotidian."[4]

Some of the most fundamental questions imbedded in the history of women, work, and religion over the past sixty years are vocational questions. What is woman's "place"? What meaning do women find in the work they do? What gifts do women have, and how can they be developed? What work do women choose? What purposes do women's work serve?[5] The word *vocation* comes from the Latin *vocare,* meaning "to call." A vocation literally means a "calling." The term has deep roots in Jewish and Christian traditions, with quite specific meanings, as will be seen. Broadly understood, questions about the purpose of one's work and life are vocational issues.

Women's shifting roles must inform religious understandings of work and vocation. Indeed, theological understandings of work have changed as the nature of work itself has shifted in different historical and cultural situations. Francis Schüssler Fiorenza points out, for example, that the medieval conception of work took for granted a hierarchical social structure with limited vocational mobility. Work within one's social position had meaning because it contributed to the community in a social order ordained by God. The idea of work as ascetic discipline and calling emerged in the sixteenth, seventeenth, and eighteenth centuries with the development of a middle class. Work required self-control and industry and demonstrated virtue and success.[6] It is important, then, to be attentive to how the social context is influencing theology, to sift out what is positive and faithful from what is harmful and spiritually misguided. It also is important to enable participants' own sense of the meaning of their work to emerge, to inform and critique and be informed by the tradition. One must give attention to different social groupings, including gender and class. Theological appraisals of work based only on the experiences of one group can misconstrue the meaning of work for other groups and allow social bias to unduly influence the theology of work. Thus, it should be noted that my analysis begins a process of reflection that must expand beyond the American situation and must be nuanced to include more in-depth study of class, racial, and ethnic differences. What follows is an exploratory venture.

Hearing Women's Vocational Questions

As church and culture had for so long emphasized the home as women's "place" and her highest calling, women moving into the paid work force (and particularly those choosing to pursue careers) naturally struggled to define themselves and the value of their work. Those vocational questions can be heard with particular intensity in women's debates about feminism, work, family, and faith in the 1960s. These debates offer a glimpse into the kind of vocational questioning that accompanies women's changing economic and social roles. Although each historical and cultural context shapes vocational questions in particular ways, I would argue that women today continue to revisit fundamental questions about their place in the home and outside it, about their desire to develop their gifts, about how to juggle their multiple commitments and identities.

In *The Feminine Mystique* (1963), Betty Friedan stated that American women were in an identity crisis. They had been stripped of the chance to do important work, locked into their roles as "happy" housewives. This was, really, a spiritual crisis. Women were not able to develop their full selves; they perhaps did not even know who they were. For according to Friedan, work was the avenue to self-realization and self-transcendence:

> One sees the human significance of work — not merely as the means of biological survival, but as the giver of self and the transcender of self, as the creator of human identity and human evolution. . . . And work can now be seen as the key to the problem that has no name. The identity crisis of American women began a century ago, as more and more of the work important to the world, more and more of the work that used their human abilities and through which they were able to find self-realization, was taken from them.[7]

Mrs. James Arnold, a Catholic woman from Oregon, did not see it that way. Women would not solve their "identity crisis" by working outside the home. Mrs. Arnold wrote in a 1964 letter to *Commonweal* magazine: "Glassware is glassware — if washed at home or in the laboratory. I would suspect the housewife running naked and screaming through suburbia might also run naked and screaming through the office, laboratory, or factory *if* her frustration is induced by the tedium of her daily existence."[8] In Mrs. Arnold's view, tedium was a feature of human life, not just of women's lives in the home. She spoke out of her own experience. For ten years before her marriage, she had worked as a research librarian. She described herself as a "careerist" who "lived in emotional bankruptcy" during that time of her life. Mrs. Arnold believed that a deeper spiritual issue lay at the root of women's unhappiness.

Fulfillment, and one's deepest sense of identity, rested in the trust that God would make meaning out of one's tedious, everyday activities:

> What is that Catholic woman to make of all this? . . . The Catholic woman will realize, with Caryll Houselander, that " . . . Nothing is complete but His will, and that completes all our seemingly unfinished, interrupted, useless actions on earth." . . . If we are to have a new mystique, both feminine and masculine, let it be a very old one of individual dependence on God. Let these "decisions" be made with the help of the Holy Spirit, acknowledging our dependence and duty to God, through prayer, and, yes, certainly more frequent Communion, and a fervent awareness of God's love for each of us. Fulfillment is not dependent on the *what* (kind of work), but on the *how* (it is done) — for whom, and in what spirit.[9]

Another Catholic woman, Jean Holzhauer, however, feared that Mrs. Arnold's theology would result in passivity and a narrow view of women's place. Holzhauer argued that women have diverse callings and thus need diverse opportunities to respond with their gifts. Dependence on God did not mean that one surrenders choice and responsibility. She dialogued with both Friedan and the Catholic tradition: "Mrs. Friedan's research indicates that the dose is not good for all women. Why should we expect it to be? Not all religious are suited for contemplative life, not all are suited for active duty in the classroom or surgery. The wrong assignment frequently results in conventual disaster. Laywomen, too, need diversification of opportunity; personal talents and requirements survive marriage as they survive other vows."[10] Thus, Holzhauer drew from the familiar Catholic example of vocation — nuns — and found parallels with laywomen's situations. Marriage and motherhood could not be women's only vocational options outside of the convent. Vocation had to correspond to individual gifts, drawing these gifts out into opportunities for service.

To some women the domestic vocation seemed incompatible with a professional life. Mary Freeman described the conflict: "Sex and career pull together for a man, and in some ways for the woman who works to bolster family income. For the woman who works to express herself, the two roles are in full conflict."[11] Seeing that conflict, some women rejected domesticity and remade themselves so as to be successful in the male "public" world. Faced with a perceived decline in her significance and identity in the home, stated Freeman, some women "made a bitter but clean decision to turn in all personal values for the public ones prevailing in a man's world. She ruthlessly amputates all parts of her psyche in the way of her career."[12] Freeman's comments show a kind of spiritual estrangement and loss of identity.[13] Women who looked to the workplace for self-realization ironically had to cut off part of themselves. They could not find themselves either in the "female" home or in the "male" public world. They were caught in between the domestic ideal of womanhood and emerging feminist ideals.

Guilt: An Excursus

Friedan argued that women who sought to escape an exclusively domestic life for self-realization or to contribute in "important" ways to the world ran into guilt at defying convention and religion. The move out of the home was particularly difficult for Catholic women, she wrote, as the feminine mystique was enshrined in church teachings, images of Mary, and programs such as those of the Family Life Bureau.[14] Friedan wrote: "Women of orthodox Catholic or Jewish origin do not easily break through the housewife image; it is enshrined in the canons of their religion, in the assumptions of their own and their husbands' childhoods, and in their church's dogmatic definitions of marriage and motherhood."[15] She cited a Family Life Bureau manual that connected sterility to work outside the home and quoted a Catholic woman who capitulated: "It is more difficult for a Catholic woman to stay emancipated. I have retired. It will be better for everyone concerned if I am just a housewife."[16] The woman had retired from the state board of the League of Woman Voters after pressure from her priest, her husband, and her daughter's school psychiatrist.

There was some truth to Friedan's point about guilt. Regardless of religious background, many women felt guilty as they deviated from the 1950s ideal of the happy housewife. Yet women from traditions such as Catholicism, which strongly advocated women's domestic mission, faced a particularly complex spiritual tension.

In the 1950s, for example, Dolores Huerta became a political activist working for Latino voter registration and community improvement. She knew that domestic life would not fulfill her. Yet embedded in Latino Catholicism, married to her second husband, and then the mother of seven children, she not surprisingly found it difficult to say so: "I knew I wasn't comfortable in a wife's role, but I wasn't clearly facing the issue. I hedged, I made excuses, I didn't come out and tell my husband that I cared more about helping other people than cleaning our house and doing my hair."[17] Huerta was coming up against what Friedan called the "problem with no name," a problem that undoubtedly contributed to the failure of Huerta's marriage. She divorced in 1961.

She went on to build the United Farm Worker movement with Cesar Chavez.

In 1963, Jean Holzhauer described the intense guilt and self-criticism experienced by Catholic women who desired work — or even a vocation — outside the home:

> Catholic women are bewildered. The majority, to be on the safe side, stick to the interpretations of permissible "vocations," and when intelligent American Catholic women are discontented with being the "heart" of the home to a point just this side of suicide, they blame themselves and their sinful natures. It is amazing how many Catholic women castigate themselves for "not being a really good wife and mother," when all they really want is a chance to put their training and ability to work.[18]

This vocational questioning and guilt likely afflicted most sharply educated middle- and upper-class women, who had the greatest choice about working outside the home, who less easily could cite economic need as their rationale for wage work, and who more likely found self-development and creativity in their jobs. At the same time, working-class women from cultures that strongly endorsed women's domestic roles, such as Dolores Huerta, also struggled.

Work and Self-Realization

The debates of Catholic women about Betty Friedan and feminism poignantly reveal their vocational dilemmas — the intricate attempts to bridge religious tradition with new roles and opportunities or to hold on to tradition in the face of change that looks misguided. Because most religious teaching about women's vocations focused either on vowed religious life or on women's maternal nature, women often lacked language to speak about their vocation outside the home and convent. They struggled to put their desires for meaningful nondomestic work within a theological framework.

In reality, Friedan made a kind of spiritual argument for women's work outside the home. Such work was meaningful, she wrote, because it realized women's true selves and in the process gave women self-transcendence. Work used and developed human talents. Work provided a deep identity that went beyond finite existence. Through work, women contributed to the world in ways that carried on. They were producers. They helped to shape the world. On the other hand: "Housewives who live according to the feminine mystique do not have a personal purpose stretching into the future. But without such a purpose to evoke their full abilities, they cannot grow to self-realization."[19] Ironically, of course, Friedan discounted reproduction as a path of self-transcendence. Yet what is important at this juncture is her argument that work contributes to women's self-realization and self-transcendence.

Those arguments are actually not far from Catholic teaching on work. In his 1961 encyclical *Mater et Magistra,* Pope John XXIII wrote: "That a man [sic] should develop and perfect himself through his daily work — which in most cases is of a temporal character — is perfectly in keeping with the plan of divine Providence."[20] John Paul II too emphasized the subjective meaning of work. Work has meaning finally because the worker is a person, "capable of deciding about himself [sic] and with a tendency to self-realization."[21] Self-realization need not mean selfishness. Rather, human beings have a fundamental, created identity. God calls them to realize the fullness of those created selves. Work is one important human activity that, while it also can demean, has the power to realize and even perfect the self.[22] The American Catholic bishops similarly asserted the moral and spiritual import of work as a means of self-realization: "All work has a threefold moral significance. First, it is a principal way that people exercise the distinctive human capacity for self-expression and self-realization."[23] That work should involve self-realization, then, is a point shared by Friedan and Catholic teaching. The differences lie in questions about the true nature of the female self and that which constitutes "self-realization" for women.

For John Paul II, domestic labor realizes women's selves in a fundamental way. It is not the only vocation for women, of course; the church long has asserted the greater perfection of the vocation to virginity. Yet motherhood is a highly regarded calling built into women's created nature, leading to self-discovery and self-realization: "Motherhood implies from the beginning a special openness to the new person: and this is precisely the woman's 'part.' In this openness, in conceiving and giving birth to a child, the woman 'discovers herself through a sincere gift of self.' "[24] Women are physically and psychologically oriented to motherhood. They thus have particular spiritual gifts, a "special communion with the mystery of life" and a greater capacity than do men of "paying attention *to another person*" (italics in original).[25] Mothering work, then, in the church's perspective, is deeply fulfilling and self-transcending.

Friedan, on the other hand, warns that women's role in biological reproduction and child-rearing can become a "forfeiture" of the self. Under the power of the "feminine mystique," women seek to live through their children, become more and more "infantile" themselves, and finally almost "destroy" their children in the process. They do not perceive a choice beyond motherhood.[26] Friedan, by no means the most radical of feminists,[27] represented an important countervoice for religious women debating the meaning of their changing work roles.

In addressing questions raised by these voices and countervoices, it is important to consider religious women's own reflections on their work. Listen to this plea by Frances Ayvish, published in *U.S. Catholic* in 1975:

> The parable of the talents states clearly that a Christian has a duty to develop the talents God has given to him *or her*....
>
> If we believe in the progressive unfolding of the kingdom of God, in the forward movement of history, then it seems to me we must believe that the movement to free women to use all their talents is part of God's plan....
>
> Balancing both a career and a family is like walking a tightrope. ...Why then struggle at all?
>
> Because for some of us, not to use our talents would amount to a kind of death. Secondly, there is tremendous need for Christian witness in the world. It is not necessary actually to preach Christian values, but one must be a witness to them where they need application today — in the working world. For many women, remaining at home and tending to families, church, and neighbors is a vital and rewarding life. But there is also a great need to have Christian

women at the heart of the decision-making process, or else we shall find ourselves living in an environment hostile to Christian values and to the very idea of the family, which is at the center of a woman's concerns.[28]

Ayvish, drawing on the parable of the talents (Matt 25:14–30), argued that God commands women to develop the gifts given to them. It is a matter of "self-realization," but more strongly a question of life or death. The development of talents brings life to the self; the alternative, not using one's talents, brings a kind of death. Moreover, the individual's use of gifts benefits society and participates in God's plan. Ayvish still portrays the family as women's central concern. Yet some women can best serve the family by influencing social and economic structures that ultimately shape culture and policy.

Ayvish illustrates the position of many women who felt torn between two calls — family and work outside the home. To Ayvish, these were not actually opposing vocations; they were complementary and mutually enriching. Women had gifts that called for development outside of domestic life; at the same time, such vocations could bolster — rather than disrupt — familial well-being. God called, even commanded, women to use their gifts both within and outside of the home.

In my view, the domestic vocation must be safeguarded and cherished, but so too can one affirm other forms of work. The conflict between these two vocations should not concern women's spirituality, nature, or virtue, all of which are compatible with various private and public ventures. Women's socialization, their experience of motherhood, and, yes, even their nature may well give many women certain insights into humanity and the rhythm, mystery, and sacrality of life. To be sure, society would not want to lose such gifts. Yet there also are important theological reasons why women should be encouraged to develop their various gifts in public work outside the home. For one thing, such work can contribute to the common good, as can domestic labor. Society needs its members to contribute to the whole as best they each can. Moreover, certain talents do not find development in the work of child-rearing. Women's gifts must be identified in each individual, rather than being determined a priori. Gifts point in vocational directions. In fact, a person's gifts can correspond with a range of vocations, each of which might be a path of humanization and self-realization. One cannot walk down all of those paths, and so the range of vocations must be weighed in light of the deep passions of the individual, the potential for service in a given context, and practical circumstances.

The real conflict comes with the needs of children. Because public policy and the structures of the workplace have not adequately responded to women's increased labor force participation, parents face inflexible work demands and inadequate childcare options. Women's increasing work outside the home, then, does carry moral and spiritual implications, for it affects children's well-being. Yet women should not bear the sole responsibility for these moral and spiritual stakes. The church must evaluate the justice of workplace structures and gender relations within the home. It must seek to create as much space as possible for both the "self-realization" of adults who feel called to work outside the home, and the protection and education of children. There always will be limitations and conflicts. Yet religious institutions need to state the ideals and work toward them. The structures of work and childcare are more human when they allow male and female parents the opportunity to develop their gifts and talents — and to serve society — both within the home (a sphere of labor still undervalued for men) and outside the home.

Religious Language

While it is important to look at women's changing work roles though the prism of vocation, it must be emphasized that Catholic women generally do not resonate with that term. In part this is an issue of language; laity often describe their work (and their lives) without using the traditional religious terminology more common in church documents and academic works of theology. There still may be points of deep resonance between the lay sense and traditional theological concepts. For example, Joyce Harvey believes that God gave her gifts that enabled her to be a social worker:

I'm sure that part of my being a social worker has to do with the gifts I have from God. Even on this job [state division of medical assistance] when I don't normally do social work, I've ended up talking to people who have problems and sometimes probably ended up bringing God into the conversation, or at least brought my God-attitude into the conversation . . . being good to people and having respect for self. I definitely believe that my religious attitude, direction, influences what I do at work.[29]

It never occurred to Harvey to consider her work a vocation, but perhaps a "gift from God."[30]

In fact, Harvey's understanding of her work does resonate with the meaning of *vocation*. She looks to the talents that she has and sees them as gifts from God. As she uses them in service, she comes to understand her work itself as a divine gift. One could say that a vocation is just this kind of gift, to which a person responds and into which she grows. As the American bishops wrote in their reflection "Called and Gifted for the Third Millennium": "The laity's call to holiness is a gift from the Holy Spirit."[31] The church needs to listen for women's own sense of having a purpose, being gifted, being drawn, or simply doing a good job with faith in something higher. Women — like laity in general — may not use traditional theological terminology. They still offer important insights about what it means to struggle with vocational questions in a changing context. At the same time, concepts such as *vocation* may help women to reflect more deeply on their work and their lives. Religious terminology should not be jettisoned but can be gently introduced as a tool for reflection, offering language where people may not have words.

Laity and Secular Work: Vocation?

Part of the discomfort with religious language such as *vocation* is a substantive problem. As already mentioned, Catholics long have associated *vocation* with vowed, celibate ministry. Many find it strange to link their secular jobs with the word *vocation*. The church reinforces this idea even today; "prayers for vocations" at Mass usually request men for the priesthood, not lawyers or secretaries. It is true that the Second Vatican Council emphasized the calling of the whole People of God. Yet the conciliar message still needs to be heard, assimilated, and believed by the laity. Mrs. Arnold had a point when she noted the importance of finding grace in the mundane. The complex question that laity still face is how the various, seemingly secular, mundane spheres of their lives — including their jobs — relate to God. This question becomes particularly relevant to women as they expand rapidly into jobs beyond the service professions traditionally linked to women's piety and virtue.

The Christian tradition holds resources to counterbalance a separation of faith from secular work. Protestant reformer Martin Luther (1483–1546), for example, emphasized the value of mundane tasks. He glowingly described a man changing his baby's diaper, an "insignificant and despised" task that nevertheless is pleasing to God when done in faith. Faith looks upon

> all these insignificant, distasteful, and despised duties in the Spirit, and is aware that they are all adorned with divine approval as with the costliest gold and jewels. It says, "O God, because I am certain that thou has created me as a man and hast from my body begotten this child, I also know for a certainty that it meets with thy perfect pleasure. I confess to thee that I am not worthy to rock the little babe or wash its diapers.... O how gladly I will do so, though the duties should be even more insignificant and despised. Neither frost nor heat, neither drudgery nor labor, will distress or dissuade me, for I am certain that it is thus pleasing in thy sight."[32]

In Luther's view, the task itself does not matter; faith in the God who gives the vocation and trust in God's will does. "God, with all his angels and creatures, is smiling — not because that father is washing diapers, but because he is doing so in Christian faith. Those who sneer at him and see only the task but not the faith are ridiculing God."[33] Secular work does not save, but is part of one's earthly vocation, done in faith and in service to the neighbor.[34] Indeed, this idea of a worldly calling, particularly as it developed within the Calvinist branch of the Reformation, may have unintentionally propelled the development of the capitalist economy, as sociologist Max Weber famously argued.[35]

Born about twenty years after Luther's death, the Roman Catholic bishop Francis de Sales also counseled laity to embrace their secular vocations. In numerous letters to lay women and men, de Sales set out to persuade laity that they could be devout in the world. Devotion was not a rigid program of piety suitable only for monks and priests, but rather devotion was "simply true love of God," love enflamed, seeking ardently to do God's will.[36] Devotion could be exercised in a variety of vocations and should be adapted to people's different circumstances and temperaments:

> When he created things God commanded plants to bring forth their fruits, each one according to its kind, and in like manner he commands Christians, the living plants of his Church, to bring forth the fruits of devotion, each according to his position and vocation. Devotion must be exercised in different ways by the gentleman, the worker, the servant, the prince, the widow, the young girl, and the married woman. Not only is this true, but the practice of devotion must also be adapted to the strength, activities, and duties of each particular person.[37]

Luther and de Sales, then, both made important moves to democratize notions of vocation. All could claim a vocation, not just the monks and clerics of the church. They rejected a heroic sanctity, recognizing instead the meaning and holiness possible in every person's life, including the day-to-day tasks of work in the family and outside the home. The idea of lay vocation gained some force in the twentieth century, when lay movements in the pre–Vatican II decades claimed their apostolates and the Second Vatican Council asserted the holiness of lay work.[38] Catholic teaching in the latter part of the twentieth century has done much to correct the tradition's neglect of the lay vocation, particularly through the documents of the Second Vatican Council. The Council freely referred to lay work as a vocation and made clear that all were called to holiness: "It is therefore quite clear that all Christians in any state or walk of life are called to the fullness of Christian life and to the perfection of love, and by this holiness a more human manner of life is fostered also in earthly society."[39] Faith obliges Christians to carry out "earthly responsibilities," according to the *vocation* of each one."[40] Conciliar documents refer to marriage and family life as a vocation, a "lofty calling" from God.[41] In a beautiful image drawn from the kitchen, the Council specifically affirmed the religious worth of public work in the secular world: "The characteristic of the lay state being a life led in the midst of the world and of secular affairs, laymen are called by God to make of their apostolate, through the vigor of their Christian spirit, a leaven in the world."[42] The secular vocation, then, has the power to lift up society, as yeast, mixed invisibly through dough, raises bread.

These understandings of lay vocation and faith can powerfully affirm the meaning of even seemingly insignificant tasks at secular jobs. They provide an important corrective for laity who associate the term *vocation* only with vowed religious life — inviting them to look again at the meaning of their work in the world. And yet they do not adequately respond to the lay dilemma, raised anew by women in the work force. Are all jobs religiously relevant? Are all vocations?

It is easier to see the helping professions such as teaching, social work, and nursing as vocations. They involve direct human contact and service. They also, incidentally, have been associated with women's work. One recalls the 1950s Grail Council on Service Careers, which encouraged women to enter professions such as teaching and nursing. Even as recently as 1995, Pope John Paul II described service as woman's vocation: "For in giving themselves to others each day, women fulfill their deepest vocation."[43] Women may find it particularly difficult to see their secular jobs as "spiritual," much less as a vocation, given the traditional emphasis on women's place in the home and in service jobs. Moreover, many jobs simply perform a necessary function; they have little intrinsic meaning or creativity. A female mail sorter stated pointblank: "No, there's nothing that interesting about my job that relates to my religion."[44]

Material Pursuits and Spirituality: Tensions Resurface

For women who work in financial fields, questions about spirituality and work take on another level of complexity. The financial indexer who sits at her computer all day alone finds it difficult to relate her job to her faith. Kathy Petersen Cecala explains:

> I think of teachers, doctors, nurses, social workers — people whose workaday lives involve some worthy human contact. There is some potential in those occupations, I think, for affecting the lives of others in a positive way, winning grace through the practical application of the commandment of love. But behind my computer, as an indexer for the nation's foremost business newspaper, there seems little opportunity for my faith to play any sort of role in my work, which deals primarily with the world of money: the intricacies of corporate finance and international exchange rates.[45]

For Cecala, the distance between her faith and her work stems from a lack of direct human service, weak workplace community (note the hint of isolation as she sits behind her computer all day), and a perceived gap between money and spirituality. Indeed, many women and men would not equate a job that focuses on wealth accumulation as a vocation. One lay Catholic man, a financial consultant, stated: "I don't think of my job as a vocation. It's just a job. I work in the financial world. I don't see my job as helping people in a spiritual way. I see myself helping people safeguard their wealth. I don't see my job as an avenue for exercising my faith; I try to find other avenues."[46] As women increasingly break into the business world, they face this same dilemma. I would argue that the spiritual tension is even more complex for women, who long have been portrayed as the humanizing force protecting against materialism.

This situation should raise questions that too frequently religious groups sweep under the rug or dismiss with simplistic sermons, questions about how Christians should regard wealth and the use of material goods.[47] Women often have been accused of materialism for taking jobs outside the home. Questions about the worthiness of secular work, then, take on particularly tangled dimensions for women. Cecala continues: "And I am, to be truthful, attracted by it all.... There's something seductive, compelling about the great game of Wall Street.... And yet, probably because of my strict Catholic upbringing, it's a fascination I feel guilty about, like a sexual perversion of some sort, something forbidden and ultimately wrong. I worry that my growing fascination with money and business — and accompanying sense of materialism — is impeding my spiritual growth."[48]

The spiritual enervation and human deprivation that materialism engenders should be a concern. Classic spiritual teachings constantly sound warnings about the effects of attachment to material goods (hence, the vows of poverty taken by religious). There is much to be learned here. On the other hand, people who have responsibility for dependents cannot and should not live like monks. They have a responsibility to provide for the material needs and long-term human development of those entrusted to them, with an eye not only for the present but also for the future. Theirs is the task of "stewardship." Theirs is a different vocation, one that necessarily involves concern for money and goods. The fine line, then, is between responsible "stewardship" and irresponsible consumption, between appropriate care of intimates and disregard for the wider community. It is the difference between wise use of money and attachment to it. This is a very difficult, even "seductive," line to tread. Spiritually, it may be particularly problematic for women, who have not been trained to see their material pursuits as part of a womanly vocation and holy call. The moral tension between stewardship and materialism should remain a concern; the particular religious criticisms of working women's "materialism" are inappropriately directed at one gender.

Moral Ambiguity of Work

Women in professions outside the financial sector also express concern about the moral ambiguity of their work. The ethical grayness of secular jobs contributes to lay hesitation about the concept of *vocation*. An engineer, Nancy Haegel wrote: "I do live, though, with a certain ambiguity about the work. Scientists and engineers can look with both pride and dismay at the results of their handiwork, and for many of us in academic research, the pride and dismay are hopelessly intertwined." Haegel did have moments when she felt her job turn into a calling. Those moments came when she taught (teaching, incidentally, being a traditionally female helping profession), when she could share exhilarating moments of breakthrough discovery with her students: "I love the 'Eureka' moments, seeing students' eyes light up . . . when they make a discovery of their own. . . . For me, sharing those moments with students transforms work and career into service and vocation. On the good days, it's enough."[49]

Women holding jobs outside of the "helping professions" show the uneasy fit between traditional notions of spirituality and secular work. Most jobs have some morally ambiguous elements. How one's work will be used often cannot be predicted. Well-intentioned endeavors can yield unforeseen negative consequences. One works within large systems and structures over which one has very little control. (Many of these concerns apply too in religious work and helping professions, although the stated purpose of such jobs may be more clearly laudable.)

I would propose a middle road between heroic sanctity (vocations are elite paths distinct from everyday work) and a blanket spiritualization of all work. Secular jobs can be part of a person's human vocation; one even can encourage laity to "redeem" their work (to use the phrase of the YCW) and in small, invisible ways, like yeast dissolved into bread dough, to humanize their corner of the world. Yet the moral and religious ambiguities of secular work demand careful examination. While secular work is necessary and can be religiously meaningful, work also can participate in ethically questionable purposes. The word *vocation* should be used critically so as not to elevate that which may have little to do with God's purposes. The dissonance between the idea of vocation and particular jobs may actually be good, for it reminds workers that no particular job can fulfill the entirety of God's purposes for one's life. It may be more helpful to think about vocational *moments* within one's job.

Work and Suffering

The ambiguity of work stems partly from the fact that work can produce intended or unintended suffering. Suffering can result from how one's work is used (e.g., human injury, environmental harm); this was Nancy Haegel's concern. Work conditions them-selves also produce human suffering, as the following example shows. Laura I. entered the United States from Mexico, her home country, in 1985 at the age of about twenty. With three young chil-dren to support, she earned a living picking berries and cucumbers and working in the canneries in Oregon's Willamette Valley area. She recalled: "It is very hard work. By the time it was ten o'clock in the morning I would just raise my eyes and say, 'God, just give me the strength to finish this row, to get to the end, and make a little bit more money.'...I was struggling to survive. Eighteen to twenty dollars a day to buy diapers, milk...to put food on the table for me and my children."[50]

To call Laura I.'s job a "vocation" can sanctify and romanticize a demeaning situation. This kind of religious gloss on demeaning work encourages people to accept poor conditions. Karl Marx, of course, powerfully raised this issue during the industrialization of the nineteenth century. As women move increasingly into the mod-ern workplace, many working for unequal wages and few benefits, one must raise the question anew.

The Judeo-Christian tradition long has acknowledged that suf-fering is a dimension of work for both women and men in our fallen world. Genesis 3 describes this suffering as a punishment from God. Eve would endure pain in her childbearing labor, while Adam would toil to find sustenance from the earth:

> To the woman he said,
> "I will greatly increase your pangs in childbearing;
> in pain you shall bring forth children...."
> And to the man he said,
> "...cursed is the ground because of you;
> in toil you shall eat of it all the days of your life;
> thorns and thistles it shall bring forth for you;
> and you shall eat the plants of the field.
> By the sweat of your face
> you shall eat bread
> until you return to the ground." (Gen 3:16–19)

In other words, human pride brought pain in procreation and production. Overreaching human capabilities, idolizing humanity, distorts the original goodness of human creative action. The biblical text unfortunately casts this suffering as a rather vindictive divine punishment, yet it still expresses a vital truth about the human vocation. The human being is called to work, to cooperate with God's creativity. Work thus signals the human relationship with the divine; it is a kind of covenantal sign. Work should be a means of respectfully discovering, enjoying, and stewarding God's good creation. Yet sin infiltrates the structures of work and individual actions, distorting work's good purposes. Work entails suffering. As many women confirm, work is no unmitigated joy, nor should one expect it to be.

Part of the suffering of work stems from injustices and human neglect built into the structures of the modern workplace. Religious groups too often have glossed over these structural injustices. Equating work with vocation can be dangerous when it sanctifies human structures, bureaucracies, and abuses of power. This is the critique that Joan Martin brings to Protestant understandings of vocation in her study of slave women in the antebellum period. Martin takes issue with the Lutheran and Calvinistic notions of vocation that became dominant in the Protestant traditions: "By placing an unambiguously positive notion on work as calling and vocation, as a theological belief with ethical consequences for obedience and duty without criticizing the social relations of the changing political economy, the tradition was left with no theological or moral recourse for challenging exploitative work."[51] Evaluating Catholic theologies of work, Francis Schüssler Fiorenza makes a similar point: "An abstract theology of work can be put to ideological use or used to satisfy ideological needs. Theological affirmations of the positive meaningful nature of work can serve to minimize the *de facto* negative qualities of work with its dehumanizing fragmentation."[52] At the same time, one witnesses to an important truth when one asserts the goodness of work as a divine gift and calling. This witness stands in constant contrast to oppressive realities.[53] As Schüssler Fiorenza continues: "Yet this very theological affirmation of the positive meaning of work can also serve as an ideal which judges this present fragmentation. It can be the symbolic and conceptual force behind a social critique."[54]

Luther and de Sales took for granted the social and economic order of their day, and their notions of vocation reinforced that order. A twentieth-century lay leader such as Dorothy Day (cofounder of the Catholic Worker) addressed questions of work and vocation from a far more critical standpoint. Day sharply criticized what she saw as the dehumanizing effects of modern industrial capitalism. From her support of strikers in the labor disputes of the 1930s to her arrest with migrant worker supporters in the 1970s, Day stood for the "the fundamental truth that men should not be treated as chattels, but as human beings, as 'temples of the Holy Ghost.' When Christ took on our human nature, when He became man, he dignified and ennobled human nature."[55]

Just work does not reduce persons to means or tools. One might heed the warning of textile worker Sarah Bagley, who witnessed the dehumanizing effects of industrialization in the nineteenth century. Bagley stood with all those who "are not willing to see our sex made into living machines to do the bidding of the incorporated aristocrats and reduced to a sum for their bodily services hardly sufficient to keep body and soul together."[56] While work may well entail toil, God does not call people to dehumanizing work. This kind of critical perspective on vocation is essential.

Overidentifying with Work

Necessary too is a strong understanding of identity and human personhood that is more fundamental than any job. For women like Laura I., it is vital to know who and whose one is, so as to stand over against the dehumanizing aspects of work. For middle- and upper-class women too, identity can be a deep spiritual concern. One recalls that Friedan referred to "the identity crisis of American women," which she said began as women were deprived of important work. Friedan called work the "creator of human identity," "the giver of self and the transcender of self," and a means of "self-realization."[57] Such thinking does respect the enormous capacity of work to shape the self. Yet it also gives work a dangerous power to destroy identity. As women move into new economic roles, they face important questions of identity.

To completely equate work (or worse, any particular job) with one's human vocation can lead to spiritual crisis. Work gains too much power as a source of fulfillment and self-understanding. A particular problem results when workers lose their jobs, retire, or step out of the workplace to take care of children. They often feel a vacuum of meaning and a sense that they are failures or somehow not as valuable as they were in the workplace. Work can be a vital part of one's vocation, but it is not the whole.

In the productive mentality that dominates industrialized societies, many people too quickly rely on their external works to prove who they are. As accomplishments build, the self may diminish, too closely identified with exterior expectations and too little nourished in its own right. When failures come, the self has little ground upon which to stand. This is not a plight specific to women, but it is one that women increasingly are encountering as they advance in the workplace. While the idea of vocation affirms the religious significance of work, an affirmation needed by many women, vocation also can be misused. One can misapply the term *vocation,* giving workaholism or insecurity or simple ambition a religious rationale and making it more difficult for women to affirm other aspects of their lives. Work must be kept in perspective. One does well to recall the Reformed caution about works righteousness, which manifests itself today in a secular guise.

A theology of vocation responsive to women's changing work roles, then, must carefully distinguish sources of personal identity. Too often, work becomes the source or even the whole of who a person is and what she is worth. The external expectations of the employing system dictate how people act and, more seriously, the kind of people they should become. It sets the standards of "success." The problem is not just that, for example, women in competitive work environments become more competitive. The problem is that competition may define them, shape their views of themselves and others. The external structures get internalized and occasionally sanctified. Similarly, women who are treated harshly and denied dignity at work may internalize that treatment. Even women who understand their primary work as motherhood can overidentify themselves with their work. This leads to emptiness and confusion when children leave home or when mothering work does not fulfill as expected. Vocation does not mean that one *is* one's work.

Vocation, on the other hand, always relates work to an ultimate source of being, God. One's identity comes most fundamentally from God, who is known as Creator and source of all life, through which all "live and move and have their being" (Acts 17:28). What people do at work can participate in God's creative purposes, but work activities never constitute one's being in God's eyes. Here one does well to recall John Paul II's insistence on the priority of the subjective over the objective meaning of work. As he wrote in his 1981 encyclical "On Human Work," work has value primarily because of the personhood of the worker rather than the material outcome of the work: "The basis for determining the value of human work is not primarily the kind of work being done, but the fact that the one who is doing it is a person. The sources of the dignity of work are to be sought primarily in the subjective dimension, not in the objective one."[58] The person's identity exists prior to work and infuses work with meaning. This theological perspective also may help to correct the undervaluation of women's unpaid labor in the home and community. Value need not be equated with market value.

Nor does one lose the tension between divine ways of being and the demands of work life. A vocational person may compete, but she has some framework to keep the competition from unduly shaping her worldview. A woman who must work under poor conditions may not be able to quit or overthrow the system. Yet she gains perspective on her work situation rather than internalizing it. If vocation means that one is called by God, then responding with love and responsibility to that call is the ultimate measure of success. Work can cause pain and joy, moral confusion and moral development, but it does not threaten one's fundamental identity and relationship with God.

Some women do find a new sense of worth and humanity through their work. For example, one married woman who labored in support of the United Auto Workers in the 1930s remarked: "I found a common understanding and unselfishness I'd never known in my life. I'm living for the first time with a definite goal. I want a decent living for not only my family but for everyone. Just being a woman isn't enough anymore. I want to be a human being."[59] Work can give women purpose and a fuller sense of who they are. Work can help women to discover and develop talents that they never knew they had. Work can reveal dimensions of one's identity that otherwise might go unnoticed. For some women, work provides a community that nurtures a deep sense of self.

However, if self-understanding is too dependent on one's job and others' estimations, then identity has a tenuous foundation. Workplace failures and disappointments take away from the self. One's identity becomes dependent on institutions and bureaucracies that often fail, manipulate, or overlook individual needs. If the workplace environment undermines dignity, women workers need tools to resist and to sustain a conviction that they count, that they are worth something. An identity grounded in one's worth as a being created and loved by God goes far deeper than any work experience. Work then becomes an expression and development of identity and a means of sustaining life and families, but not the entirety of who one is.

Vocation: Reconsidering the Concept

Work is best understood as part of the human vocation — not the whole of it, nor irrelevant to it. Work is one dimension of a fuller human vocation and fundamental identity. One must resist using the idea of vocation to legitimate work and workplace structures that demean the human being or to dictate to women a narrow range of acceptable roles. Because human beings are created with diverse gifts, they flourish most fully when they can choose responsibly among multiple works those that enable their particular talents to develop and serve the common good. Thus, I propose a critical understanding of *vocation* that emphasizes created identity, human dignity, and responsible discernment.

Put simply, the word *vocation* refers to God's purposes for human life. God creates the human being in the divine image (Gen 1:27). This is the fundamental human identity; this is who we are. God calls this created being to its fulfillment, to abundant life, to happiness, to service. This is the human vocation. How one defines the end toward which God draws the human being depends on one's fundamental theological beliefs and reflects different theological emphases. Paul's Letter to the Galatians states: "You were called to freedom, brothers and sisters" (Gal 5:13). Ignatius of Loyola (1491–1556) writes in the *Spiritual Exercises:* "Human beings are created to praise, reverence, and serve God our Lord, and by this means to save their souls."[60] Thomas Aquinas (1225–74) describes the end of the human being in terms of perfection or divinization: "The last end of all things is to become like God."[61] Individuals and communities will articulate the ends or purposes of their lives in different ways; what is important is some implicit or explicit understanding of why they are here. In the broadest sense, God's purposes for human life constitute vocation.

Human beings then respond to this general vocation in particular situations. Scriptures describe numerous instances of God calling individuals for specific tasks. The prophet Isaiah says, "The Lord called me before I was born, while I was in my mother's womb he named me" (Isa 49:1). One sees here the integral relationship between identity and vocation. Yahweh names the prophet whom he calls to bring Israel back. In each particular time and place, God calls individuals and peoples to offer their labor and talents in service. Most people may not be called as directly or as specifically as was Isaiah, yet each person can choose to respond in a range of ways within her or his context. To respond to that call is part of the process of claiming one's identity. One hears one's name spoken by God; vocation is a response to who one is, in the totality of one's life.

Christian theology teaches that baptism offers sacramental grace to move a person, guided by the Holy Spirit, in a path of Christian discipleship within the community of the church. Human beings must continually discern God's purposes for their lives, seeking wisdom and guidance in the scriptures, in prayer, in religious tradition, reason, community, and conscience. This is the human task of discernment. Hence, vocation, identity, and discernment are intricately connected. Human beings recall and decide who they are as they name that to which they are called.

The Practice of Discernment

As social change widens choice for women, women need to grow in the practice of discernment. They face deep choices about how they use their time, the location of their primary mission, expanding career opportunities, diverse family configurations, religious options, and social commitments. They have various — and often competing — vocational pulls. They encounter ethical and spiritual questions about how to spend their time, how to act in the workplace, how to take care of their children. They face questions such as: Should I take this job? How should I care for my children while I am at work? How should I respond to unethical pressures at work? Should I take on a time commitment to my children's school, to the local parish, to a political organization? Discernment is a process of choosing in accord with the divine will for one's life. It is a deeply personal practice. At the same time, one discerns best with the support of a community and in prayerful conversation with scriptures and traditional wisdom. Along with a revived understanding of lay vocation, religious groups need ways to guide women in discernment.

Discernment is the process whereby one prayerfully seeks to become more free from distorting perspectives and thus more able to glimpse what is good, to glimpse the will of God: "Do not be conformed to this world, but be transformed by the renewing of your minds, so that you may discern what is the will of God — what is good and acceptable and perfect" (Rom 12:2). Discernment, then, is a countercultural practice, calling for perspective beyond the particularities of our circumstance and culture. As Frederick Buechner writes: "There are all different kinds of voices calling you to all different kinds of work, and the problem is to find out which is the voice of God rather than of Society,

say, or the Superego, or Self-Interest." In discerning one's vocation, one needs to look within to one's gifts and desires and
outward to the needs of the world. "The place God calls you to is
the place where your deep gladness and the world's deep hunger
meet."[62]

Discernment implies the ability to see to the heart of things. The
discerning person has wisdom, perception to distinguish between
the Spirit of God and false prophets (1 John 4:1). Discernment
is a process of transformation; God gives wisdom and revelation
"as one comes to know him, so that, with the eyes of your heart
enlightened, you may know what is the hope to which he has
called you" (Eph 1:17–18). Thus, discernment is a fruit of growing intimacy with God. It is a gift of God. As the person comes
to know the divine, she sees more clearly the life into which God
beckons her. Discernment must be tentative and humble, respecting the divine Mystery and the human being's limited vision. Still,
as scripture notes, there are pointers to indicate whether one is
looking in the right direction. The fruits of the Spirit (love, joy,
peace, patience, kindness, generosity, faithfulness, gentleness, and
self-control) offer testimony to the rightness of one's discernment
(Gal 5:22–6:5).

Scriptures also describe discernment as an active human process.
It is a "testing," a way to sift out good from bad. All must test
their own work (Gal 6:4). One should "test everything, hold fast to
what is good" (1 Thess 5:21). Here discernment is a way of looking deeply into one's life, choosing the good, clinging to the good.
Discernment, then, presumes moral choice. Human beings are created with freedom. Although weakened by the fall, they retain free
will. They can and must make choices throughout life. When con-
fronted with choices, the discerning person seeks to act in accord
with the divine will, with good, with justice. In Ignatian terms, one
judges all things in light of the purpose for which we have been
created, to love and serve God. To discern, then, involves some
judgment about the divine will and the end of human life. Discernment is not a technique, but rather a theologically loaded spiritual
practice, sharpened by prayer, scripture study, and engagement
with a faith community.

Choosing a Path

As women gain options in education, employment, and family commitments, they need to make vital decisions about their lives. Women's debates about vocation show how they can struggle with this choice. In 1964 Jean Holzhauer wrote:

> Mrs. Arnold is quite right to insist on acknowledgment of dependence on God in making decisions. For the believer it is the only possible position. It does not, however, preclude choice of individual means of sanctification or of work. Indeed, it requires such choice, to be made in accord with conscience and abilities, not necessarily in accord with what other people say.[63]

Holzhauer argued, then, that discernment of one's calling is a deeply personal task that involves moral responsibility and awareness of one's gifts. External expectations are secondary. She implicitly put cultural and religious authority at a distance, prioritizing individual conscience and choice in the discernment process.

The debate between Holzhauer and Arnold continued, for example, as they wrestled in particular with the contemporary meaning of Mary's "fiat." The "fiat" was essentially Mary's "YES" to God; she would bear Jesus, the Christ.[64] Mrs. Arnold saw Mary's "fiat" as an embrace of motherhood as God's will for her life:

> I am a convert, and perhaps have overlooked something in the life of Our Lady, who, I supposed, was to be the model of Catholic women, and whose Fiat, I thought, was our guide to daily living. Perhaps she did, after all, hire a loving substitute mother to teach the Child to love; and did she pay this person from her earnings from Caesar? the Jews? What was, I wonder, her profession, for which she was "gladly" paid — for surely she must have been "fulfilled"?[65]

Mrs. Arnold contrasts the unselfishly accepting, maternal Mary with the professional career woman who hires others to care for her children while seeking her own fulfillment. Holzhauer, however, quickly objected. Mary's "fiat" is a model, she asserted, but it

need not restrict women to the domestic sphere. Holzhauer broadened the range of situations in which women could, like Mary, say
"YES" to God: "So far as I know, modern women may utter their
'fiats' over the cradle, the lecture podium, the automatic washer,
the wheel of a car, the kitchen range or the desk — or over all of
them. We often do."[66]

Discernment is the moment of pause before the uttering of a fiat.
Discernment can be understood as a process of learning to what
to say yes and to what to say no.[67] The psychologist JM draws
this insight from her work as a psychologist. As a psychologist, "I
try to help people know what they want to say yes to . . . especially
women. It can be an act of courage to say yes."[68] After much
struggle with the church, JM has come to think of Mary differently,
substituting the passive Virgin with the woman who said yes, who
made a choice. The Annunciation (Luke 1:26–28), when a puzzled
Mary gives her "yes" to the announcement that she will bear the
son of God, takes on a special significance for JM.

Women today can choose their paths and configure their lives
to a greater extent than most other periods in history. For more
educated and professional women with a high degree of choice,
discernment is a process of "composing a life," to use the title
of Mary Catherine Bateson's book about women's lives.[69] Out of
the multiplicity of paths open, one consciously pieces together a
path. Or, to use a musical metaphor, one writes a song, choosing
what will be the dominant melody and what will be background
harmony. Will a job or career consume most of my energy? Will
motherhood, or friendships, or other pursuits be central? Will I
risk leaving my job and going back to school to pursue a different field? Will I speak up about a workplace injustice, even if that
means risking my job and my family's income? Each choice closes
off other paths. Indeed, in discernment one faces one's own multiple desires, conflicting senses of identity and vocation, projected
hopes for the future. Discernment, then, is a process of coming
to terms with choice, responsibility, and limits. This may be a
frightening process, fraught with internal conflict and ambiguity.
Nevertheless, it is a profoundly ethical and spiritual process that
affirms moral choice and reaches deep into a person for her core

convictions and views of the world. In the end, a woman may make her choices with a degree of ambivalence, grief for the paths closed combining with hope for the choices made. In the absence of a clear and convincing pull toward a certain path, she simply may pray for wisdom and ask for strength to make her choice and live it out well.

To frame this task in terms of "discernment" infuses women's lives with a theological and spiritual perspective — and some different tools or approaches to decision-making (e.g., one could explore Ignatian discernment of spirits). Decision making becomes a process of naming oneself, one's fundamental identity, and naming that to which one is called, the range of choices that fit with one's vocation. At the same time, this study shows that many women do not experience choice in their lives. They may be constrained by economic pressures and social expectations. They lack a sense of agency. Many women described their lives as "one thing leading to another," the accumulation of circumstances and small decisions with no clear direction from the outset. One may perceive choices in retrospect, but perhaps not in midstream. Taking these realities into consideration, how does one think about discernment?

I would advocate a dual-pronged approach. On the one hand, it is important to affirm freedom and responsibility. Work raises numerous choices, some small and some large. Spiritual guidance should enable people to make choices more and more freely, less bound to cultural expectations and distorting human passions. It should help people to claim those paths that best reflect their truest identity and that best respond to God's purposes for life. This discernment is not a one-time event, but rather a process of becoming grounded in the scriptures and the wisdom of tradition, walking with a community, using intellect and prayer to see rightly, and forming habits of the will that facilitate the making of good choices.

Second, the church needs to support women who find little room for choice in their lives. Discussions about discernment must not overlook the fact that women — particularly poor women — often have little choice about work. Yet as spiritual guides such as

Francis de Sales taught, human beings can be devoted disciples in any circumstance. Women may not have a choice of jobs or the luxury of choosing to work or stay at home with children. Their choice may be simply a choice to love God fully in the present circumstances. Every person has the freedom to love or not to love. These theological truths should not serve as a justification for relaxing vigilance on social issues; religious institutions and individuals must still work to secure justice, education, safe and dignified working conditions for all. Moreover, one must be very careful in the discernment process not to equate passivity with obedience to God's will, as Kathleen Fischer notes in her book about spiritual direction of women:

> Certain false conceptions of God's will can reinforce cultural conditioning in women. One such conception equates God's will with external authority; finding God's will then means trying to measure up to that outer authority rather than developing a sense of inner authority. Women can mistakenly think they are living out God's will when they are merely living out a cultural pattern of conformity or helplessness.[70]

Yet women in this study have shown the importance of finding agency and spiritual sustenance even in constrained situations.

Discernment ultimately should serve to realize one's humanity — whatever one's circumstances. For the most fundamental vocation is the calling to be a person, as John Paul II writes. Work participates in that calling: "These actions must all serve to realize his humanity, to fulfill the calling to be a person that is his by reason of his very humanity."[71] Neither circumstances nor nature absolutely dictate one's vocation. That would deny human freedom and dignity. Indeed, to decide about oneself is a mark of being a person, in the words again of John Paul II: the worker is "a subjective being capable of acting in a planned and rational way, capable of deciding about himself [*sic*] and with a tendency to self-realization." The practice of discernment becomes critical as women workers confront vocational questions and, as will be seen, increasingly face time constraints and conflicts.

Chapter Four

Sanctifying Time

Liturgical Perspectives on Work, Seasons, and Fragmentation

By the end of the twentieth century, women had gained tremendous opportunities for professional and educational advancement. The career woman had emerged as an important ideal. Yet women continued to take primary responsibility for the family, with increasing numbers of mothers working full-time while raising young children. Women's growing tendency to combine employment and family roles, noticeable by the 1970s, increased substantially through the 1980s and 1990s. In 1975, both parents held employment in about 36 percent of couples with children under the age of six. In 1985, that number had risen to nearly 52 percent.[1] By 1998, nearly two out of three mothers of preschool children held down jobs outside the home.[2] It was no wonder that social scientists concluded in the late 1980s: "Time has become an increasingly scarce — and valued — commodity for parents. As growing numbers of women maintain their employment during the years of childbearing and child-rearing, a greater proportion of the labor force will be wrestling with work-family cross-pressures."[3] Women bore the brunt of those pressures. They faced "role overloads and strains," a "life cycle squeeze," and uncontrollable "time pressures."[4]

Religious institutions have not appreciated the time pressures that increasingly have besieged women as they juggled employment and domestic labor. They have not addressed the moral and spiritual implications of the "overwork that plagues many Americans, especially married women."[5] The structures of work have

111

not adjusted adequately to women's larger presence. For example, women who seek to balance work and family by working part-time usually earn a lower hourly wage and fewer benefits than do full-time workers. They "will most likely be relegated to the bottom part of the female labor market — the service, sales, and clerical jobs where the majority of women part-timers reside."[6] Nor has the division of labor within the family sufficiently adapted to women's increased work outside the home. Women still spend far more time than do men in childcare and domestic chores, even when both work full time. Women are, so to speak, in a real time bind.

Women's changing work force participation, combined with continuing cultural expectations regarding women's primary role at home, put enormous pressure on women's time and consciences. For example, women's changing work patterns squeezed the time available for volunteer activities, a reality that carries serious implications for religious institutions that long have depended on women's volunteer labor. Some women volunteered less, others volunteered at particular seasons in their lives. Some women tried to "do it all" and faced exhaustion, spiritual enervation, and a strong sense of fragmentation. Moreover, women's expanding economic opportunities combined with the professionalization of many church and charitable tasks to raise new questions about whose time and labor was compensated and why.

As more spheres compete for women's time, women must discern how to use their time. This is not simply a "practical" question, but rather involves values, priorities, self-understandings, and assumptions about fulfillment and justice. How one spends time not only reflects who one is but also shapes the person one will become. Left with little thoughtful religious guidance on how to make such choices, women creatively seek to make sense of their hectic lives; some redefine their church involvement and sense of vocation in the process. Spirituality remains a vital source of meaning for many women in the midst of time pressures. Still, women grapple with questions of guilt, selfishness, exhaustion, balance, and a profound experience of fragmentation.

In responding to this situation, I propose three theological avenues to explore: a seasonal perspective on vocation; the recovery of Sabbath-keeping, and a eucharistic spirituality that finds grace in the fragments.

Guilt: An Excursus

As women sought to do more and more and faced their own limitations, many felt a sense of moral or spiritual failure. Time constraints merged with cultural and religious ideals of goodness, femininity, success, and holiness to produce guilt. For even as women from 1960 onward increasingly combined employment and child-rearing simultaneously, the "model" woman who managed everything effortlessly looked over their shoulder. For example, Joyce Jackson seemed to be able to do it all. Featured in the Methodist magazine *Together* in 1965, thirty-six-year-old Mrs. Jackson held down a job as a kindergarten teacher, mothered four children between the ages of one and fifteen, and still served as a pillar of the Brentwood Methodist Church in Wintersville, Ohio. She directed the church choir and was treasurer of the Woman's Society of Christian Service. Mrs. Jackson represents other women who continued to hold up local churches amid their home and work responsibilities. Amazingly, though, Joyce's husband remarks: "I have never heard Joyce say she was tired, nor have I seen her look tired. I know of no challenge or responsibility she has turned down."[7] So, as women's time constricted, Joyce is held up as the model religious woman who does it all, refuses no request, and shows no strain.

Real women did show the strain. Many tried to be like the depiction of Joyce Jackson. They tried to do it all. Women's traditional socialization in service and relationship heightened their pressure and guilt. As social worker Elena Lucas noted, many women "did not know how to say no to people." Lucas was a social worker and leader in the United Farm Worker movement in the 1960s and 1970s. She described her exhaustion as she and her husband tried to establish the first UFW Service Center: "And I worked such long hours, during the nights and on the weekends...but I just didn't know how to say no to people. I got very skinny. Sometimes I'd have thirteen or fourteen people waiting for me to do different things for them. It was just impossible. . . . I was burning out." Lucas saw that women's time was stretched differently than was men's, as women had continued expectations within the family despite their new public roles (and particularly so in Latino culture): "They [men] have the support of their wives and families, but most of us women have to work against our husbands and all of the services they expect."[8]

An avid volunteer in retirement, Ruth Grant also struggled with saying no as she tried to reduce her extensive community volunteering:

> I'll never cut down where the church is concerned because I love my church and that will always be first. . . . God has been very good to me. . . . I have to give something up, otherwise I won't have the time to do it. . . . I'm feeling how you've been programmed when you were younger growing up. . . . Don't say no because that's selfish, maybe my parents ran that into the ground a little bit. I'll confess to you, I won't confess to my priest. I want to be a little selfish, how about it?[9]

Dolores Huerta wrestled with guilt as she undertook a public vocation while simultaneously mothering eleven children. Cesar Chavez and Huerta began organizing farm workers full-time in the Delano, California, area in 1962. Three years later, the National Farm Workers Association (NFWA) joined with Filipino American workers in a strike against grape growers. Huerta was central to the strike and the organizing campaign. She traveled up and down the West Coast, often leaving her children with other organizers or foster parents. She recalled her strong guilt feelings:

> I had a lot of doubts to begin with, but I had to act in spite of my conflict between my family and my commitment. My biggest problem was not to feel guilty about it. I don't anymore, but then everybody used to lay these guilt trips on me, about what a bad mother I was neglecting my children.[10]

Latino culture and Catholicism surely contributed to that guilt, as they so strongly emphasized women's roles as mothers. Motherhood was a sanctified vocation; failure as a mother diminished one's purity and womanhood. Yet Huerta did not reject her faith and cultural tradition. She adapted them. She prayed. She bargained with God. She used traditional Catholic piety to validate an untraditional public role. She herself was not certain of the legitimacy of this spiritual maneuvering, although it worked for her:

> The way I first got away from feeling guilty about neglecting my family was a religious cop-out, I guess. I had serious doubts about whether I was doing the right thing, giving kids a lousy supper so I could go to a council meeting. So I would pray and say, if what I was doing wasn't bearing fruit, then it would be a sign that I shouldn't be doing it. When good things came out of my work, when it bore fruit, I took that as a sign I should continue and the sacrifices my family and I were making were justified.[11]

Like many women, however, Huerta continued to question whether she could justify her work outside the home.

Time: A Spiritual Issue

Clearly, women have to make difficult decisions about how they organize and value their time. These decisions about time actually involve choices about competing goods and ideals of womanhood. Time is not simply a pragmatic issue; though often unrecognized, it is a spiritual dilemma. What value should one give to productivity, to reproductivity, to leisure? How can women, socialized to give their time freely, learn to steward their time and say no to unjust or unwise uses of their time? How find a center amid multiple, competing demands on the self?

As human beings are finite creatures, time is a limited quantity. Time takes on a sacred character; it is a gift. As Dorothy Bass asserts in her book *Receiving the Day,* God the Creator is the giver of time. God creates the day and the night (Gen 1:1–5). Time, then, is not something to be controlled, but received: "To know time as a gift is to know that its basic rhythms and inevitable passing are beyond our control."[12] How people use the gift of time both shapes and reflects their understandings of who they are, the things they cherish, and the social circumstances that circumscribe their lives. For many women, time has become simply something to divide up, to schedule. Time must be parceled out among work, family, friendships, self, and — perhaps — church or other volunteering activities. The structures of the workplace convert time into a measure of productivity. Women punch time clocks. They have to meet deadlines. They live through their date planners. Professional women seeking advancement must log quotas of billable hours; they race against tenure clocks. There is no time to "receive" time; it must be managed, accumulated, divided, battled. This is a fractured sense of time.

Psychologist JM, for example, described her experience of time pressures as she did a clinical psychology internship in the early 1980s: "It was intense. I was working with schizophrenics, and I had a one-year-old at home. I was just so stressed. It was awful. I really didn't want to do that kind of schedule for the rest of my life. I tried to knock it down some, with some success. While I was doing my dissertation I worked twenty hours a week, with a hospitalized population."[13] JM completed her doctorate in 1984. She went on to work part-time (i.e., about thirty hours a week) for the next fifteen years, occasionally finding herself working more than full-time hours but then saying, "This is crazy," and scaling back.

Workplace structures and the time squeeze on working parents exert tremendous pressure toward what James D. Whitehead calls "compulsion," or time "obsessively focused." It is "unfree time...unholy because we are possessed by a contemporary demon, a compulsion that distorts our awareness and compels our energy into unbalanced behavior."[14] American workers are driven to produce, putting in rising numbers of hours (roughly thirty-six more hours at work per year in 2000 as compared to 1990). They log far more hours than their European counterparts, exceeding even the hard-working Japanese.[15] Time is compressed, space for leisure (time simply to be) constricted. Women add on top of that their unequal share of domestic labor. Contemporary workers need ways to recover time, to push against the pressures that make them compulsive and exhausted. Religious traditions hold much wisdom regarding the meaning of time, the seasons of life, and balance in ordering multiple tasks. This wisdom should be brought into conversation with women's own reflections.

Liturgy and Time

One of the most important ways in which religious traditions respect time is through liturgy. Liturgy is a way of marking time as holy. Communities set aside specific times for worship. Christians celebrate their main weekly liturgy on Sunday. Jews begin their weekly *Shabbat* observance at sunset on Friday evenings. Muslims designate Friday as their sacred day. Daily prayer too sanctifies time, rendering it to God. Daily prayer or *salat* is, for example, a central practice of Islam. Muslims have an obligation to pray five times daily facing Mecca.[16] The Christian "liturgy of the hours," or "divine office," similarly sets aside specific times during the day — for example, sunrise (lauds), dusk (vespers), and night (compline) for scripture reading and praying of the psalms. The Second Vatican Council noted: "The divine office, in keeping with ancient Christian tradition, is so devised that the whole course of the day and night is made holy by the praise of God.... The purpose of the office is to sanctify the day."[17] Saying the liturgy of the hours long has been an integral part of monastic life and an expectation for ordained priests, and since the Second Vatican Council more common among laity. It also is an important practice in some Protestant traditions, particularly among Anglicans. Moreover, just as liturgy marks off times during the day and week for prayer, so too the Christian church follows the "liturgical year." It thus recognizes different seasons within the year (Advent, Christmas, Epiphany, Ordinary Time, Lent, Easter, Pentecost).

What this structuring of time does is invite the individual to step into a story larger and wider than her or his individual life story. Time is marked off to commemorate sacred history, to renew life, to refresh community, and to sanctify the ordinary. Too often, the contemporary productive mentality makes prayer more difficult. Prayer seems like a "waste of time," an unproductive activity that requires an uncomfortable stillness. Liturgy builds prayer into schedules, signifying its rightful place among other "productive" activities. By praying with the movements of nature — sunrise and sunset, or winter and spring — the community also affirms the connection between the created world and God. It patterns its own life according to a larger rhythm of life.

Such insights could aid women trying to provide some order and wholeness to their scattered, hectic days. Their individual stories need not be orderly, but rather they are as one day in the larger history of God's love for humanity. When human time is put into the perspective of God's time, our harried lives take on a larger meaning and integrity. As Psalm 90 proclaims: "From everlasting to everlasting you are God.... For a thousand years in your sight are like yesterday when it is past, or like a watch in the night" (Ps 90:2, 4). This way of seeing time helps us to step back from the particularities of our schedules. While the time clock, the production deadline, and the children's soccer schedule all still exert their pressures, they do not ultimately define the meaning of our days or our selves. The God who breaks into time in Christ ultimately defines that meaning. Sacred time encompasses and sanctifies ordinary time.

Contemporary writer Kathleen Norris sees parallels between liturgy and women's work. Like liturgy, women's work must be done day in and day out with a repetition that could be drudgery. Yet, says Norris, like the repetition of the liturgy it also can be transformative, life-renewing, and revelatory. In a lecture entitled "The Quotidian Mysteries: Laundry, Liturgy, and 'Women's Work,'" Norris stated: "It is a paradox of human life that in worship, as in human love, it is in the routine and the everyday that we find the possibilities for the greatest transformation.... We have the power to transform what seems meaningless — the endless repetitions of a litany or the motions of vacuuming a floor."[18] Work is like the movement of time; it is repetitious, necessary, bidding us with the break of day. In a poem called "Housecleaning," Norris writes:

> I could use some sleep.
> What I do must be done
> each day, in every season,
> like liturgy.[19]

Norris, a Protestant, is deeply informed by her experiences in Benedictine monasteries. Indeed, liturgical prayer is a central part of the Benedictine vocation. The Benedictine tradition also encourages a balance of time spent on work, prayer, and rest. Such a sense of moderation expresses duty, prudence, and humility. Time cannot be harnessed; the rhythm of life must be respected.

While liturgy can integrate faith throughout the day, week, and year, it also must be recognized that regular prayer done at particular times may be more suited to the monastic context than to contemporary lay life. Rigidly scheduled prayer can become another pressure, another thing to add to already full schedules. Yet prayer can be adapted in light of time constraints and family schedules. Noting the pressures of modern life, for example, the Second Vatican Council introduced a measure of flexibility into the schedule of the liturgy of the hours.[20] Just as the Second Vatican Council considered the reality of contemporary life in modifying the divine office, so too it is important to take seriously the time demands already pressing on women. At the same time, a structured way of praying may be the only way to make sure that faith gets built into a busy schedule. Some working women find that daily prayer gives a calming order and grounding to the day. Psychologist JM, for example, taps into a Web site on her palm pilot to pray the liturgy of the hours in between patients.

The Daily Examen

Perhaps a simple form of daily prayer, a brief daily "examen," would be well suited to working women today. Engineer Nancy Haegel describes her practice:

> I quiet myself, at the end of what is always a long and busy day, and go very slowly, meditatively, prayerfully, through the day — each person and encounter, each activity and incident. I ask myself two questions: Where was God, and where were the opportunities to serve?[21]

The daily examen is a central part of Ignatian spirituality, a means of self-reflection, discernment, and reorientation. Ignatius of Loyola emphasized the importance of regular meditation on one's relationship with God. He built into the first week of the Spiritual Exercises two modes of self-examination, a "Daily Particular Examination of Conscience" and a "General Examination of Conscience." These practices have been adapted for particular individuals and contexts, and contemporary spiritual writers have proposed simplified versions.[22] This is in keeping with the spirit of Ignatius, who envisioned his Exercises as a flexible guide for retreatants.

Haegel's practice is a form of daily examen. This spiritual exercise centers a person in the midst of busyness; it can be an important practice for working women juggling work, family, and the needs of the self. It reminds one of one's fundamental relationship with the Creator, the giver of all gifts. It provides a moment for taking stock. Where was God in the many moments of this day? How did I use the gifts that God provided today? Where did I feel anxious, decentered? Where did I fail to act in a spirit of love and service? The examen does not necessarily require large amounts of time, but it does provide a regular way to examine the rhythms of one's life and discern patterns. Women may want to use the examen to uncover trends in how they use their time — and why. This affirms the sanctity of time; it is a gift to be received and used wisely.

Seasons of Vocation

As women's social and economic roles change, women and religious institutions would do well to consider seasons of vocations across a lifetime. How women use time — and how they are religious — changes as their lives unfold. Many women travel on winding paths. They work at different jobs, moving in and out of the work force as their family responsibilities require. They do not necessarily set out on a work path, but their vocation (or, I would argue, vocations) emerge from a retrospective — not a prospective — position. One thing leads to another. Work experiences build on one another, leading to different identities and even careers. Mothering and volunteering skills lead to work paths later in life. Jobs and families yield in quieter, later years to church involvement and spiritual intensity.

Mary Parella looks back and now sees God's hand directing her life through varied jobs and her role as a parent:

> When I look back at how my career developed, it didn't. It happened.... It's a zigzag line...I think there was direction given to me in my work life. I am where I am because of an accumulation of experiences, none of which did I know were happening while I was going through it.... I feel in my faith and in my heart of hearts that somebody led me through it. I don't think it was all accidental.... This had a plan. I didn't know the plan. I firmly believe that I was led this way. I was there for the kids, I was close by when they needed me to be.... This definitely was not accidental.[23]

From this retrospective position, she clearly sees herself having a vocation to raise her children: "My vocation was my family. As I look back on it, the only thing that counts in my life, I think, is what we create as a family."[24] If one is to talk about vocation with women workers, one must be able to consider vocation as a "zigzag line," full of varied steps and stops and leaps, a path that evolves over the course of a lifetime.

Developmental psychology yields important insight into the varied life tasks that must be undertaken at different stages. When combined with a theological perspective, such research stands to contribute much to pastoral ministry with women workers.[25] Joann Wolski Conn, for example, brings a critical perspective on developmental psychology to the analysis of women's spirituality. She asserts that relationality is an important component of each life stage, that spiritual and psychological maturity entails both intimacy (traditionally defined as a feminine quality) and autonomy (traditionally defined as a male virtue).[26] Such an insight could help women struggling to balance and integrate family ties with desires for independence, ambition, and "self-realization." The tension between independence and relationship expressed by so many women is a natural part of the human personality. It is not an either-or, a conflict to be overcome, but rather part of the process of living, necessary for growth. Multiple vocational pulls can simply reflect the multifaceted quality of human personhood. Human beings grow by incorporating love and work, by integrating relationships and independence, by struggling to affirm these various dimensions of mature life.

Pastoral psychologist James Fowler also offers perspective on the seasons of life. He writes: "When we consider the dynamics of faith in our lives, we sense that at each of the crisis points of our lives and at each of the expected or unexpected turning points of our lives, we face a time when our ways of making meaning and the patterns of our trust and loyalties are subject to testing and change."[27] Life transitions are, in effect, vocational turning points. These are moments of discernment when one must ask anew how to live out one's vocation, "the response a person makes with his or her total self to the address of God and to the calling to partnership."[28]

Vocation, then, is not a rigid appointment, determined once and for all. Rather, it entails choices at every life stage, new opportunities to enter more deeply into one's created being and to respond more fully to God in the concrete circumstances that present themselves. This is not to say that vocation does not involve permanent commitments. It can and often does. Yet at each life stage one chooses again to live those commitments — and how to live them well.

It is important to take a longer view of a lifetime, seeing it as a whole. There are seasons in life. And there are seasons of vocation. As the biblical writer of Ecclesiastes hymns:

> For everything there is a season,
> and a time for every matter under heaven
> a time to be born, and a time to die;
> a time to plant, and a time to pluck up what is planted.
>   (Eccl 3:1–8)

Yet when imbedded in the particular moment with its multiple demands and time conflicts, one may forget this wisdom. Life may appear fractured, when actually wholeness emerges over the course of a lifetime (and, more completely, at the end of history, in an eschatological perspective).

A seasonal perspective becomes particularly relevant when one considers that women's life spans have been increasing. In 1900, women in the United States had an expected life span of forty-eight years. In 1930, that number had risen to sixty-one years. By 1970, women could anticipate a lifetime of nearly seventy-five years. By the late 1990s, it was nearly eighty years. The lengthening life span meant that women had more and more time beyond their childbearing years, time they increasingly spent in the labor force. Moreover, as the gap between male and female life expectancies widened (from two years in 1900 to about seven by the close of the twentieth century), and as rates of divorce increased, women had to prepare financially and emotionally for some period of life alone.[29]

Thus, more women have come to have a season of time that can be devoted to education and employment. In the early 1960s, that period tended to start when a woman reached her mid-forties, when children began to leave the home. Women often went back to school or gave more energy to work or volunteer activities during this season of their lives. By 1990, women were delaying marriage and childbearing, devoting their twenties and sometimes early thirties to work and education. Changes in life expectancy and patterns of marriage raise new questions about how women use time. New choices and different seasons of women's lives have emerged.

Several women reported increased volunteer activities in later times of their lives, after work responsibilities decreased or children left home. For example, MK recalled that she did not volunteer during her forty years of work as a telephone operator: "I had all I could do to get up and go to work."[30] In retirement or after children were grown, time became more available. It was after she retired that AB, the financial manager for construction companies, brought her work skills into the church, serving on the Parish Finance Council even at age ninety!

Harriet White (b. 1918) was an active church volunteer as she raised three children, worked, and cared for her mother. Yet her most intensive volunteering occurred after her three children were grown. A parishioner at St. John–St. Hugh Roman Catholic parish in Roxbury, Massachusetts, White sewed vestments for priests, helped church youth groups, worked church bazaars, served on the parish council, held the post of secretary of the mothers' club, and volunteered at the Boston Food Bank. She now volunteers only for church-related activities. Volunteering is a social network for her; church and the priests are "another family" for her.[31] Church activities can offer important sources of community at this later life stage.

Like White, Ruth Grant now gives almost all her volunteering time to her church. Her story also shows the seasons in women's lives, how their use of time varies at different life stages. Grant stepped out of the work force when her son was born in the 1946. When her son began school, she worked full-time as a legal secretary in New York. When she was nearly fifty years old, Grant got a degree in broadcast journalism. She then moved to Roxbury, a poor section of Boston, and worked as a legal secretary, administrative assistant, and a newscaster until her retirement in 1985.[32] Grant began most of her volunteering after she retired at the age of sixty-two. She has been on the boards of a neighborhood initiative and the Boston Archdiocese Office of Black Catholics. She taught office skills at the South End Settlements and lectors in her parish. She definitely feels the strain of balancing time in the midst of her heavy community involvement:

> I am so surprised. You enjoy doing it [volunteering] but it's work. . . . You get involved because you want to make it better. . . . I'm going to try to make Roxbury respectable. So you roll up your sleeves and you go out there. And it is really a lot of work and a lot of things go undone, because that means you have to go to a lot of unexpected meetings and it is very time-consuming. It makes it very very hard sometimes when you want to do other things.

Grant does want to do other things. She considers herself a black historian, and — at the age of seventy-seven — hopes to write two books: "One would be about God's great men of color, and one about God's great women of color."[33] Thus she begins a new chapter in her lifelong story of work.

Some women grow in their faith and find community through church activities, once their family and work obligations lighten.

After recounting the hectic responsibilities of raising her children and caring for aging parents, Mary Parella says:

> Now I actually have time to think about my faith. Maybe that's what the difference is. Maybe there's a little more time for me now. I never would have gotten involved in the Committee or become a Eucharistic Minister with all the kids at home, with everything else that was going on. Now I am ripe for that. I have a time in my life that I can do that. And I don't volunteer anywhere else.[34]

These accounts indicate that women do not face an absolute conflict between work, family, and religious activities, but rather that different roles take prominence in different seasons of their lives. Religious groups may benefit from women's work experiences, but the benefit will come in different life stages. Annette Kane, former executive director of the National Council of Catholic Women, confirms this reality. The average NCCW member is in her fifties or sixties; the group has difficulty attracting younger women who are often juggling work and family. Indeed, the organization's Web site announces its new Membership Mentoring Program, to combat "declining membership due to women in full-time employment."[35] Kane notes, however, that older women can be a tremendous resource for religious groups: "Women seem to be retiring younger. . . . There they are in their parish. They have all this energy and a lot of expertise, and they are the ones that step forward when a job needs to be done. We hope to pull them into our organization."[36]

Employment and family responsibilities develop skills and confidence that women may bring into church activities in later middle age and after retirement. Several women who saw no connection between their faith and their work ended up using their work skills in service of the church in their later years. The integration of work, family, and religious life may appear over the course of a lifetime. The pieces that did not seem to fit, the zigzag line, eventually looks like a path — at least for some women. A seasonal perspective affirms the multiplicity of endeavors that can give service and express the human relationship to God. This perspective — a biblical one — resonates too not only with the dynamics of a human life but also with the particular situations of contemporary women.

Sabbath

As women increasingly take on demanding jobs and professional careers and combine them with child-rearing, they describe
themselves as hectic, burned out, exhausted, strained. JM, the psychiatrist, was "just so stressed." Elena Lucas was "burning out."
Mary Parella said that she had little time to think about her faith
while she raised her children. As women increasingly hold down
full-time jobs while simultaneously caring for children, the pace
of life accelerates. Sociologist Arlie Hochschild writes: "As masses
of women have moved into the economy, families have been hit
by a 'speed-up' in work and family life. There is not more time
in the day than there was when wives stayed home, but there is
twice as much to get done. It is mainly women who absorb this
'speed-up.' "[37]

Recovering the Jewish and Christian traditions of Sabbath keeping would give women permission to slow down. The Sabbath
also offers women important perspective on their work and identity. The Sabbath (*Shabbat*) is central to Judaism and, though less
prominent, an important element of Christianity. Jews honor the
Sabbath as a gift from God and a divine commandment; it is a time
to stop working, to worship, and to simply be. Christians too set
aside a Sabbath Day, designating Sunday rather than Saturday as
a day of worship. The Gospel of Mark shows Jesus interpreting
the Sabbath as a gift for humanity, even as he moderates strict
legal interpretations of the Sabbath: "Then he said to them, 'The
Sabbath was made for humankind, and not humankind for the
Sabbath; so the Son of Man is lord even of the sabbath' " (Mark
2:27–28).

Contemporary Jewish and Christian practice varies, of course.
Reform Jews interpret the rules of Sabbath keeping more loosely
than do Conservative and Orthodox. Many Christians have lost
any sense of the Sabbath. Religious organizations actually encourage work overload; they rely on those who cannot say no. As union
organizer Mary Baker recalled: "I tell you . . . what a priest told me
many years ago. He said: 'I'll tell you, you take the busiest person
in the parish and you get more work out of them than you do

anybody else!' "[38] Given Western culture's emphasis on productivity and in light of women's increasing participation in the labor force, it is time to reclaim the gift. The Sabbath can be a center of wholeness, a way to reclaim one's fundamental identity in God, and a means to affirm the whole of life as vocation.

Through Sabbath keeping, time is sanctified and human beings remember the work of God and their own creatureliness. The Book of Exodus commands: "Remember the Sabbath day, and keep it holy. Six days you shall labor and do all your work. But the seventh day is a Sabbath to the Lord your God; you shall not do any work — you, your son or your daughter, your male or female slave, your livestock, or the alien resident in your towns" (Exod 20:8–10; see too Deut 5:12–15).[39] The Sabbath day, then, affirms the human dignity of all, including the slave and the alien. Even animals are to rest; all that is created gives honor to God and to themselves by observing the Sabbath. Sabbath keeping puts human work and all human standards of evaluating work in perspective. The practice is a mark of humility; one's work is limited and ultimately not of the utmost importance. At the same time, keeping Sabbath is a bold imitation of God: "For in six days the Lord made heaven and earth, the sea, and all that is in them, but rested the seventh day; therefore the Lord blessed the Sabbath day and consecrated it" (Exod 20:11). In the creation of the world, God worked. One can assert that God continues to work in creation, as this passage from Ignatius's *Spiritual Exercises* expresses: "I will consider how God labors and works for me in all the creatures on the face of the earth; that is, he acts in the manner of one who is laboring. For example, he is working in the heavens, elements, plants, fruits, cattle, and all the rest."[40]

Core to the meaning of the Sabbath is freedom. Dorothy Bass observes: "In Deuteronomy, the commandment to 'observe' the Sabbath day is tied to the experience of a people newly released from bondage. Slaves cannot take a day off; free people can.... Sabbath rest is a recurring testimony against the drudgery of slavery."[41] As women become more and more significant economic producers, they run the risk of enslaving themselves to economic values, technology, and workplace definitions of success. In the

early twentieth century, sociologist Max Weber warned that industrialization had left workers locked in an "iron cage."[42] Devoid of
the former religious sense of calling, they drove toward productivity without even knowing why. Women risk finding themselves
in that same iron cage today. Sabbath keeping may provide a key
out of the cage. For as Jewish theologian Abraham Joshua Heschel
writes in his classic text, the Sabbath offers an independence from
technical civilization: "to set apart one day a week for freedom,
a day for being with ourselves, a day . . . of independence of external obligations, a day on which we stop worshipping the idols of
technical civilization, a day on which we use no money."[43] The
Sabbath is "the exodus from tension, the liberation of man from
his own muddiness, the installation of man as a sovereign in the
world of time."[44]

Bass also notes that observing Sabbath means not only resting
from work but also abstaining from shopping, which depends on
others' work.[45] Hence, Sabbath keeping could be an antidote to the
consumerism of contemporary culture, a consumerism that drives
productivity and threatens the environment. In other words, the
Sabbath through its emphasis on our creatureliness rescues human
beings from a ceaseless cycle of production and consumption and
gives respite to all of creation.

While Sabbath keeping affirms human freedom and the sanctity
of rest, it also must not be interpreted so as to minimize the sanctity
of work during the rest of the week. Evelyn and James Whitehead
cautioned of the dangers of dichotomizing time into secular and
holy, *chronos* and *kairos*, "in the emphasizing of the holiness of
a particular day (Sunday) to the neglect of the 'daily holiness' of
other times."[46] The Sabbath teaches us that time is a gift, one
we receive each day. The Sabbath should be, in Heschel's words,
"not a depreciation but an affirmation of labor . . . a sequel to the
command: *Six days shalt thou labor, and do all thy work.*"[47] The
Sabbath should affirm the holiness of work, a sharing in God's own
creative activity, as well as rest, a time of reconnection to the whole
of life. The Sabbath reminds us of an identity and relationship with
God that goes deeper than any work we do.

Toward a Eucharistic Spirituality

As women more and more juggle simultaneous employment and family responsibilities (including, increasingly, single parenthood), they describe feeling scattered, broken, divided. Time seems forever chopped up into scheduled pieces; women feel diffused into multiple roles and selves. Amid these multiple roles, these multiple selves, women wonder "Who am I?" and "Where is my center?" This is in part a time pressure, but it goes deeper. It becomes a more unsettling question about whether one *is* only this or that role. Women search for wholeness, for a core identity of center that connects the various roles. And they seek meaning in the midst of the scatteredness.

This sense of fragmentation, of course, is not just a recent development. In 1955, best-selling author Anne Morrow Lindbergh, wife of the famous airman Charles Lindbergh, poignantly described fragmentation as an inevitable part of womanhood, a kind of centrifugal force:

> To be a woman is to have interests and duties, raying out in all directions from the central mother-core, like spokes from the hub of a wheel. The pattern of our lives is essentially circular. We must be open to all points of the compass: husband, children, friends, home, community; stretched out, exposed, sensitive like a spider's web to each breeze that blows, to each call that comes. How difficult for us, then, to achieve a balance in the midst of these contradictory tensions, and yet how necessary for the proper functioning of our lives.... How desirable and how distant is the ideal of the contemplative, artist, or saint — the inner inviolable core, the single eye... how to remain balanced, no matter what centrifugal forces tend to pull one off center; how to remain strong, no matter what shocks come in at the periphery and tend to crack the hub of the wheel.[48]

Nor is the experience of fragmentation limited to women in the paid work force. Homemakers too balance multiple roles, as this woman explained: "No matter what our career, we all have periods of fragmentation when we feel we are out of control, even when we desperately try to stay in control. The full-time mother

can feel parceled out as teacher, nurse, psychologist, nutrition-
ist, caterer, interior designer, social director, financial planner, and
even taxi driver."[49]

Yet the increase of women in the paid work force and resulting time constraints undoubtedly exacerbate the experience of
fragmentation. Many women seek an integrative center. A law professor and mother wrote: "I try not to live in two worlds: a world
of work and a world of home; a world of prayer and faith and a
'real' or 'modern' world. I try to make one world."[50] Fragmentation calls for discernment, a constant sifting to find what is at the
center, what is most meaningful. The indexer for the *Wall Street
Journal*, Kathy Petersen Cecala, drew this insight from her work:

> Seeing the corporate world on the scope that I see it in my everyday
> work — broken down into many, many tiny fragments and facts,
> intricate detail — gives me an interesting perspective on life. Just as I
> sort through vast amounts of data, trying to pinpoint what is essen-
> tial, what is valuable, so too does my life — as a busy commuter, as
> a wife, as a Catholic — present myriad moments and experiences,
> which must be sorted through to determine what is meaningful,
> what is important.[51]

Given the persistent and multilevel experience of fragmentation
in the twentieth century, it is no surprise that recent scholarly and
popular descriptions of spirituality focus on integration. According to leading spirituality scholar Sandra Schneiders, for example,
spirituality is "the experience of consciously striving to integrate
one's life in terms not of isolation and self-absorption but of
self-transcendence toward the ultimate value one perceives."[52]
Theologian Anne Carr writes that Christian spirituality involves an
experience of grace through which people "experience themselves
lifted beyond previous levels of integration by a power greater than
their own, by the Holy Spirit."[53] Bradley Holt emphasizes the integrative character of spirituality as an antidote to an individualistic,
therapeutic notion of spirituality: "Christian spirituality includes
more than an introspective search for psychological health; ideally
it integrates relationships to God and creation with those to self
and others."[54] Implicit in this theme of integration is a broadened

understanding of spiritual life, as Philip Sheldrake writes, not "limited to a concern with the interior life but seek[ing] an integration of all aspects of human life and experience."[55]

Integration also emerges as an important theme in the popular spirituality-and-business movement. The new heralds of transformed work seek to bring a greater sense of values and vision into business, to instill more humanity and connectedness in the workplace. They want workers to see themselves and co-workers as whole persons, to look at the bigger picture of what life means, to "live for a higher truth."[56] People are not just cogs in the wheel of a business; rather, they are "spirit" possessing deep inner power. The spirituality-and-business movement reacts against a fragmentation that so many workers experience. It seeks instead an integrated relationship among work, personal values, and other aspects of life. The International Alliance for Spirit at Work, for example, states: "We support the growth of spirit in the consciousness that weaves our daily world together, from the kitchen to the boardroom."[57] Organizers of an international symposium on spirituality and business write: "A deep sense of spirituality enables one to see the unity of all beings; leads one to live authentic lives congruent with one's values; and guides us to spend one's life in service to humanity and all life on earth."[58]

These understandings of spirituality rightly point to the desire for wholeness, relatedness, and integration so deep in the spiritual life. Yet women's own reflections point to an alternate moment in Christian spirituality, one focused not so much on the goal of integration but rather on grace in the fragments. Following the lead of Deborah Smith Douglas, who had an epiphany as she watched the bread broken at Mass, I will call this a eucharistic spirituality.

A Catholic, Deborah Smith Douglas described her harried, scattered daily life as she struggled in the early 1990s to care for two daughters, work, and hold chaos at bay: "I have begun to notice, in a rueful sort of way, how often Jesus in the gospels seems as harried and distracted as a mother. He is forever trying 'to get away to a quiet place' and is forever delayed and interrupted by the needs of other people, people he loves."[59] She describes a yearning to integrate all these strands of life, for a sense of wholeness and order. Finally, an experience of the Eucharist gives her new perspective on the meaning of her daily activities, a way to appreciate grace in the fragments:

> Perhaps it is the endless shopping-cooking-serving labor of feeding my family that so draws me to the stories of Jesus feeding people. Perhaps it is my own need to be fed by Jesus that so draws me to the Eucharist. A family meal is at the center of the sacrament — bread broken, wine poured out.
>
> At any rate, it was at the Eucharist that an insight was given me that may help in my struggle against the entropic forces that regularly disintegrate my life.
>
> As I watched, the priest...proceeded to break the consecrated wafer into a corresponding number of pieces.... All that remained of its original integrity was a heap of fragments on the plate. "My life is like that," I realized....
>
> The fractioning of my days is not likely to end any time soon. But perhaps — by a miracle of grace, by the grace of God — I can come to see myself not as meaninglessly disintegrated but as broken and given like bread, poured out like wine.[60]

Catholics carry a sacramental imagination,[61] reinforced by the liturgy, week after week. A eucharistic spirituality, then, may come quite naturally for them. Yet the Eucharist also can be a powerful symbol for meaning-in-fragmentation for Protestants. Perhaps women are drawn to the imagery of feeding, baking, and cleaning, tasks traditionally assigned to them. A woman attorney published a poem in the evangelical magazine *Daughters of Sarah,* in which she queried whether it wasn't a woman who baked the bread that Jesus broke, and a woman who made the wine that he poured out:

> And afterwards, did a woman come
> To clear the cup; to mop...
> To gather every scattered crumb
> Of broken body, broken bread?
> Did a woman, coming to clean the room,
> Find a grace in the fragments left behind....[62]

And thus one comes back to the theme of liturgy as sanctifying time and bringing meaning to fragmented lives. Indeed, a eucharistic spirituality both responds to an important contemporary experience and draws upon the deep wisdom of the tradition. A eucharistic spirituality affirms the presence of God in the fragments of human lives. This is an incarnational spirituality that takes account of human brokenness. Human beings are limited; we cannot be and do all things. We are called in many directions. We search for identity in many places that cannot possibly provide it. We are scattered. Yet through faith one affirms that God can enter into those pieces, can sanctify them and make them into food for others. Indeed, God becomes our own brokenness. Grace pierces our world. While human beings long for integration, while we long for wholeness, we nevertheless can live in hope where we are. The hidden God finds a way into the pieces and in an unseen way makes them holy.

This is, then, a holiness for busy, scattered people going in a million directions. This is a holiness for women who call themselves "jugglers," "distracted," "disintegrated," "parceled out," and "walking on a tightrope." To be clear, this vision of spirituality in no way works against the pull to centeredness and wholeness so important to the spiritual life. Yet it recognizes an important spiritual moment in the process of waiting for divine fulfillment. The choppy, incomplete experience of life reminds us that human efforts do not save, but that grace binds life together in an unseen way. Theologian and pastor Dietrich Bonhoeffer made a similar point when he wrote from prison during the Holocaust, facing the realization that he would not be able to fulfill a full life: "this fragmentariness may, in fact, point towards a fulfillment beyond the limits of human achievement."[63]

A eucharistic spirituality does its best to keep the whole in vision, even as one hopes and believes that God works in the incomplete fragments. For example, during the Mass the community prays for unity, recognizing that the church is not yet one but still is in the presence of the Holy Spirit. In the *epiclesis,* the community asks that the Spirit transform the bread and wine into the body and blood of Christ "so that those who take part in the Eucharist may be one body and one spirit."[64] In our current state, though, we are fragmented.

Poignantly, Pierre Teilhard de Chardin wrote about his own experience saying Mass alone in the desert. Because he had no bread or wine or altar, he offered up all the labor of the world:

I, your priest, will make the whole earth my altar and on it will offer you all the labours and sufferings of the world....I will place on my paten, O God, the harvest to be won by this renewal of labour. Into my chalice I shall pour all the sap which is to be pressed out this day from the earth's fruits...above all, those who in office, laboratory and factory, through their vision of truth or despite their error, truly believe in the progress of earthly reality and who today will take up again their impassioned pursuit of the light.[65]

Christ becomes present in that work, which is a fragmentation that becomes the Body of Christ. And in the midst of that human brokenness and dispersion is the hunger for unity that cries out to God from the fragments: "This bread, our toil, is of itself, I know, but an immense fragmentation; this wine, our pain, is no more, I know, than a draught that dissolves. Yet in the very depths of this formless mass you have implanted — and this I am sure of, for I sense it — a desire, irresistible, hallowing, which makes us cry out, believer and unbeliever alike: 'Lord, make us one.' "[66]

A eucharistic spirituality hopes for unity and wholeness, but perceives Christ's presence in the fragments at this very time. A eucharistic spirituality does not propel one feverishly into productivity. Rather, it counters a Catholic works-righteousness or its equivalent — a secularized Protestant work ethic. One waits humbly, looking up at the broken bread and saying, "My life is like that." Indeed, the liturgy affirms that the bread that becomes the body of Christ is that which "earth has given and human hands have made." The bread is our lives and our work, in all of their pieces, broken and transformed. One does not rush up to fix the bread. One simply receives it in faith: "Only say the word and I shall be healed."[67] The healing, the wholeness, is what one hopes for, but it is not a condition of Christ's presence. Christ is really present in the fragments of the bread. And one can return each Sunday, or each day, to those fragments, the repetition of the liturgy reminding us that our lives are still fragmented and yet Christ is still there, in our ordinary time.

Chapter Five

Models of Holiness for Women Workers

Defining Sanctity

A Spiritual Vacuum: Where Are the Models?

Elisabeth Schüssler Fiorenza, a feminist biblical scholar and theologian, recalls her high school experience in the mid-1950s:

> Our images of ourselves, our problems as young women, and our goals for life were totally different from the images of the female saints that were preached to us. The lives of the saints presented more of a hindrance than a help in finding our own self-destiny. These stories stressed suffering, sexual purity, submission, out-moded piety, and total obedience. They were anti-intellectual and anti-erotic; they told about many nuns and widows and some queens, but rarely did they speak about ordinary women.[1]

One can imagine this teenager, dreaming of what she might become, hearing stories of holy women she would not want to emulate. The dissonance must have been tremendous. Indeed, her resistance to those stories undoubtedly helped to forge her own vocation as a feminist theologian.

Now Schüssler Fiorenza does not represent all women, to be sure. She is a highly educated, professional academic. Yet many women share her story — in varying degrees of intensity. As women increasingly have pursued professional growth, higher education, and identities outside of either the home or the convent, too often they have lacked religious models. Like Schüssler Fiorenza, many have not seen themselves in the models presented for women by the church. Where are the holy people who run harried between work and family responsibilities? Which saint stands as a model for the woman sitting at a desk in a government office, worrying because her child is running a fever at home? Which female saints navigate their way with integrity through competitive structures? Which negotiate for pay raises and better working conditions? Which saint guides the woman who picks strawberries for eighteen dollars a day and wonders if she should return home to her abusive husband?

Models provide life stories that open up for others to enter into. They are conversation partners as people go along their own paths. Within Catholicism, saints are presented as prominent models, exemplars of holiness and faithful living. Orthodox Christians also look to the saints as models or icons. Icons image the divine; they actually draw human beings closer into the divine life. The Protestant imagination may find it helpful to speak in terms of stories or narratives. With the lack of models, women also lack narratives that help to make sense of their changing social and economic roles. Stories can be powerful means of integrating experience within a framework of meaning. As Protestant theologian Bonnie Miller-McLemore writes: "Possessing no strategy or story to reconcile the public world of work and the private world of mothering, many women have the 'feeling of always doing something wrong.' "[2] Models provide life stories that offer perspective on one's own.

Models also are people to follow. For example, a labor union organizer, Mary Baker, describes the influence of models in her life. Raised as a Baptist, Baker later converted to Catholicism. She saw her mother observe the Sabbath on Sundays, even preparing the Sunday meal the day before. She also found in her girlhood church in the late 1920s a strong working woman who became a role model for her. Miss Lulu Craig Wessel was a bookkeeper for Georgia Petrified Brick and Clay Company, a widow in her early forties with no children. Baker recalls: "And I used to see her going along early in the morning, going to work, real dignified lady, drivin' a fine car. I visited her home and in the meantime she would pick me up and take me home. She was just my idea of a fine person, someone you want to pattern yourself after."[3] That is an apt description; a model is someone you would pattern yourself after. Or, as the National Council of Catholic Women put it, one tries to "mirror" the admirable qualities of a model, in their case, Mary.[4]

Diverse religious traditions — including Christianity, Islam, Hinduism, and Confucianism — affirm the power of models to shape piety and virtue.[5] And yet as women have assumed new social and economic roles, they often have lacked relevant religious models. Indeed, they may face a paucity of models of any kind. Best-selling author Laurie Beth Jones wrote *Jesus, CEO* (1995) because she "found it disturbing that nearly all leadership and management books are written by men. Yet women are the fastest-growing segment of business owners in this country. . . . With the business world changing so rapidly and so drastically, it seemed to me that we need creative and innovative role models now more than ever before."[6] Jones, a marketing executive, describes Jesus as the ultimate role model for both female and male leaders. Jesus embodies what Jones calls the "Omega management style," which incorporates both the male "Alpha" and the female "Beta" ways of using power.[7]

Obviously such language seeks to translate Jesus into highly secular terms. Jones does seem to respond to some of the particular difficulties that women workers describe. She paints Jesus as a model, for example, because he "believed in himself," "guarded his energy," "worked through his fears," and "did not despise the little things."[8] Yet she also risks diluting the gospels into popular, self-help, success culture. Jones casts Jesus as a "turnaround specialist," and she encourages leaders who "must be able to rise above controversies, jealousies, petty personal attacks" to take inspiration from Jesus who "rose above it all."[9] Women workers need a more critical effort to bring out of the faith models for contemporary living.

Women do seek role models in popular culture. Oprah Winfrey, for example, is a model to countless women who watch her television show, including its segment "Remembering Your Spirit." Women's magazines promote a wide range of models — from the Cosmo woman to the Good Housekeeper. Yet where are the religious models for contemporary working women?

Models define the good or successful or holy woman. This is a task that religious institutions should not leave to popular culture. They must look closely at women's real, contemporary situations, and with women seek to identify spiritual models for a new context. This means looking deep within religious traditions and thinking anew about how to understand models and holiness. If the church does not attend to these questions, women workers likely will find themselves more and more distant from existing notions of spirituality. Some will look outside the churches, some will do their own theological maneuvering, and others will lose the hope that their lives might be holy.

Modeling as Evangelism

Scriptures point to the importance of models, people who serve as examples of holiness or faithfulness. Modeling is a kind of evangelism. The Pauline author writing to the community at Thessalonika shows that models inspire others to faith. These others then may become models themselves: "And you became imitators of us and of the Lord, for in spite of persecution you received the word with joy inspired by the Holy Spirit, so that you became an example to all the believers in Macedonia and in Achaia" (1 Thess 1:6–7). The Second Letter to the Thessalonians actually calls on the beloved to serve as models of a work ethic, an example for the idle to imitate:

> For you yourselves know how you ought to imitate us; we were not idle when we were with you, and we did not eat anyone's bread without paying for it; but with toil and labor we worked night and day, so that we might not burden any of you. This was not because we do not have that right, but in order to give you an example to imitate. For even when we were with you, we gave you this command: Anyone unwilling to work should not eat....Brothers and sisters, do not be weary in doing what is right (2 Thess 2:17).

Models are important because they witness to the faith in a diversity of circumstances. The Letter to the Hebrews recounts the faith of the ancestors: Abel, Enoch, Noah, Abraham, Isaac, Jacob, Moses, Rahab the prostitute, unnamed women. Their faith inspires the faith of the Christian disciples: "Therefore, since we are surrounded by so great a cloud of witnesses, let us also lay aside every weight and the sin that clings so closely, and let us run with perseverance the race that is set before us" (Heb 12:1). Indeed, as they run, the faith of those who come before propel them forward even as they keep their eyes fixed on the ultimate model, Jesus: "...looking to Jesus the pioneer and perfecter of our faith..." (Heb 12:2).

Saints and Sanctity

And yet too many women today cannot find in the ancestors of faith guides for their everyday life, including work. Too many female ancestors remain unnamed. Too many have been made into caricatures of feminine piety. Contemporary women might yearn for a "cloud of witnesses" to surround them as they seek to be faithful in new circumstances. Yet many see more of a spiritual fog. Catholic women have particular difficulties — and particular opportunities to find models.

Because saints have been presented as such significant models within Catholicism, it is important to explore their potential to serve as holy guides for contemporary women. Indeed, the canonization process itself does much to define "spirituality" or "sanctity." When the church canonizes, it selects models of holiness. It defines a faithful and exemplary life. Saints are not the only models of holiness in the tradition, but they have been prominent, reinforced through devotional literature (particularly the "lives of the saints") and the liturgy. Devotion to the saints declined after 1960, at least among whites in developed Western societies. As sociologists Weinstein and Bell conclude: "It is undeniable that there has been an overall great decline in the role of cult and of saints as intermediaries between the faithful and their God."[10] The Second Vatican Council downplayed the veneration of the saints as it sought to emphasize a biblical spirituality; this is but one of several factors accounting for the decline. On the other hand, saints have not vanished. Hispanic piety still retains a place of honor for the saints, as do many Asian and African cultures. Indeed, the present pope John Paul II has canonized more than four hundred saints and beatified more than twelve hundred blessed persons.[11] Saints retain importance as models for many people, and their potential is still rich. Indeed, this exploration of saints as models should be useful across denominational and even religious lines. As Jesuit John A. Coleman writes: "In his *Systematic Theology,* Paul Tillich claimed that Protestant theology needed a thorough rethinking of the problem of sainthood; [Lawrence] Cunningham argues that Catholic theology is no less in need; and... the resources available to a search for a new kind of sainthood are even more ecumenical than current attempts at intra-Christian dialogue would imply."[12]

One problem, however, is that most saints identified within the Christian tradition are not lay. Indeed, as Ann Astell points out, the church's definition of sanctity long has favored cloistered or clerical vocations.[13] André Vauchez attributes this fact in part to a shift in understandings of sanctity in the late Middle Ages: "The criteria of sanctity were to become more and more extraordinary... visions, revelations, exchanges of heart, anorexic crises, and other mystical and paramystical phenomena.... This evolution led inevitably to the disappearance of the modest and useful movement of lay sanctity, a victim of the dual processes of clericalization and spiritualization of religious life which characterized the final centuries of the Western Middle Ages."[14] In other words, the most perfect spiritual life grew further and further from the reach of ordinary laity. Holiness was equated with miraculous deeds and extraordinary mystical experience. Feminist theologian Elizabeth Johnson notes that definitions of holiness enshrined in the canonization process have distanced spirituality from everyday life:

> The term "heroic sanctity," used in official church language as a criterion for those whose cases are tested for canonization, reflects a value given to a certain kind of spiritual achievement, attained by intrepid acts and buttressed by miracle. It customarily points to such deeds as witnessing to the point of bloody martyrdom, or engaging in the white martyrdom of stringent asceticism, or experiencing a radical conversion from which one does not turn back,

renouncing family and material possessions.... Traditional "lives of the saints" are filled with such titanic acts. Noble they may be, but their telling within a tradition of holiness interpreted along the lines of hierarchical dualism serves to reinforce the "unsaintliness" of those who do not measure up to these epic proportions.[15]

There was, then, a fundamental conflict between the renunciation of family and material goods common among saints and the reality of lay lives, particularly those of women. Within the canonization process, models of holiness became extraordinary and distant from lay life. Work — an ascetic activity at best or a distracting involvement with the material world — did not rank highly in conceptions of holiness. There are, of course, exceptions. Saint Joseph, carpenter, (adoptive) father of Jesus and husband to Mary, is regarded as the patron saint of workers. A "Prayer to Saint Joseph for the Spirit of Work" reads:

> Glorious Saint Joseph, model of all who pass their life in labor, obtain for me the grace to work in a spirit of penance to atone for my many sins; to work conscientiously, putting the call of duty above my own inclinations; to work with gratitude and joy, considering it an honor to use and develop by my labor the gifts I have received from God; to work with order, peace, moderation and patience, without ever recoiling before weariness or difficulties ... all after your example, O Patriarch Joseph![16]

Joseph could be a model of both worker and loyal family man. Yet none of the women interviewed for this study indicated that they looked to Joseph as a model or conversation partner in prayer. Perhaps Joseph has simply taken a back seat in the tradition, overshadowed by his wife, Mary, and son, Jesus. Or perhaps the fact that he is male makes Joseph less relevant to contemporary women.

The Problematic Presentation of Women Saints

Laywomen who were not celibates found themselves in a peculiar position. On the one hand, like all laity they had a certain subordinate place in the hierarchy of holiness. On the other hand, the church strongly affirmed women's maternal role. This was a holy role, a vocation, a sacred task. After all, the most powerful female model for Catholics and Orthodox, Mary, was Mother. This was a strong model and affirmation for laywomen. Yet the model was complicated, for Mary also was the Virgin Mother — an impossible model for ordinary women to imitate. As women embraced motherhood as a holy vocation, they also entered into sexuality, a necessary but lower realm in the eyes of the church. Pope John Paul II, for example, repeated this long-held understanding of the relationship between holiness and sexuality: "Virginity or celibacy . . . bears witness that the Kingdom of God and His justice is that pearl of great price which is preferred to every other value no matter how great. . . . It is for this reason that the Church, throughout her history, has always defended the superiority of this charism to that of marriage, by reason of the wholly singular link which it has with the Kingdom of God."[17] It is not surprising, then, that married women are the least represented group among canonized saints, a fact that feminist theologian Elizabeth Johnson attributes to the "dualist assessment that to be female is a handicap, but to be a sexually active woman renders one almost incapable of embodying the sacred."[18]

Real women who aspire to be mothers necessarily put themselves on a "lesser" spiritual path, according to church tradition. Christian Duquoc asserts that the conceptualization of Mary, the Virgin Mother, as model has served "to keep the ordinary Christian in second place."[19] Mary's perfection is inimitable. Many theologians and philosophers have grappled with the problematic aspects of Mary as model. Writing in the mid-1970s, for example, Marina Warner noted that Mary is, paradoxically, defined both as wholly unique and as "the model of Christian virtue." She is a model who continually frustrates those who would seek to imitate her, leaving them in a position of "hopeless yearning and inferiority." Warner concluded: "Mary cannot be a model for the New Woman."[20]

Moreover, the presentation of other women saints, like the presentation of Mary, tended to emphasize qualities such as submission, purity, long-suffering, selflessness, and dependency. These qualities stand at odds with many of the qualities demanded of women in the workplace and aspired to by many contemporary women. Meanwhile, hagiographical literature and church teachings do not emphasize the vision, initiative, independence, courage, and self-assurance of saints such as Catherine of Siena or Teresa of Avila; their virginity and mysticism become elevated instead. Johnson asserts that the "stories of the saints function as a means of ecclesiastical control. They...inculcate virtue that is unattractive and even oppressive to any woman whose goal is mature adult personhood."[21] In short, the presentation of women saints has amounted to "meager feast for women's souls."[22]

How have Catholic women in the twentieth century responded to this "meager feast"? Some have bracketed off their faith from their everyday lives, including work. Others have tried to make sense of traditional models, particularly Mary, in their present circumstances. This involves a theological process of adapting existing models for a new context, a process that has received inadequate attention by theologians and church leaders. Other women, when faced with the "meager feast," have simply pushed back from the table. They have left the church or distanced themselves from institutional religion in general.

Compartmentalization, or Living with Irrelevance

The lack of models for laity in general and contemporary women in particular presents a dangerous pastoral situation. Models convey the idea that the church values particular ways of living; they highlight certain spiritual paths. Yet few models officially sanctified by the church show work in the world as a spiritual path — and fewer still reveal this path for women. In reality, women saints have been leaders, managers, preachers, teachers, and innovators. They have begun religious orders, built hospitals, resisted powerful critics, negotiated with popes and politicians. Yet their saintliness seldom is linked predominantly with their work or leadership. This paling of work in the lives of great women in the tradition encourages contemporary women to compartmentalize their working lives from their faith. Work seems irrelevant to faith, or uncomfortably dissonant with the values women learn in church.

The reality is that women find themselves in new, demanding social and economic roles with little guidance about how to fit these new roles into traditional religious frameworks that, however, remain important sources of identity and community. No wonder women describe an experience of fragmentation. No wonder many compartmentalize these two seemingly unrelated areas of life; compartmentalization is a useful strategy for living with dissonance.

The problem, however, is that compartmentalization weakens the transformative power of faith. The church loses relevance and faith loses its power to inform and transform all aspects of life. The individual, too, lives with a hollow feeling that one's everyday life lacks meaning — or at least meaning that is strongly affirmed by one's religious tradition. This is a terrible inferiority complex that the church has laid on laity, and women in particular. It is an unfaithful rendering of the gospel. For while the gospels do relativize all human activity in the face of the awesome news of salvation, the gospels also reveal the good news through the ordinary. The sacramental tradition of Catholicism affirms this revelation.

Moreover, the values of the industrialized workplace may indeed be in tension with Christian values. People need ways to relate their fundamental convictions about the world to the concrete situations in which they live and work. Good models would help to guide workers, to challenge them, to provide another perspective on the taken-for-granted values of the workplace. If women find few models at all, however, they are likely to compartmentalize their faith and uncritically accept the workplace for what it is. The community of the church must reflect on what would constitute a model of holiness in the contemporary workplace.

Adapting Models

At the same time that the church suffers from a lack of public or identifiable models, it also is important to explore how some women are piecing together models from the tradition. Particularly for Catholics, search for and retrieval of models within the tradition is a vital part of maintaining religious identity. Mary is the most central model presented to Catholic women; thus, critical reflection about Mary and women's varied interpretations of her is crucial.

Some Catholic women clearly have retained a deep devotion to the Blessed Mother. African American Catholic Ruth Grant found Mary in 1945, when she was in her twenties. She saw Mary as "the greatest woman in the world," and she sought to be like her. Grant shows that models teach different things at different stages in life (or history). In her twenties, Grant "learned from the Blessed Mother the greatness and beauty of humility, which I don't think I had enough of when I met her." Now in her seventies, Grant learns from Mary how to surrender to God's will, relinquishing her desire to control her grown children.[23]

Other women found the presentation of Mary to be distant or even oppressive. They discarded her as a model; they either actively opposed what Mary represented or they simply "didn't relate" to her. One recalls novelist Mary Gordon's experience; Mary was "a stick to beat smart girls with." Gordon rejected Mary as she came into adulthood in the 1960s "in order to hold on to the fragile hope of intellectual achievement, independence of identity, sexual fulfillment."[24]

Women also adapted Mary in light of their social and economic roles, emphasizing characteristics demanded by the new situations. The Virgin Mary became more independent, less submissive. The meek domestic paragon became an advocate for the woman breaking into the male-dominated world of barbers. Mary had a voice. She intervened for the marginalized. The meaning of Mary varies widely depending on the theological beliefs and the historical and cultural context of the interpreter. As one Catholic woman put it, Mary can seem like "a plastic template that can be adapted to the culture of any age."[25] Indeed, descriptions of Mary reveal the varied meanings of this one model. In the late 1940s and early 1950s the Young Christian Workers, for example, appealed to Mary as the model of womanhood: "We can have no better model of womanliness than our Blessed Mother, for in her God has shown us the womanly nature in all of its fullness and beauty."[26] The National Council of Catholic Women designated Mary, "Our Lady of Good Counsel," as their patron saint. The NCCW called on women to mirror her admirable qualities — her compassion, fidelity, purity, prudence, and wisdom — as they gave themselves in service to the needy.[27] In 1966, Jesuit Richard McKeon held Mary up as a model management consultant. He described Mary's "courtesy," "pleasing personality," "punctuality" (particularly interesting!), "keen intellect," "efficiency," "service," and "humility."[28] While the NCCW description emphasized purity and charitable service, McKeon's later portrayal of Mary added to the traditional gentle qualities some very well suited to industrial success: punctuality, efficiency, and intellect.

While clearly Marian devotion has changed over the years, it is not dead. As Ann Astell points out: "The much deplored lack of an independent female standard, of a realized womanly ideal and positive role model, has prompted considerable new interest in the person of Mary."[29] Indeed, Astell points to the importance of Marian devotion in twentieth-century lay movements such as Focolare and Schoenstatt, both of which emphasize "the Christian calling to be an *altera Maria,* a living apparition of Mary, an *apparitio Matris.*"[30] Writing in 1982, Mary Gordon also described a movement to retrieve Mary:

> Life has changed. The most interesting and sophisticated thought by feminists now sees that in rejecting those things that were traditionally thought of as female, we are going with the male system of values that rates them as inferior.... It is this impulse to re-examine and to understand in a deeper way the history of women, female genius, female work, often anonymous, hidden, uncredited, to look for new values that are not simply male values dressed for success, that is leading women back to Mary.[31]

A Woman Caught Up in a Mystery

Born in 1940, AC grew up in New York in the 1950s surrounded by public displays of Marian devotion — May processions, block rosaries, prayers to Our Lady of Fatima for the conversion of Russia. Mary was held up to girls as a model of purity and womanliness. As she attended parochial schools, AC found that the nuns used Mary to keep order and to promote an ideal of the chaste woman: "The nuns chided us by saying 'Mary doesn't like girls who chew gum or wear sleeveless blouses, or "soul kiss" their boyfriends.'" AC graduated from college and married in 1961; she gave birth to her first of four children a year later. With three children under the age of six, she studied for a master's degree and began part-time work as a librarian. Mary hovered as the model wife and mother, a model that clashed with the reality of domestic life and the pull of the workplace:

> We were to emulate her as the perfect wife and mother, the "heart of the home," loving, humble and docile. As a young wife I wondered why Mary needed to be a perpetual virgin. Didn't she have feelings for Joseph, want to be physically close to him? As a mother of four small children, how could I identify with a perfect mother with one perfect child? What kind of role model could Mary be for me when I yearned to use my talents in the workplace as well as at home?[32]

The hagiographied Mary seemed distant from AC's own life situation. She reflected:

> The church has always held her up as the best model for women to emulate, but for some reason, that has never really resonated with me. The Mary of the Gospels seems real (what mother could fail to identify with the worried Mary looking for her missing twelve-year-old Jesus? "Where have you been?! Didn't you know I've been looking all over for you?") but I wonder how these few biblical references support the accretions and adulation of later ages.[33]

AC recognizes that new images of Mary are now being promoted, but she remains careful about constructing a Mary who is not real. She hesitatingly comes to her own peace about Mary as model: "In contemporary times, efforts have been made to present Mary as a strong woman, a different model from those of the past. But, like the queenly Mary of medieval days, the managerial Mary of the twenty-first century doesn't ring true to me. I think I prefer to honor her as a woman caught up in a mystery greater than her understanding but who struggled nonetheless to be faithful to her unique calling. So, perhaps, after all, she *is* a model for me as a woman who tries to be faithful to *my* individual calling."[34]

Models as Ideals of Spirituality

As women wrestled with the tradition, as they identified or con-
structed faithful models, they inevitably were engaged (mostly
unknowingly) in a process of defining holiness, faithfulness, or
spirituality. This is, indeed, a central task for women and for
the church as a whole. Unfortunately, as it has identified models
for women the church has defined spirituality too narrowly and
ignored the complex challenges that new social and economic roles
present women. The task at hand is to redefine spirituality for the
context of the everyday, including work and family. Women — as
well as laymen across several religious traditions — express a great
hunger to do so.

Clearly, definitions of holiness are influenced by historical context and social bias. Duquoc warns that definitions of sanctity
can strongly reflect relative historical assumptions and the bias of
those in power: "Models are not only ways; they can often become
obstacles. By stereotyping holiness they overvalue the forms of the
past and do not encourage the innovatory force of the Gospel."[35]
On the flip side, canonization also can promote social transformation. This is perhaps why Cape Verdean Catholic woman Margaret
Fortes ardently supported the canonization of Martin de Porres.[36]
De Porres was a symbol of interracial justice; his canonization also
affirmed the holiness of blacks and other races.

It is critical, then, to carefully reflect on the tradition and the
contemporary situation, discerning where wisdom lies and how
to guide the community in a new context. In each new historical
and cultural situation, people enter into a dialogue with traditional models. However, the church has given little theological
attention to, and scant guidance of, this dialogue. The dialogue is
actually a complex theological and spiritual process, as the church
has acknowledged. In his 1975 exhortation on evangelization, for
example, Pope Paul VI made this apt statement:

> The question is undoubtedly a delicate one. Evangelization loses
> much of its force and effectiveness if it does not take into consid-
> eration the actual people to whom it is addressed, if it does not
> use their language, their signs and symbols, if it does not answer

the questions they ask, and if it does not have an impact on their concrete life. But on the other hand, evangelization risks losing its power and disappearing altogether if one empties or adulterates its content under the pretext of translating it.[37]

Women are now, as in other eras, creatively engaging in this process of translation. Yet this process needs theological guidance and attention. The church as a whole has much to learn from women's negotiations with existing models. At the same time, women must be equipped to undertake this delicate task with a critical eye and the necessary knowledge.

Fruitful Directions

The church needs to articulate a spirituality for the everyday that responds to the hungers expressed in popular culture, but that also can critically connect these desires to models and wisdom within religious traditions. Specifically, women need models with whom they can converse in a dialectical conversation that will yield a holy perspective on work and life. Women today look for those models and conversation partners in many places — talk show hosts such as Oprah Winfrey are important examples. There is nothing wrong in this; accomplished and respected women in all fields offer examples of what women can be, how women can live and work gracefully. Yet women need to be critical in choosing models, remembering that as they gravitate to models they are choosing what it means to live a good life.

While the workplace and popular culture can provide helpful models, religious women also need connections to their own heritages of faith; as JM said: "I need a connection to this incredible legacy!" I would advocate a fresh look at "ordinary" lay people who will not be canonized by the church, but who show us what it means to try to be faithful in the everyday. They may include parents, co-workers, employers and employees, children, friends, parishioners, teachers, secretaries, bus drivers, and nurses. To see the holy in "ordinary" others enables us to see the holy in our own ordinary selves.

As women move into more professional roles, religious women also may serve as models or at least sisters on a common journey. Long before most women could hope for such educational and professional opportunities, sisters received training and served as leaders in education, health care, and ecclesial spheres. Sisters must be credited with educating large numbers of Catholic young women and, like the nun who prompted Janet Riley to enter law school, encouraging them toward professional accomplishment. They also worked with the poorest of the poor, putting their skills at the service of those in need — a good model of vocation. Moreover, while many women growing up saw nuns as a different species (one thinks, for example, of Mary Gordon's experience), sisters actually faced issues parallel to the ones confronting women outside of religious orders. Just as women faced sharp questions about their vocation and fulfillment outside of the home, so too did sisters encounter clerical resistance as they pursued work outside of their traditional teaching and social service roles. One recalls Mother Caspary's firm stand in 1967: She would encourage her sisters to develop their own talents in a wide diversity of work. This kind of independent vision, discernment of talents, professional zeal, and clarity in the face of powerful opposition presents a model that could inform many other working women. Of course, women in and outside of religious orders also need to assess the immediate effects of their changing work lives; in both cases, shifting vocations deeply impact important institutions, such as the family, schools, social services, and parishes. Care for these institutions, however, must be shared creatively and flexibly by both women and men.

One can look within the Catholic tradition to recover and see anew a host of faithful who can talk with women and point them in good directions as they navigate new terrain. What follows is an exploratory venture into what must be a much larger task.

Imaging Mary

For Catholic women, Mary remains a central model that must be addressed. Recognizing that the presentation of Mary has done damage to some, I still would argue for a recovery of Mary as model. In reality, despite the ambivalent effects of Mary, she provides a central feminine image of holiness that many Protestant traditions lack. Miller-McLemore writes about her experience in mainline Protestantism: "A great deal that I have learned about exhaustive self-sacrifice, sinful self-assertion, the trappings of embodiment, and the place of women and mothers in biblical stories and religious traditions — even the Protestant dismissal of Mary's role as mother of God and of feminine images of the deity — serves me very poorly indeed."[38] Two directions seem particularly fruitful for recovering Mary as model for women in the contemporary context. One is a focus on Mary's "fiat." The second is the example of Mexican devotion to Our Lady as a strong, compassionate woman who seeks justice.

Mary's Fiat

Mary was a woman who gave her "fiat," her "yes" to God. Picture her situation. She was a teenager, not yet married to Joseph. An angel appeared to her and told her that she would bear the Messiah. Mary did not understand what was happening to her. She did not know why God was calling her to this vocation. Mary was "perplexed" and "afraid" (Luke 1:29–30). She needed to be assured that "nothing is impossible to God" (Luke 1:37). She faced a moment of discernment. Not fully seeing what lay before, she chose to say yes to God: "Here I am, the servant of the Lord; let it be with me according to your word" (Luke 1:38). This was a statement of faith that enabled Christ to come to life within her.

Catholic women in the twentieth century were moved by Mary's fiat. Mrs. Arnold called Our Lady "the model of Catholic women" and her fiat "our guide to daily living"[39] Women debated how they could imitate Mary's fidelity in their own particular life contexts. Did women follow Mary only by saying yes to motherhood? Or could they respond to God's call in other ways? Could they be faithful lawyers, engineers, union activists? The psychologist JM gravitated to Mary's fiat, relating it to her own life's work. For she helped women discern to what they would give their "yes," a courageous act.

In my view, God calls each person to the fullness of life. How one lives out that call can vary widely, just as each individual is created differently and given her or his own name. Perhaps to some God gives a very specific path at a point in time. Most can respond to God by walking along one of a number of different paths. What is most important is that — no matter the particular path, no matter the confusing or painful steps along the way — we find it in us to whisper a yes to God. Mary stands before us as a model for this task.

To emphasize Mary's fiat rightly puts the focus on Mary's fidelity to a surprising God. She was, as AC put it, a "woman caught up in a mystery beyond herself." She could have said no to that mystery. Yet, with fear and trembling, she accepted a path that she did not understand. Out of that act, divine life entered history in a way that Mary could not have grasped. This is a very human, and very powerful, model of faith. As Christian Duquoc notes, we need to turn our attention to "just what does make Mary a saint: her faith, a model that is relevant to all Christians."[40]

"A Powerful Woman"

Mexican devotion to Our Lady of Guadalupe may well serve as a guide to women seeking strong, holy female models. For women such as Laura and Sister Esperanza, Our Lady is a powerful woman who *stands* at the foot of the cross, shows compassion to the suffering, and speaks to the people in a language they can understand. This image of Mary combines strength and compassion, qualities that have too often been divided by gender. As Esperanza, a Mexican sister who worked in the United States with migrant workers, explained: "There is a beautiful strength in the Mexican women.... It is a strong devotion to Our Lady." Devotion to Our Lady reminded women workers of their dignity and strength: "They say to me, *'Stabat Mater.'* Women tell me, 'Our Lady was standing — *stabat mater.* She wasn't whining at the cross. She was on her feet.' Sometimes I would say, 'How can you endure this?' And they say, 'Like our Lady, she was *standing* at the foot of the cross.' "[41]

The text of the "Stabat Mater" poem begins: "The mother stood, in sorrow and in tears, by the cross as her Son hung from it." Mary stands at the foot of the cross, pierced with sorrow. Yet her grief and compassion have power. Mary, the source of love, inspires others to love of Christ. Again, from the "Stabat Mater" text: "O Mother, source of love, let me feel the strength of this sorrow so that I may mourn with thee. Make my heart blaze with love for Christ the Lord so that I may please him!"

Depictions of Our Lady of Guadalupe show this same model of power and compassion. La Virgen de Guadalupe is the most important saint in her culture, says Mexican American Laura I.: "To us, and to me, she reflects what a powerful woman she is. To get all these masses of people getting together and coming into a church or celebrating that day for her is amazing. And what can I think about her when she moves almost the whole world? To me it is powerful." At the same time, Our Lady remains an understanding *co-madre* (co-mother): "I always think that if I wanted to ask God for something and it is related to my family, I will always go to La Virgen and pray, 'You're a mother of God and you went through the same thing we're going through with our children. We're here. Please help us. Through you, we know that your son is going to hear that we're praying and we're looking for some answers.' "[42]

The historicity of Our Lady's appearance in Mexico has been debated. According to traditional accounts, she appeared as a dark-skinned woman in Tepeyac in 1531 to an indigenous named Juan Diego. She spoke to him in his native tongue, expressing solidarity for the oppressed Mexican people, who then were under Spanish conquest. What seems clear is that over the past four hundred years a tradition of Marian devotion has emerged that unites the Mexican people's struggles for independence and cultural respect with this figure of Mary as advocate and compassionate power. As pastoral theologian Virgilio Elizondo writes, "Her presence is not a pacifier but an energizer which gives meaning, dignity, and hope to the peripheral and suffering people of today's societies."[43]

This understanding of Mary shows the impact of culture on understandings of holiness. Whereas out of the Mexican culture

Our Lady emerges as a powerful advocate, in Mary Gordon's 1950s and 1960s American experience Mary seemed like "a stick to beat smart girls with." Whether women who do not come out of the Mexican culture could relate to the tradition of Our Lady of Guadalupe is unclear. However, the qualities of Mary emphasized in this tradition — the power, compassion, and justice — certainly could inspire women seeking to be faithful amid changing social and economic roles. Moreover, Our Lady of Guadalupe remains so important to Mexican and Mexican Americans in part because she communicated to them in their own language. Mary, then, is a model with whom one may converse.

Recovering Other Models from the Tradition

Recovering other, less well known, models from the tradition also will be helpful. For while Mary is a very prominent and important model, she has been overlaid with many charged meanings. Some women find her to be an ambiguous or untouchable model. It will be helpful to look to other women in the tradition. For example, French mother and saint Jane de Chantal (1572–1641) could be a model for women who struggle to find their vocation amid competing pulls and who yearn to feel spiritual in the midst of hectic domestic responsibilities.[44] Jane was widowed at a young age, left to raise four children and run an estate alone. Jane knew the pain of grief; she lost two children and her husband. She also knew what it was like to be busy, feeling scattered and exhausted. Jane was a woman of great devotion who yearned to give herself fully to God. In her context, she understood that to mean entering a convent. Jane felt torn between her responsibilities for her children and the administration of her estate, and her growing desire to live as a nun. While she yearned for a more heroic vocation, she gradually (with her confidant Francis de Sales) learned to define vocation in terms of love, not a particular path. Her struggle to live devoutly in the midst of busyness offers contemporary working women a model. Her life also illustrates the seasons of women's vocations. Although Jane desired to enter a convent, she learned patience, learned to see her present situation as a call from God. Later in life, after her domestic duties lessened, she and Francis established the Visitandine religious order in 1610. The order was designed for women who needed some flexibility due to domestic responsibilities or ill health; these women could not commit themselves to more strict religious orders. Hence, Jane's own experience as a mother later bore fruit in a different vocation as the Mother Superior of a religious order. Each vocation had its own time. Still, they were integrally connected — not fragmented pieces of a life but (when seen in retrospect) seasons of vocation that unfolded into one another.

Of course, every model has limitations. Jane's spirituality was forged in the context of an aristocratic lifestyle; she was an upper-class woman with an estate. Salesian spirituality has been critiqued for its uncritical acceptance of courtly life.[45] Her notion of vocation speaks poorly to women in unjust social or economic situations, as it tends to promote acceptance of one's social location. Moreover, much as Jane tried to embrace motherhood and administration as her vocation, she still translated her holy desires into the establishment of a religious order. She was, perhaps, caught in the Tridentine formulation that celibacy was the more perfect way. In any case, discernment of paths was comparatively limited in Jane's worldview, a fact that reflected her social context and her understanding of God's will. There is a difficulty in translating any "model" into a different historical and cultural context. Theological and historical-contextual sensitivity must guide the translation process. Still, there is potential here.

Dorothy Day and the Catholic Worker

Where Jane de Chantal is limited as a model, Dorothy Day offers an alternative vision. Whereas de Chantal uncritically accepts her aristocratic milieu, Day trenchantly critiques the materialism and moral compromise of twentieth-century America. Where de Chantal builds little room for social resistance in her notion of Christian obedience, Day embraces a countercultural vocation that refuses to equate the status quo with God's will. Seeing their stories side by side shows that, indeed, women need multiple models from various contexts; different figures from the tradition model pieces of a spirituality needed by contemporary women workers. De Chantal is the gentle model seeking to live devoutly in the present moment, learning to love the everyday vocation in which she finds herself. Day is the fierce model challenging the system, embodying a spirituality of resistance that calls comfortable assumptions into question.

Much has been written about Dorothy Day (1897–1980), cofounder of the Catholic Worker movement.[46] Here I will look at two angles of her life that may serve as a much-needed model to women moving increasingly into the workplace. First, she insisted on the human dignity of the worker and sharply resisted the dehumanizing effects of work. Second, her faith propelled her in public as well as private vocations. She would not have seen a dichotomy between personal religiosity and public work; rather, she connected public and private in an integrated life and faith.

In 1933, in the midst of the Great Depression, Day began the Catholic Worker movement in New York City together with French philosopher Peter Maurin. Day was a New York journalist with leftist leanings who had converted to Catholicism. They published the *Catholic Worker* newspaper, supported labor, and opened houses of hospitality and farming communes for the poor, unemployed, and homeless. By 1942 Catholic Workers were running thirty-two houses of hospitality and twelve farms in the East and the Midwest.[47] Day thought that workers' problems ran deep. Workers needed far more than tools to integrate their faith and their work. Work was fundamentally flawed; faith had to resist the capitalist structures that demeaned workers and undermined Christianity. She wrote in 1936: "Workers have to defend their rights as individuals and Christians against a system which makes the Christ-life practically impossible for large numbers of workers."[48] Day fed the unemployed, she stood with striking workers, she camped out in jail with California farm workers. She prayed for more leaders to stand with the workers in their "struggle with Mammon."[49]

Day offered a realistic, not sentimentalized, picture of Christian faith. Love is not easy, yet it is the only answer to the indignities and suffering of the modern world. She wrote: "Love is indeed a 'harsh and dreadful thing' to ask of us, of each one of us, but it is the only answer."[50] Love happens in the little things. Day did not promote a heroic sanctity, but rather a roll-up-your-sleeves saintliness that gives service to individual people — difficult as they may be. Day upheld community as a vital aspect of spirituality and a means of social renewal: "We have all known the long loneliness and we have learned that the only solution is love and that love comes with community."[51] Day knew that forming community is immensely difficult as well as joyful. She lived with people's frailties, not eschewing the little, ordinary works of love. Yet her emphasis on love did not result in a private spirituality. Day was a journalist, labor advocate, antiwar demonstrator, civil rights supporter, and sharp social critic. Hers was a public witness.

While she was deeply committed to social justice, Day did not join the church because of its social teachings. Rather, she joined the church because there she found Christ, and, "like all women in love, I wanted to be united to my love."[52] She compared prayer to the experience of falling in love: "But more and more I see that prayer is the answer, it is the clasp of the hand, the joy and keen delight in the consciousness of that Other. Indeed, it is like falling in love."[53] Day expressed her spirituality, then, in terms of intimacy. Her experiences as a lover and mother (she had one daughter, Tamar) shaped her perceptions of God and the human person. To be a mother was to co-create with God: "God is the Creator, and the very fact that we were begetting a child made me have a sense that we were made in the image and likeness of God, co-creators with him."[54] Yet Day did not fall into a dichotomy between private, feminine spirituality and public, male action.[55] She "never seemed to cast the mother in her and the worker in her in any opposition. She took it as a given that she had a distinctive voice to speak to questions of public and social policy precisely because of her being a woman and mother."[56] In these ways, then, Day bridged the private, domestic ideal of womanhood and her public vocation.

Returning to the Cloud of Witnesses

It would be foolish to try to identify a single model for all women. Women find themselves in very different situations. Class, ethnicity, education, region, and age all influence the particular shape of women's work and the questions that women entertain. Women's work takes many different forms, and varies too across the seasons of a single life. What I have proposed thus far is meant only to jump-start the imagination, so to speak. Women figures from scripture, from the tradition, laywomen, religious women, missionaries, martyrs, mystics, mothers, managers — all these can serve as models to women stepping into new economic and social roles. The church as a whole can lift up models, assist with the translation process, and encourage women to identify themselves with holy persons. Yet each woman will seek out models for very particular situations and different dimensions of herself. Rather than proposing a single model, what is better is to return to the scriptural image of the "cloud of witnesses" (Heb 12:1).

We are surrounded by ancestors who sought to be faithful in their particular circumstances, all holy souls, who walk with us. The multitude of witnesses allows us to draw upon different models for various parts of ourselves and our work. The model a woman turns to when she gives birth may not be the same model she turns to in the midst of salary negotiations. For example, AC explained that she looks to many different sources for guidance in her work life:

> As director of a public library I strive to provide good service to our patrons, worthwhile programs to the community, and a fair and equitable environment for our employees. Working with boards, the public, unions, and contractors requires a spirit of cooperation and constant efforts at problem resolution. Where do I look for moral and ethical guidelines to apply to the work situation? Who are my spiritual models? The Ten Commandments and the spiritual and corporal works of mercy that I learned in childhood provide a basis for right actions. Reflecting on the Gospels challenges me to grow in love and to conform my interior attitudes with my actions. I look to the social teachings of the church on justice and labor to apply gospel values to contemporary issues. I draw inspiration from the lives of the saints and other holy figures, especially those who

struggled with doubt, ambiguity, and temptation (Thomas, Nicodemus, Augustine), those who spoke courageously to the powerful (Thomas More, Catherine of Siena), and those who lived a life of humble service to others (Dorothy Day, Mother Teresa, Thérèse of Lisieux).[57]

Women need multiple models, as their lives have many dimensions and they are always unfolding in a new social context. Thus, the "cloud of witnesses" is an apt image.

Models as Mothers, Teachers, Companions

It is not that one should exactly imitate the "cloud of witnesses." Rather, this image conveys the communion and support at the heart of the church. Models surround us and point to something beyond themselves. We may seek to follow the witness, but imitation of the witness is not the primary aim. Seeing, and walking toward, that to which the witness points is the goal. Models help us to see. Models help us to take our own steps from our own starting point toward life in God.

Thus, this discussion takes us to a somewhat different perspective on models of holiness. Let us return briefly to Mary as model. Some women did not consider Mary as a model, but rather as a companion. These women emphasized connection and intimacy, either because they would not put Mary on a pedestal or because they felt that their context was too different from Mary's to try to imitate her. Mary Parella said: "I realized she was the mother of the Lord and therefore let me get close to her and talk to her about things and ask her for help. I felt connected to her, not that I had her as a role model, because I don't think that's the right term. But I felt a connection to her."[58] Eileen Farrell too spoke in intimate terms: "The Blessed Mother is my friend."[59]

Thinking of models as friends similarly conveys that communion at the center of Christendom. Indeed, Christians affirm the "communion of the saints." This is a companionship among the living and the dead, brought together in unity in Christ. As the Second Vatican Council document *Lumen Gentium* stated: "Exactly as Christian communion between men [*sic*] on their earthly pilgrimage brings us closer to Christ, so our community with the saints joins us to Christ.... It is most fitting, therefore, that we love these friends and co-heirs of Jesus Christ who are also our brothers [*sic*]."[60] The language of this text illustrates the church's problem in naming women models of holiness. Yet it also affirms a companionship relationship with models. Models can be friends, intimate conversation partners as women seek to be faithful in their everyday private and public lives.

The term *model* usually connotes a unidirectional relationship. Many understand a model as one to be imitated, an exemplar. This can be problematic, for it ignores variations in context and the importance of surfacing each individual's gifts and vision. As Ruth Grant advised: "Never copy someone else. You may admire what they are doing, but my goodness, have enough faith in God to say, 'Let's see what God has given me!' "[61] Or, as Johnson put it, saints as models have been used to promote "spiritual dependency" and "relationships that pivot on inequality rather than solidarity."[62] While women certainly do look for models to imitate, they also hint at a different understanding of model as friend, teacher, and mother. These images allow for more recognition of the very different life contexts of contemporary persons. For example, whereas imitating Mary may be difficult, confusing, and even unadvisable in some contemporary situations, looking to Mary as a friend, mother, and teacher allows for more of a loving, back-and-forth conversation.

A mother, for example, might be a model, but she is always a limited one. She sends her child forward into a new context that she herself will never experience. She cannot serve as a model like a template, but rather like clay, the substance of which remains while the child molds it with her own hands to give it new shape. The child honors the mother not by imitating her exactly, but by bringing her own experience in a new context into dialogue with her mother's most fundamental values and admirable qualities. One remains close to the mother, conversing and loving, while forging ahead into a new time. One may be different from a model while respecting her most important ways of being. The child carries the family forward, not just as it is, but as it will become with the child's own stamp in a new context.

Similarly, one might think about a teacher as a model who also can learn from those starting out. As Mary Parella recalled: "I would be teaching the kids about the Blessed Mother, and through your teaching you learn so much. As you are a teacher, you are being taught by your kids the same way."[63] The image of the teacher-learner presents a helpful picture of the kind of model needed today. If women are indeed in a new context, they can learn from teachers who have gone before and add their own thoughts to the body of wisdom. This kind of thinking suggests that relationships with models are more like prayer and spiritual companionship rather than imitation. It also invites contemporary women to walk forward, to bring the community of faith into a new context, yet with the whispers of those who have gone before in their ears.

Chapter Six

Pastoral Ways Forward

Spiritual Formation for a New Context

Popular images of the woman worker over the past decades offer colorful snapshots. Rosie the Riveter straddles a tank in overalls, muscles bulging, her face a picture of confidence and conviction. June Cleaver follows in the 1950s, standing in front of the oven in apron, pearls, and high heels, the picture of femininity and domesticity. The Enjoli woman who can "bring home the bacon and fry it up in a pan" appears two decades later, sporting a smart suit, high heels, and a briefcase. These snapshots tell us something about women's changing roles. They show a shift from domestic ideals to the career woman ideal, for example. Yet they also provide caricatures of the woman worker that hide the deep complexity of women's changing situations. The reality is far more complicated. Women workers can be painted in myriad ways. They look like Ruth Grant, one of the first African American legal secretaries in New York, who stayed home with her son before sharing childcare with her husband. They look like Mary Parella, who really wanted to retire from her job as a teacher when she had children, but found herself taking jobs in retail, insurance, and software while she raised her kids. They look like Dolores Huerta, driving up and down the West Coast organizing farm workers, worried and guilty about the children she had left with relatives and friends. They look like Janet Mary Riley, a single woman who broke ground as a law professor in the 1950s. They look like MK, a telephone operator for forty years.

In many ways, these real women were navigating new terrain, although they may not have realized it at the time. For they were part of an important social change in the twentieth century that

162

sharply increased the numbers of women in the work force and opened doors to educational and professional advancement. This was not only an economic, social, and cultural shift. In profound ways, women's changing work patterns also raise spiritual questions. Women have — often implicitly and even unknowingly — begun to respond to these questions. There is much wisdom in their answers. Yet there is much work still to be done, even to articulate the questions.

Religious groups today stand at an important juncture. They have witnessed the rise of women, and particularly married women, in the workplace. In many ways, religious institutions resisted this move, warned about its effects, and clung to an ideal of womanhood difficult to reconcile with women's changing roles. If not qualified, of course, this statement would be an overgeneralization. For example, while the dominant message of the Catholic hierarchy emphasized women's private, domestic, and service vocations, numerous pastoral leaders quietly supported individual women in their more public work. However, Catholic women time and again came up against an image of what is was to be a good woman, an image with which they had to wrestle as they sought jobs, juggled work and family, pursued professional careers, or fought for just working conditions. Religious groups must respond with new eyes and ears. They should not uncritically accept all that change has brought. Yet they need to walk with women and together seek meaningful work — domestic and otherwise.

Spiritual Formation

Women's changing work patterns carry enormous implications for spiritual formation today and in the future. Spiritual formation is a process of sustained theological reflection and the learning of practices to foster rightful orientation to the divine. More specifically, Christian spiritual formation turns persons toward the incarnational God in Christ, revealed and made present through the work of the Spirit in the created world. God has created each person in the image and likeness of the divine (Gen 1:26–27). Yet human beings easily forget that created identity and mar the image. Spiritual formation leads people to a deeper awareness of who they most fundamentally are in God. It attunes them to carry a keen awareness of their created identities and a loving attentiveness to the created world. Human beings are not static. We are meant to live into the image of God in our earthy, complicated everyday contexts. This is the human vocation. We are meant to be fully who we are. Moreover, spiritual formation invites people to "abide in Christ" (John 15:4) and to take on "the mind of Christ" (1 Cor 2:16), to see the world from the perspective of the compassionate Co-Sufferer and the Redeemer in whom life triumphs over death. Spiritual formation draws people into life "in the Spirit" and helps them to see that toward which God continues to call them. Christians are meant to bear witness to God in Christ, to God with us, who continues to move through the Spirit in our world. We are always unfinished, and so we always live with hope for the perfection yet unseen. Yet, here and now, with the guidance of the Holy Spirit and wise human companions, human beings can grow. This understanding of spiritual formation presumes that people can cooperate with grace to grow in faith, hope, and love. The sacred draws us to that growth in the exigencies of our particular lives in history. God remains Mystery beyond our ken, yet we can learn how to live toward (rather than away from) that Mystery.

Every aspect of our lives can form us, can turn us in a direction. Work carries enormous power to develop or demean human beings, enormous power to direct or distort human gifts and purposes. Work does form people, offering identity, purpose, a place where one belongs. Conversely, work (and its absence) can form people in misguided ways, convincing them that they are nothing, that they are only a thing, that they have no purpose, or that their lives should be directed to unworthy purposes. As women increasingly enter the paid work force, they need ways of understanding spirituality rightly, so that good and just work can be seen as an integral part of a spiritual life. They need a spirituality that helps them to resist dehumanizing work and the consumerism and anxiety that drive needless productivity. They desire balance, integration, and meaning. They seek practices that will carve out space in their busy lives for reflection, prayer, and discernment. The task of spiritual formation in the face of changing economic roles must not be neglected.

This study of women workers can inform Christian spiritual formation in several ways. First, communities of faith should aim to develop flexible vocational witnesses in the world. People should have a sense of their lives as a calling that must be lived out creatively and responsibly in all spheres of life, including work. The vocation is flexible because women (and men) have more than a single vocational realm. Home and family remains a primary vocation for many women, yet there is no reason why it must be the exclusive calling for all women. To discern one's gifts, to use them for more than self-development, to practice love and care in tangled circumstances, to create community, to hope in the midst of limited vision — these are the practices that witness to the abiding grace of God and the dignity of creation. Work demands these practices in particular ways, yet work is not the only place of vocation. Christians need to look flexibly at life circumstances, seeing the places that need tending, finding ways to witness from within the particular structures and relationships they are in at the time. They can find room for those practices on the job but also can carry those practices beyond a particular role or job.

Second, spiritual formation enables people to step back from the harried blur of everyday events to grasp the sanctity of time. Liturgy places everyday schedules into a greater, eternal perspective. Spiritual practices such as the *examen* provide regular ways to reflect in the midst of busyness, to recall that we have been given a day, to give thanks and seek to discern life-giving patterns in how we use our time. The Sabbath most of all reminds us that time is a gift and that we are more than what we do. Clearly, women grapple with a sense of fragmentation and yearn for integration. Spirituality should help women find ways to make sense of multiple roles and all the divisions that lead to a compartmentalized faith. For Christians, a eucharistic perspective offers meaning in the pieces, the divine presence breaking into our ordinary time. Spiritual formation creates people who can find grace in the fragments.

Spirituality is not a fixed "ladder of ascents" but rather a creative dialogue between the present reality and the wisdom of the tradition in an ever-restless seeking to live well with God. Models of holiness can be very important. In light of women's changing roles, however, models should be seen as conversation partners rather than as templates to be imitated. For spirituality in each new context will take on somewhat different contours. Always it involves a desire to know and love and trust the divine. Always it involves attentiveness to created life, a compassion and humility and awe. Yet the particular ways in which one embodies faith in the world must change with context. Holiness then is rooted in a community of seekers who have gone before us and who pray with us, but we together are oriented to an unseen future.

Spiritual formation should blend concrete understandings of the workplace with theologically grounded reflection in a community. The church needs processes whereby women and men reflect on their work experiences in a community, bringing their work lives into the ongoing conversation of religious groups. Ultimately, this kind of reflection challenges the faith community to be more just and to wrestle with the complexity of lay life. Laity also gain insight and inspiration to develop more faithful practices at work. This spiritual formation could occur in the local congregation, in the workplace, or in other small group settings. Each poses particular possibilities and limitations.

Consultation

The first step is to dialogue with women workers. The dialogue process will serve two main purposes. First, it will enable clergy to better understand the needs and experiences of women workers. Women face some challenges at work quite similar to the challenges faced by men. They also encounter quite specific issues and tensions at work. Religious leaders can learn important information about the impact of modern work on all people, and about the significant ways that work shapes women's lives in particular. Second, consultation should aim to facilitate theological reflection about the experience of work. Laity need space, tools, and practice in articulating the meaning of their work lives. They — and women particularly — are rarely asked to do so. They often do not know how to do theological reflection, or they may articulate their reflection in language that is not churchy or technical. Professional theologians and clergy may miss the wisdom or urgency of these reflections. Hence, co-reflection would provide laity with tools for reflection and would help church leaders to catch the meanings laypersons do articulate. Laity also may think that their lives do not provide important content for theological reflection; a mutual process of consultation and reflection sends a different message.

The consultation process would guide particular communities in shaping pastoral responses according to their own theological traditions and the specific economic situations of their members.

Women's own diverse senses of the meaning of their own work must inform theological reflection on vocation and discernment. At the same time, the tradition can provide wisdom to speak to contemporary difficulties, to address confusions in a time of social change. When searched with a careful eye, keenly aware of the present context, the Christian tradition may guide women as they undertake new roles. This conversation is a back-and-forth dialogue, a dance that aims to critique and enrich both tradition and context. One takes women's experience seriously by bringing their concerns to traditional theological resources, searching them for insight while also challenging the tradition to evolve in light of the new situation.

Local Church

Identity and Human Dignity

The local church can do much to foster the spiritual formation of women workers. First and foremost, the community of faith ideally supports human dignity, tells each individual that she or he is worth something. As one African American pastor put it, the local congregation is a place where women workers count, where a "nobody can be a somebody." Reverend Joseph L. Roberts Jr., pastor of the famous Ebenezer Baptist Church in Atlanta, for example, described in a 1977 interview the importance of church in the lives of black women workers:

> I've got women in my congregation who go out five days a week wearing white uniforms, which says they are nobody, but when they dress on Sunday morning and come to Ebenezer, they are dressed to kill, naturally. This is the only place where a nobody can be somebody. It doesn't matter to the people where they work who they are, and the uniform is a sign that they do not belong in that community, that they are only there to serve it. But when they come here, it means something altogether different.[1]

Communities of faith can offer a sense of identity deeper than one's work roles. The church community can sustain women's spirits in work situations that are demeaning and destructive. It becomes an oasis and a place of rest and reorientation. Here one is seen and known in a different light, outside of roles and uniforms and paychecks. Here, ideally, one's basic identity as a human being created in the image and likeness of God is reinforced, providing leverage against other forces.

Telling the Biblical Stories

The community of faith tells the biblical stories that relate this basic identity, the Genesis narratives, the parables of Jesus. One hears the stories too of hope and divine power leading to freedom and life — the Exodus story, the resurrection. Of course, one also hears biblical texts that seem to deny women's innate equality and freedom (e.g., "Wives, be submissive to your husbands" [Col 3:18]). The local church should be a place for authentic struggle with these texts. Interpreting scripture becomes a spiritual discipline and — as in the early church — the root of doing theology. Practices such as the ancient *lectio divina* ("sacred reading") could be done with a focus on texts about work and about women. *Lectio divina* was an important part of the sixth-century Benedictine Rule, and the medieval monk Guigo II systematized this ancient way of praying with the scriptures. The practice involves four dimensions. One reads (or hears) the scriptures (*lectio*), meditates on them (*meditatio*), prays into them (*oratio*), and rests in a wordless contemplation (*contemplatio*).[2] The practice could provide a way to wrestle and pray with scriptural texts in light of women's changing roles. In a similar vein, a Lutheran sourcebook for congregations proposes a "workplace hermeneutic" with which to read the scriptures. Texts are interpreted through the lens of workers and in relation to concrete work contexts.[3] It is important that lay women and men be given opportunities to reflect on the scriptures in light of their jobs and to share their reflections with the worshiping community. Lay people could be invited to give occasional homilies on work and to write reflections on work and faith for the church bulletin.

Liturgy and Sacramental Imagination

The congregation is a worshiping community. God becomes present in the community itself, an important sacramental sign for women who so clearly value relationships in the church, in the family, and at work. The liturgy is the central space for engagement with the Word. Liturgy also reminds us of the sacred quality of time. Moreover, the liturgy is itself a sacramental sign, patterning people into a sacramental understanding of the world. This sacramental understanding powerfully informs women trying to make sense of the mundane. In the liturgy the bread is broken, Christ made present in the fragments. God breaks into the world, in the repetitiveness of the liturgy, in the repetitiveness of work.[4]

Special liturgies for workers and prayer celebrating holy female and male workers can connect this sacramental life more explicitly to labor. Occasions such as Labor Day can be marked through worship. For example, the United Methodist Church celebrates "Labor Sunday" on the first Sunday of September. Prayers rededicate workers to their vocations: "Help us steadfastly, and as in thy sight, to fulfill the duties of our calling." Worshipers ask for discernment to see and resist the sinful and destructive elements of their jobs: "If there has been anything in our work harmful to others and dishonorable to ourselves, reveal it to our inner eye with such clearness that we shall hate it and put it away, though it be at a loss to ourselves....May there be nothing in this day's work of which we shall be ashamed when the sun has set, nor in the eventide of our life when our task is done and we go to meet thy face."[5] Prayers also raise up the unemployed and ask for just relations between labor and management.

Problematic Structures

Of course, the church presents its own contradictions. How can one discuss spiritual formation for women workers without noting that women work in problematic structures within the church? Some parishes do foster women's strong leadership, with women taking important roles on parish councils, religious education staffs, music ministry, and even as pastoral associates. As mentioned earlier, Catholic women also have moved increasingly into diocesan leadership positions. In such roles, they demonstrate the contributions that women make professionally to the church and society. However, women's leadership is not embraced within many Catholic parishes and dioceses. In general, a male pastor and male hierarchy ultimately control women's work — both volunteer and paid — within the parish and diocese. The restriction of ordination to men also is a powerful symbol and a reality of power within the church. It sends a signal that women are not equal in dignity, or not as holy, as are men (despite church arguments that try to avoid this implication). The parishes that prohibit altar girls reinforce that signal in children. Women work within a church structure that pays poorly, offers little job security, and keeps men in positions of power. This ecclesial reality forms women and girls. How do they reconcile this church experience when they enter a work force that increasingly offers women opportunity for leadership? Will this cause religious alienation, or will women negotiate contradictions through compartmentalization, adaptation, or active resistance?

Developing Confidence and Community

As women move into new roles in the workplace, they need self-confidence to take on leadership positions. In the past, many women who held leadership in the home or in volunteer activities in church, school, or neighborhood still questioned their ability to do the same in the workplace. Or they felt guilty about taking on new roles. One commentator describes this "internalization of gender-based stereotypes": "Women, for example, have identified lack of self-confidence as a major factor inhibiting their greater participation in union activities.... Women who have run PTAs, church organizations and community groups, raised vast sums of money, and involved hundreds of people in working toward a common goal maintain that they have no skills."[6] This is an important issue, about self-worth as much as competency in a new field. Even Dolores Huerta, known now as a fiery labor leader, began her labor career in 1955 only after a local community organizer bolstered her confidence: "If I hadn't met Fred Ross then, I don't know if I ever would have been organizing. People don't realize their own worth and I wouldn't have realized what I could do unless someone had shown faith in me."[7]

Women's volunteer work, including church activities, can help women gain confidence and skills to advance in the paid workplace. The community women find in both volunteer activities and the workplace also can support them and develop their confidence. For example, women report that their involvement in the National Council of Catholic Women, a federation of parish-based Catholic women's organizations, brings "relationships with other women of like values.... There is a sisterhood established, there is a support system that is unbelievable ... that you just can't get elsewhere." Moreover, participation in NCCW "enriches their prayer life ... and has developed their leadership skills which they find transfers both to the workplace and to family life. We have had a very effective leadership program over the past thirteen years that begins with the fundamentals of who am I, what are my gifts, and then how do I share my gifts with others. That provides the basic skills that you can use wherever your position is."[8]

Conversely, employment can bolster women's confidence in their leadership abilities, developing skills and self-assurance that later benefit the local parish. Mary Parella, having raised her four children, finds that her varied work experience enables her to contribute to the Renovation Steering Committee at St. Elizabeth of

Hungary parish in West Acton, Massachusetts: "The only reason I am there is because of all the pieces in my career that got me to facilities that gave me the courage to say, 'I might have something to offer this committee.' "[9]

Women can gain skills and confidence through their church volunteer activities. These can translate into professional success. Workplace experiences also can help women to take leadership in their local congregations. Yet a dissonance persists between religious ideals of work and the reality of women's work in the church. Many women are able to find communities that support their sense of worth and that develop their leadership skills, even in a church that does not ordain women. They develop creative ways to channel energy and to claim vocations when the most obvious positions of power are closed. Yet there are countless others who cannot make this negotiation, and they may be lost to the church.

Workplace Ministries

Spiritual formation and guidance in the workplace itself is another approach. The Catholic worker-priest tradition has all but died, yet workplace ministry still may be a viable ministry that now could serve female and male workers. Evangelicals, for example, encourage lunchtime Bible study groups and prayer breakfasts. Workplace chaplains reach out to employees in fast food restaurants, factories, and offices. This type of ministry holds both promise and dangers. The main promise is that workplace ministries reach workers and engage them in contextual theological reflection and spiritual companionship. Chaplains gain an understanding of the actual situations confronting workers, offer a presence in the workplace, and mold ministry around the schedules of workers. Religious groups could train workplace chaplains with special awareness of women workers' issues, especially when chaplains are to be placed in industries with high proportions of women workers (e.g., office staff, childcare, service).

Different models of workplace chaplaincy exist. The Texas-based Marketplace Ministries, for example, sees the role of the chaplain as evangelist. In operation since 1984, the organization emphasizes a biblically oriented evangelistic mode of pastoral care. The corporate chaplain is a "personal witness and a soul winner for Christ in both word and lifestyle."[10] Marketplace Ministries places over six hundred Christian chaplains in industrial settings, usually on a contract basis. Chaplains must have secular work experience as well as ministry experience because they "must understand the temptations in the workplace, the difficulties of relating faith to work, and the high demands of secular labor." Thus, the chaplain has a strong ability to relate to the worker. However, he or she may not have strong theological training. Marketplace Ministries does not require seminary training for chaplains, and the organization cautions against overintellectual approaches to ministry.[11]

The National Institute of Business and Industrial Chaplains (NIBIC), on the other hand, focuses on work-life concerns and explicitly distances itself from the evangelical approach. The organization sees the chaplain's work as "public ministry." It defines its work as "interfaith ministry to people in business and industry" and stipulates that chaplaincy is "not to be used for sectarian promotion nor as a preaching program." This is a "professional" model of workplace chaplaincy, guided by a code of ethics that emphasizes confidentiality, boundaries, and professional development.[12]

As the differences between these two alternative models highlight, there are some problematic aspects to workplace chaplaincy. First, how to protect religious freedom in a pluralistic workspace while also enabling chaplains to bring a powerful, tradition-specific vision of work and spirituality into the workplace? NIBIC tries hard not to impose religion, but chaplains could risk becoming simply another human resources department. Marketplace Ministries preserves a strong Christian identity, but risks being an unwanted or oppressive presence. There is a fine line to tread here. One would want to argue that workplace chaplains facilitate religious freedom and spiritual integration by offering outlets on the job. Yet what to some facilitates religious freedom could be seen to others as imposing religion in their work environment.

Second, the role of the chaplain is not entirely clear. Is the chaplain a spiritual guide or a tool of management? Since Austaco Inc., a major Pizza Hut and Taco Bell franchise, hired chaplains through Marketplace Ministries, the company reported a decline in annual turnover from 300% to 125%.[13] That means a more successful business. Is the lower turnover rate a natural consequence of an improved work environment? Or do chaplains serve as morale boosters in a less than ideal work situation, perhaps encouraging workers to remain in place? Chaplains may be compromised as their jobs depend on management's good will. Ideally, the chaplain would be in a position to engage in advocacy for workers, including women workers. Yet when their salaries or their positions depend on management, this reality weakens their advocacy position. In some cases, spiritual consultation in the workplace distorts authentic spirituality, turning it into a utilitarian tool for a company's economic gain.

Still, as a ministry of presence, workplace ministries remain important. Particularly taking into account the time crunch faced by women workers, schedule-sensitive opportunities for brief spiritual refreshment at lunchtime or a break could provide vital nourishment. Moreover, the opportunity to connect with colleagues on a spiritual level may be quite welcome and may provide important perspective on the implicit values of the structures in which women work.

Para-Church Small Groups

Small groups hold great potential to facilitate theological reflection on work in the contemporary situation and to nourish the spiritual growth of women workers. Small groups can offer women a safe space to reflect on their work, to articulate their own sense of meaning, to study scripture and tradition, and to build community. Small groups also are vital supports for discernment, a task that faces women as they negotiate jobs and family, confront injustices on the job, and seek meaningful work at various seasons of their lives.

Episcopal priest Whitney Roberson describes the growth of a San Francisco–based group called Spirituality at Work:

> Spirituality at Work began as an experiment: a small group of individuals whose spiritual roots lay in the Christian tradition met to explore the relationship between their work and their faith.... The conversations developed into a project to discover just how participants might create conversation "spaces" in which they could assist one another in integrating the inner life of spirit with the outer life of work, deepening their own sense of meaning and purpose as well as empowering one another as agents of reconciliation and transformation in their workplaces.... In the almost five years since that first conversation, Spirituality at Work has become a community of business professionals.[14]

Women workers wrestling with a sense of being fragmented and harried would benefit from these kinds of integrative communities.

Small groups also could engage workers with wisdom from the tradition, perspectives on labor, justice, and consumerism that can help contemporary workers to frame and direct their experience differently. For example, the Woodstock Business Conference, established in 1992, helps business executives to incorporate Judeo-Christian values into their work; to integrate faith, family, and professional life; to develop an ethical corporate culture; and to exercise a positive influence on wider society.[15] WBC introduces religious concepts, such as vocation: "The Judeo-Christian tradition sees business as a calling, a vocation ... as a business person you are a steward, entrusted with God's creation."[16] Local chapters meet monthly in cities across the country. Each meeting follows a format loosely based on the see-judge-act method. Meetings include prayer, silence, and reflection on a designated scripture passage. Within that context, members discuss a topic for the day and discern an active response to the issue in their particular contexts. Topics include: vocation, leadership styles, compensation, management in an era of globalization, and diversity in the workplace. The formation process embraces a "spirituality of engagement which is designed to move participants in 'Christian practical wisdom.'"[17]

Like the Woodstock Business Conference, the Shalem Institute for Spiritual Formation also focuses on top levels of management and draws on traditional spiritual resources. Founded in 1973, this ecumenical institute based in Maryland started the Soul of the Executive program in 1998. The sixteen-month program combines intensive retreats, monthly peer group support meetings, individual spiritual direction, readings in spiritual classics and organizational analysis, and a pilgrimage to the Holy Land. Numerous women participate. Participants must hold executive management positions in private or public organizations. Shalem makes its theological foundation clear: "The primary basis of our learning draws on the rich wisdom and practices of the classical contemplative tradition, and in particular, of Christian contemplative tradition. This long-tested spiritual heritage, which focuses on the individual's evolving orientation to the sacred in everyday life, offers significant practical application to executive leadership today."[18]

Both the Woodstock Business Conference and the Shalem Institute seek to create community grounded in a religious heritage. They attend to spiritual practices that can sustain and guide workers. While extending an open posture, each organization clearly defines its worldview. Many leaders and participants of the groups are religiously affiliated, although the organizations themselves are not directly church-related. One limitation of these groups is that neither cater to the working class. The Shalem program requires spare income and time for week-long retreats and a pilgrimage. The Woodstock Business Conference specifically targets managers. The groups maintain that they seek to reach leaders who can influence the workplace culture.

Small groups need not be limited to management, however. A benefit of this approach is its flexibility and democracy. Leadership can be shared. Small groups could give women workers — many of whom lack sufficient leadership opportunities in both secular work and parish life — real spaces for leadership. Tradition-specific groups can flourish, but so too can ecumenical and interfaith groups. Structured programs such as Woodstock or Shalem can guide small groups, but impromptu groups also are viable. Small groups can emerge out of the workplace, congregations, professional associations, or friendships. One difficulty is that small groups unattached to a congregation or structured spiritual vision may lose their moorings and disintegrate into group therapy or purely social gatherings. Still, small groups can be authentic manifestations of the church, moving into deep understanding of members' particular life circumstances, with real care, accountability, theological reflection, and supported action. Small groups, then, hold promise as a dimension of spiritual formation and theological reflection for women workers.

Public Policy Approaches

Theological visions and spiritual formation should not be divorced from attention to social structures. In order to protect human dignity and to create the possibility of vocational witness in work, religious groups also must address the structures of work itself. Theological analyses of women's work and vocation must take into account the human sin that infiltrates work and undermines human dignity. Religious groups also must seek to overcome, as far as is possible, the injustices and destructive aspects of work that only perpetuate human sin. Women, and particularly women of color, are at risk given their more tenuous position in the work force, due in part to their adjusting work commitments to fit family responsibilities. They have less leverage against powerful employers, accumulate fewer years of continuous experience, and build fewer financial resources.

While overall women have narrowed the pay equity gap since 1980 (when it hovered about 59 percent, as it had for twenty years previously), they continue to earn only about 72 cents for every dollar men in similar positions earn. Women of color face a wider wage gap. By the end of the twentieth century, black women earned 65 cents for every dollar men overall earned; Hispanic women earned a mere 52 cents.[19] In addition, some economists attribute much of women's relative gains in pay equity to men's falling wages rather than to increased wages for women.[20]

Women's promotion to high-level leadership also still falls short. According to a congressional study, by 2000 women constituted about 47 percent of the American labor force but occupied only 12 percent of managerial jobs. Moreover, the wage gap for female managers actually widened between 1995 and 2000 in industries such as communications; finance, real estate and insurance; retail; and entertainment.[21] Debates continue, of course, as to whether gender discrimination or women's preference for family-friendly jobs (or a combination of these factors) accounts for the discrepancies.

One piece of good news: some evidence showed that the "feminization of poverty" slowed and even began to reverse itself in the 1990s, at least among whites, perhaps due to gains in women's earning power.[22] Furthermore, the passage of the 1993 Family and Medical Leave Act, which guarantees twelve weeks of job-protected, unpaid leave to parents upon the birth or adoption of a child, so long as they work for a company with fifty or more employees, provided some — albeit quite modest — relief to working mothers.

Religious groups need to exert influence on the structures of work so as to limit their demeaning aspects and develop their life-giving potential. If spirituality is to be understood as related to public life, as I believe it should be, then spiritual formation should equip people not only to address the individual meanings of their own work but also to critique or transform social and economic structures that undermine human dignity. The ideal of work as part of the human vocation, the understanding of discernment as a component of a free life of faith, and a sense of justice should propel people to critically look at the impact of work on women's lives. Thus, I would argue that spirituality flows out into public policy issues, although I would not say that the Spirit dictates any one solution to most complex public dilemmas.

While churches' primary mission is to witness to the good news of salvation, careful involvement in public policy also falls within a religious calling. When it comes to providing for women's well-being at work, churches have a role, albeit a complicated one. Specific policies have a range of effects, many unforeseen, and people of faith can differ on policy recommendations. For example, Catholic groups — including Catholic women's organizations such as the National Council of Catholic Women and the National Coalition of American Nuns — took divergent positions on the Equal Rights Amendment. Positions varied both according to empirical judgments about the effects of protective legislation on women's well-being and according to theological judgments about women's nature and vocation.[23] The stance taken by religious groups on any public policy issue depends both on empirical knowledge and theological perspective.

Several religious groups have attempted to respond to policy questions about women and work. As one examines recent examples of policy statements by Christian and Jewish groups, a consensus emerges in the endorsement of pay equity, equal opportunity, and antipoverty efforts. For example, in its study paper "All the Livelong Day" (1988), the Presbyterian General Assembly in 1988 integrated social analysis and theological reflection to critique the devaluation of women's unpaid labor: "Today the concept of work is drastically different from the idea of vocation that Calvin promoted. The value of work has come to be measured by money earned, not by its contribution to the well-being of society." Noting that women's unpaid work in child-rearing, homemaking, and volunteering receives little valuation, the paper continued: "To regain the essence of Calvin's concept of vocation where we are called to serve humanity through our work we will need to redefine what is considered 'good' work.... Work would be measured by its benefit to the household of God, not by monetary compensation."[24] The paper is a good example of how religious groups can reach deeply into their own specific theological heritage to address contemporary social and economic situations.

"All the Livelong Day" endorsed pay equity, welfare reform, and improved childcare. It noted that women do the majority of volunteer church work; given women's increased rate of paid employment, "it is imperative that church volunteer work be distributed more equitably between men and women." Because women juggle heavy demands of work and employment and are socialized to be "obliging": "Pastors should be particularly sensitive to the burden of the double day when they assign extra work to women staff. In addition, sessions should not expect volunteers to pick up the work of paid staff when budget and staff reductions are made." Moreover, the report raises the question of whose labor should be compensated and whose performed on a volunteer basis.[25]

The United Methodist Church in 1992 similarly called for greater appreciation of the economic and social value of women's labor, including volunteering: "Often the productive labor of women is ignored in economic statistics, reinforcing the impression that work done by women is peripheral, of secondary importance, even dispensable."[26] The church endorsed pay equity and the eradication of workplace discrimination:

> Women's earnings are an indispensable share of the incomes of more and more families. Families headed by women are the fastest-growing segment of the poverty population and now represent 75 percent of all individuals in poverty. Many mothers must support their family on their income alone; a significant portion of these mothers are women of color. Thus, the elimination of wage-based sex and race discrimination in the labor force is an important element in ending the "feminization of poverty."[27]

Another resolution critiqued the segregation of women into lower paying and "certain stereotyped job fields."[28] Like the Presbyterian paper, the Methodist resolutions also draw on their own specific theological traditions. The Methodists resolved to develop ministries to workers, the unemployed, and the underemployed, and "in the best tradition of Wesleyan inclusiveness, design settings in which to hear their stories, survey their needs, affirm their diverse gifts, and nurture their leadership skills."[29]

The Central Conference of American Rabbis, representing Reform Judaism, similarly condemned pay inequity and the feminization of poverty in a 1984 resolution. The rabbis pledged support for the Equal Rights Amendment and legislation incorporating principles of economic equity for women.[30] A later resolution specifically called on Jewish congregations and other Jewish organizations to move toward greater realization of these ideals, to ensure their own female employees pay equity and equal opportunity in hiring practices.[31]

In their 1986 pastoral letter *Economic Justice for All,* the American Catholic bishops argued that tax policies and social welfare should support — not discourage — parents who choose to work at home caring for their children. At the same time, they denounced unjust treatment of women in the paid work force. Pay inequity and discriminative practices in promotion and job classification contributed to women's poverty: "Wage discrimination against women is a major factor behind these high rates of poverty.... [Women] find themselves in jobs that have low status, little security, weak unionization, and few fringe benefits. Such discrimination is immoral and efforts must be made to overcome the effects of sexism in our society." In the bishops' view, a lack of adequate childcare, flexible work schedules, and benefits for part-time employees compounded the discrimination against women workers. They did not present childcare as solely a woman's issue, but rather one crucial for all working parents. The bishops called on employers, government, and private agencies to improve the quality and affordability of day care. They also supported more generous "parental leave policies" to give new "parents" greater job security.[32]

Economic Justice for All also tackled the issue of time. The bishops lamented the eclipse of leisure: "Some of the difficulty in bringing Christian faith to economic life in the United States today results from the obstacles to establishing a balance of labor and leisure in daily life." This balance was critical to social, political, educational, and cultural structures of society — and most particularly to the family. Time outside of work helped to nurture marriages, develop relationships with children, and build up the community groups (e.g., parish, schools, and neighborhood organizations). Indeed, the bishops understood leisure time as important to a Christian vocation, even a countercultural stance: "For disciples of Christ, the use of leisure may demand being countercultural. The Christian tradition sees in leisure, time to build family and societal relationships and an opportunity for communal prayer and worship, for relaxed contemplation and enjoyment of God's creation, and for the cultivation of the arts which help fill the human longing for wholeness." The bishops advocated shortening the work week, particularly for working parents.[33]

Such statements put women's work issues on the religious map. They are helpful in that sense, particularly if they involve consultation, study, and follow-up discussions with the larger church body. The problem is, many such religious statements either offer quite general ideals about which few people would disagree, or they put the church's public credibility behind quite specific policy recommendations that can be disputed by people of good will. Generally, such statements combine with lobbying efforts around particular pieces of proposed legislation. For example, the United States Catholic Conference has lobbied to increase funding for childcare in the federal budget.[34] In lobbying, there is always the danger that a moral ideal will get simplistically translated into a specific legislative end. This is one of the inherent difficulties of religious involvement in public policy. The point stands, however, that attention to public policy can be a dimension of spiritual formation, as one must consider the powerful ways that social structures and law shape individuals' self-understandings, sense of dignity, and human welfare. Public policy also impacts workers' abilities to care for their families, a central issue for women as well as men, and one important to religious institutions that look to the family as a central space for spiritual development and piety.

Theological Education

If ordained and lay ministers are to be prepared to address the issue of work, then theological education must tackle the question. Seminary and adult education courses in disciplines such as spirituality, practical theology, history, sociology, pastoral counseling, preaching, evangelism, and liturgy need to address work and, specifically, women's and men's particular experiences of work (in the home and outside it). Thus, religious leaders will have some training in wrestling with the real concerns of workers.

Seminaries should be important training grounds for pastoral leadership that can address the contemporary situation of work. First, students should become more aware of the seminary itself as workplace. Within the school, they can notice dynamics and structures that influence human welfare, for good or for ill. They might become more attentive to women's particular roles within their seminary contexts — in jobs as secretaries, administrators, professors, and custodians. I also would propose the development of courses on work where students analyze diverse contemporary work situations, deepen their understanding about historical changes in work roles, wrestle with theological issues, and strategize about faithful and effective pastoral responses to workers. Such courses should be interdisciplinary and attentive to gender, racial, class, and cultural differences. Classes could offer particular foci on women's changing economic roles. Students could go out to interview women workers, and women could dialogue with the class as guest speakers. The pedagogical and pastoral aim: for students to engage in contextualized theological education with workers themselves. Students also could be placed in field education sites in the workplace, under supervision. In concurrent theological reflection, they would surface issues specific to women workers in diverse jobs and careers. Theological schools can contribute to the preparation of local pastors, workplace chaplains, spiritual directors, small group facilitators, and public religious leaders attuned to the issues raised by women's changing economic roles.

Conclusion

Women's changing work patterns ripple out to pose numerous theological and spiritual issues. This book has grappled with a selected cluster of these issues as they have arisen in one, albeit highly diverse, faith community. It is my belief that these questions about vocation, identity, discernment, time, and holiness will remain vital to the spiritual development of women and men today — across religious traditions. The ability of religious groups to make sense of work carries enormous consequences. The survival of religious institutions will be affected, as will the character of Christian spirituality. A public spirituality will not thrive if economic activities are bracketed from faith. As women increasingly take active roles in the labor force, religious institutions neglect their own mission and relevance if they cannot guide and understand these enormous changes.

As we have seen, women negotiate changing economic and social roles in quite diverse ways. No one pastoral response will meet this complex turn. It is vital that religious groups discern their responses in continuous conversation with women and the core theological visions of their traditions. Religious groups need to prepare ministers — both ordained and lay — for this important pastoral task. The church needs spiritual guides who can walk with women as they encounter new tensions, define their identities, wrestle with vocation, and seek to live faithfully with God. This is the work of forming the people of God in the exigencies of history, a work that requires both keen social analysis and theological creativity. It is the work of our hands.

Notes

Introduction

1. "Twenty Facts on Working Women," U.S. Department of Labor Women's Bureau, *www.dol.gov/dol/wb/public/wb_pubs/fact98.htm*; "Figure 1. Women's Labor Force Participation and Business Cycles: 1940–1997," U.S. Census Bureau, *www.census.gov/population/www/documentation/twps0032/fig01.gif*.

2. U.S. Bureau of Labor Statistics, *Employment Status of the Civilian Population by Sex and Age* (Table A-1), *http://stats.bls.gov/news.release/empsit.t01.htm*.

3. Irish Catholic Bishops' Conference, *Prosperity with a Purpose: Christian Faith and Values in a Time of Rapid Economic Growth* (Dublin: Veritas, 1999), 7.

4. I am grateful to my colleagues at Boston University School of Theology who raised this point during a faculty research colloquium focused on this project.

5. Michelle Conlin, "Religion in the Workplace: The Growing Presence of Spirituality in Corporate America," *Business Week* (November 1, 1999): 152. See too Daniel Akst, "When Business Gets Religion," *New York Times* (October 4, 1998): 5, and David Dorsey, "The New Spirit of Work," *Fast Company* (August 1998): 125–34.

6. Stanley M. Herman, *The Tao at Work: On Leading and Following* (San Francisco: Jossey-Bass, 1994), and Laurie Beth Jones, *Jesus, CEO: Using Ancient Wisdom for Visionary Leadership* (New York: Hyperion, 1995).

7. See, for example, Judi Neal, "Begin Again," *Spirit at Work* (February 1999).

8. There are important exceptions, including, notably, the Presbyterian statement "All the Livelong Day: Women and Work," Joint Report of the Council on Women and the Church and the Committee on Women's Concerns, Reports to the 200th General Assembly of the Presbyterian Church USA 42.040–42.252a, 1988.

9. Barbara Welter, "The Cult of True Womanhood, 1820–1860," *American Quarterly* 18 (summer 1966): 151–74.

10. Carl Degler describes African American women's situation after Emancipation: "For black women, in short, the patterns of work begun under slavery still prevailed, owing to poverty and discrimination against blacks of both sexes." See Carl N. Degler, "Women," in *Encyclopedia of American Economic History: Studies of the Principal Movements and Ideas,* vol. 3, ed. Glenn Porter (New

York: Charles Scribner's Sons, 1980), 993. For fuller depictions of African American women, work, and the family in the nineteenth century, see Jacqueline Jones, *Labor of Love, Labor of Sorrow: Black Women, Work, and the Family from Slavery to the Present* (New York: Basic Books, 1985).

11. As cited in Welter, "The Cult of True Womanhood, 1820–1860," 173.

12. Ibid.

13. Nancy F. Cott, *The Bonds of Womanhood: "Women's Sphere" in New England, 1780–1935* (New Haven: Yale University Press, 1977), 5.

14. Friedrich Engels, "The Origin of Family, Private Property, and State," in *The Marx-Engels Reader*, ed. Robert C. Tucker (New York: W. W. Norton, 1978), 744.

15. Whereas working men often disdained the clergy and parish activities, many women in nineteenth-century Europe "found in their hours spent at church almost their only release from household drudgery. In Catholic parishes a host of confraternities, catering for both the spiritual and the social needs of their members, made an important contribution to their often meager recreational life, as well as giving them a feeling of power and usefulness that extended beyond the home" (Hugh McLeod, *Religion and the People of Western Europe 1789–1970* [Oxford: Oxford University Press, 1981], 31).

16. According to Mary J. Oates: "While the administrative experience acquired in charity endeavors did not impel Catholic women to political action to the same extent as it did their Protestant counterparts, participation in the numerous associations and auxiliaries legitimated their advance from the confines of the home and eased the transition to wider spheres of female labor" (Mary J. Oates, "Catholic Laywomen in the Labor Force, 1850–1950," in *American Catholic Women: A Historical Exploration*, ed. Karen Kennelly, C.S.J. [New York: Macmillan, 1989], 86).

17. McLeod, *Religion and the People of Western Europe 1789–1970*, 33.

18. Leo XIII, *Rerum Novarum*, nos. 13, 42, in *The Papal Encyclicals 1878–1903*, ed. Claudia Carlen (Wilmington, N.C.: McGrath Publishing Co., 1981), 244, 252.

19. Pius XI, *Casti Connubi*, no. 74, in *The Papal Encyclicals 1903–1939*, ed. Claudia Carlen (Raleigh, N.C.: Pierian Press, 1990), 402.

20. Pius XI, *Quadragesimo Anno*, no. 71, in *The Papal Encyclicals 1903–1939*, 426.

21. Alice Kessler-Harris, *Out to Work: A History of Wage-Earning Women in the United States* (New York: Oxford University Press, 1982), 260–61. Heavy manufacturing such as steel or automobile production — almost exclusively male occupations — suffered most during the 1930s. By contrast, light industry, clerical, and service jobs (in which women had been segregated) rebounded more quickly. The Depression also spurred the establishment of new social service agencies that needed to be staffed. Ironically, Kessler-Harris points out, women during

the Depression years benefited from previous discrimination and sex segregation, in that they were spared the worst unemployment.

22. Pius XI, *Quadragesimo Anno,* no. 71, 426.

23. Pope John Paul II, *Laborem Exercens,* nos. 1, 115, and 3, in *The Papal Encyclicals 1958–1981,* ed. Claudia Carlen (Wilmington, N.C.: McGrath Publishing Co., 1981), 299, 323, and 300.

24. National Conference of Catholic Bishops, *Economic Justice for All* (Washington, D.C.: United States Catholic Conference, 1986); see, for example, nos. 111, 97, and 32, pp. 56, 50, and 17.

25. See, for example, *From Words to Deeds: Continuing Reflections on the Role of Women in the Church* (Washington, D.C.: United States Catholic Conference, 1998).

26. Pope John Paul II, *Familiaris Consortio* ("The Role of the Christian Family in the Modern World") (Boston: St. Paul Books & Media, 1981), no. 23, p. 40.

27. Pope John Paul II, *Laborem Exercens,* nos. 92, 91, *The Papal Encyclicals 1958–1981,* 318.

28. See, for example, John C. Haughey, *Converting 9 to 5: Bringing Spirituality to Your Daily Work* (New York: Crossroad, 1994).

29. Dorothee Sölle with Shirley A. Cloyes, *To Work and to Love: A Theology of Creation* (Philadelphia: Fortress Press, 1984).

30. For helpful resources related more to the nineteenth-century context, see Joan M. Martin's book *More Than Chains and Toil: A Christian Work Ethic of Enslaved Women* (Louisville: Westminster John Knox Press, 2000), which gives a theological examination of the experiences of African American women in the antebellum period, and Eleanor J. Stebner, *The Women of Hull House: A Study in Spirituality, Vocation, and Friendship* (Albany: State University of New York Press, 1997), which explores connections between spirituality and the work and community life of settlement house women. Both books engage predominantly with Protestant theological perspectives.

31. See Bonnie J. Miller-McLemore, *Also a Mother: Work and Family as Theological Dilemma* (Nashville: Abingdon Press, 1994).

32. Mary Stewart Van Leeuwen, *Gender and Grace: Love, Work, and Parenting in a Changing World* (Downers Grove, Ill.: InterVarsity Press, 1990).

33. Patricia Mary DeFerrari, "Theologies of Work in the U.S. Grail: The Founder's Vision," in *American Catholic Traditions: Resources for Renewal,* ed. Sandra Yocum Mize and William Portier (Maryknoll, N.Y.: Orbis, 1997), 96–111.

34. See, for example, sociologist David Martin's *A General Theory of Secularization* (Oxford: Basil Blackwell, 1978), and Steve Bruce, ed., *Religion and Modernization: Sociologists and Historians Debate the Secularization Thesis* (Oxford: Clarendon Press, 1992).

35. Max Weber, *The Protestant Ethic and the Spirit of Capitalism* (New York: Charles Scribner's Sons, 1958), 181–82.

36. David Martin, for example, describes these "broad tendencies" as "fairly well established." However, Martin goes on to analyze varying cultural contexts within which these so-called "universal processes" play out. See *A General Theory of Secularization,* especially chapter 1. Martin later revised his thinking about the salience of the European model of secularization, coming to see the European experience as the exception rather than the rule.

37. See, for example, Peter L. Berger, "Protestantism and the Quest for Certainty," *Christian Century* (August 26–September 2, 1998): 782–96. Berger explains his reversal of opinion on the relationship between modernization and secularization: "The big mistake, which I shared with almost everyone who worked in this area in the 1950s and '60s, was to believe that modernity necessarily leads to a decline in religion" (782). On the state of religion in modernized societies, see, for example, Roger Finke, "An Unsecular America," in *Religion and Modernization: Sociologists and Historians Debate the Secularization Thesis,* ed. Steve Bruce (Oxford: Clarendon Press, 1992), 163. For an excellent study of the spread of Pentecostalism, see David Martin, *Tongues of Fire: The Explosion of Protestantism in Latin America* (Oxford: Blackwell, 1990).

38. See Carl N. Degler, *At Odds: Women and the Family in America from the Revolution to the Present* (New York: Oxford University Press, 1980), and "Women," in the *Encyclopedia of American Economic History,* vol. 3 (1980); Kessler-Harris, *Out to Work;* and Thomas Dublin, *Women at Work: The Transformation of Work and Community in Lowell, Massachusetts, 1826–1860* (New York: Columbia University Press, 1979).

39. For example, in his social history of American Catholicism, Jay P. Dolan touches on immigrant women's work experiences in the nineteenth century but does not study women and work in the twentieth century. See Dolan, *The American Catholic Experience: A History from Colonial Times to the Present* (Notre Dame, Ind.: University of Notre Dame Press, 1992). In his more recent book, Mark S. Massa presents an interesting description of religious women's reconsideration of their traditional labors in the late 1960s and 1970s, but he does not extend the discussion to nonreligious women. See Massa, *Catholics and American Culture: Fulton Sheen, Dorothy Day, and the Notre Dame Football Team* (New York: Crossroad, 1999), especially pp. 180–91. Debra Campbell analyzes the changing roles of laity in the twentieth century but does not tackle laywomen's shifting work patterns. See Debra Campbell, "The Struggle to Serve: From Lay Apostolate to the Ministry Explosion," in *Transforming Parish Ministry: The Changing Roles of Catholic Clergy, Laity, and Women Religious,* ed. Jay P. Dolan et al. (New York: Crossroad, 1989), 201–80.

40. See Oates, "Catholic Laywomen in the Labor Force, 1850–1950," 81–124. See also Leslie Woodcock Tentler, *Wage-Earning Women: Industrial Work and Family Life in the United States, 1900–1930* (Oxford: Oxford University Press, 1979).

41. Oates, "Catholic Laywomen in the Labor Force, 1850–1950," 82. Mary Jo Weaver also makes a broader point about the need for historical study of laywomen: "Though it is encouraging to know that American Catholic sisters are receiving some attention these days... one can still be concerned for those laywomen who have had no community to keep their memory alive." See Mary Jo Weaver, *New Catholic Women: A Contemporary Challenge to Traditional Religious Authority* (New York: Harper & Row, 1985), 28.

42. Barbara R. Bergmann, *The Economic Emergence of Women* (New York: Basic Books, 1986), 11.

43. Evelyn L. Lehrer, "The Effects of Religion on the Labor Supply of Married Women," *Social Science Research* 24 (1995): 281.

44. For examples of such studies, see Clyde Wilcox and Ted G. Jelen, "The Effects of Employment and Religion on Women's Feminist Attitudes," *International Journal for the Psychology of Religion* 1, no. 3 (1991): 161–71, and Mary Morgan and John Scanzoni, "Religious Orientations and Women's Expected Continuity in the Labor Force," *Journal of Marriage and the Family* 49 (May 1987): 367–79. Wilcox and Jelen find interesting differences among evangelical Protestant, mainline Protestant, and Catholic women. Catholic and mainline Protestant women seem to adjust their beliefs about their private family roles to fit the demands of work. Evangelical women, on the other hand, adjust only their attitudes about women's public roles, while maintaining more traditional views of private duties. Hence: "Evangelical women who work outside the home seem effectively 'double-bound' by egalitarian expectations in the workplace and traditional demands within the marital family" (170). Morgan and Scanzoni find that conservative Catholic, Protestant, and Jewish women share common attitudes about work, family, and religion more than they do with liberal women in their own religious groups. Sociologists Nancy Ammerman and Wade Clark Roof make a helpful contribution with their edited book *Work, Family, and Religion in Contemporary Society* (New York: Routledge, 1995). Yet, as a collection of quite varied essays, the book cannot offer a sustained treatment of any group of women.

45. Bradley R. Hertel, "Work, Family, and Faith: Recent Trends," in Ammerman and Roof, eds., *Work, Family, and Religion*, 116.

46. Nancy Ammerman and Wade Clark Roof, "Introduction: Old Patterns, New Trends, Fragile Experiments," in Ammerman and Roof, eds., *Work, Family, and Religion*, 6.

47. See Don S. Browning, *A Fundamental Practical Theology: Descriptive and Strategic Proposals* (Minneapolis: Fortress Press, 1991).

48. Here I take Sandra Schneiders's definition of *spirituality* as a starting point. Schneiders writes that *spirituality* is "the experience of consciously striving to integrate one's life in terms not of isolation and self-absorption but of self-transcendence toward the ultimate value one perceives," in "Theology and Spirituality: Strangers, Rivals, or Partners?" *Horizons* 13, no. 2 (1986): 266.

49. Karl Rahner, *The Practice of Faith: A Handbook of Contemporary Spirituality* (New York: Crossroad, 1992), 19.

50. Bernard McGinn, "The Letter and the Spirit: Spirituality as an Academic Discipline," *Christian Spirituality Bulletin* 1, no. 2 (fall 1993): 5. See also Philip Sheldrake, *Spirituality and History: Questions of Interpretation and Method* (New York: Crossroad, 1992).

51. Nancy A. Hewitt writes: "Those who compared the experiences of privileged and poor women in the Victorian era concluded that, if modernization occurred, it led not to the inclusion of women in a universal sisterhood but rather to the dichotomization of women along class lines into the pious and pure 'modern' woman and the prurient and parasitical 'pre-modern' women." See Nancy A. Hewitt, "Beyond the Search for Sisterhood: American Women's History in the 1980s," *Social History* 10, no. 3 (October 1985): 303.

Chapter 1: Rosie the Riveter and Ideals of Womanhood

1. Redd Evans and John Jacob Loeb, "Rosie the Riveter" (New York: Paramount Music Corp., 1942).

2. Sherna Berger Gluck, *Rosie the Riveter Revisited: Women, the War, and Social Change* (Boston: Twayne Publishers, 1987), 172–97.

3. Ibid., 228.

4. Ibid., 210–11.

5. Ibid., 41–42.

6. Leslie Woodcock Tentler, *Wage-Earning Women: Industrial Work and Family Life in the United States, 1900–1930* (Oxford: Oxford University Press, 1979). For a more optimistic view, see Mary J. Oates, "Catholic Laywomen in the Labor Force, 1850–1950," in *American Catholic Women: A Historical Exploration,* ed. Karen Kennelly, C.S.J. (New York: Macmillan, 1989). Oates argues that by the 1930s, women — including many Catholic women — attended college and gradually moved into the major professions, thus challenging "the pervasive stereotype of Catholic women as lacking in professional motivation, content with traditionally female occupations, and more accepting than other American women of socially circumscribed spheres of female activity" (82).

7. Brigid O'Farrell and Joyce L. Kornbluh, *Rocking the Boat: Union Women's Voices, 1915–1975* (New Brunswick, N.J.: Rutgers University Press, 1996), 233.

8. Maxine L. Margolis, *Mothers and Such: Views of American Women and Why They Changed* (Berkeley: University of California Press, 1984), 211.

9. Carl N. Degler, "Women," in *Encyclopedia of American Economic History: Studies of the Principal Movements and Ideas,* vol. 3, ed. Glenn Porter (New York: Charles Scribner's Sons, 1980), 994.

10. Mary P. Ryan, *Womanhood in America: From Colonial Times to the Present* (New York: Franklin Watts, 1983), 254.

11. *Doctrines and Discipline of the Methodist Church 1944* (Nashville: Methodist Publishing House, 1944), 558–59.

12. Robert B. Westbrook, "Fighting for the American Family: Private Interests and Political Obligation in World War II," in *The Power of Culture: Critical Essays in American History,* ed. Richard Wightman Fox and T. J. Jackson Lears (Chicago: University of Chicago Press, 1993), 202.

13. See Pope John Paul II, *Centesimus Annus* ("On the Hundredth Anniversary of *Rerum Novarum*") (Boston: Pauline Books & Media, 1991), no. 48, p. 71: "*The principle of subsidiarity* must be respected: a community of a higher order should not interfere in the internal life of a community of a lower order, depriving the latter of its functions, but rather should support it in case of need and help to coordinate its activity with the activities of the rest of society, always with a view to the common good" (italics in original).

14. "Statements Issued by the Archbishops and Bishops of the United States on Victory and Peace," November 14, 1942, in *Our Bishops Speak: National Pastorals and Annual Statements of the Hierarchy of the United States, 1919–1951,* ed. Raphael Huber (Milwaukee: Bruce, 1952), 112.

15. "Essentials of a Good Peace," November 11, 1943, in Huber, ed., *Our Bishops Speak,* 119. Also, Bishop John A. Duffy of Buffalo linked the American cause with women's domestic role when he condemned a city plan to provide childcare: "No patriotic endeavor that militates against the well-being of the home and the proper care of children should receive public approval. What are we fighting for in this war if not the integrity of the Christian home? We shall have lost the war if we lose the home.... We should ... return from industry the mothers of children and put them back where they belong — in the home" (cited in "Women in War Industry," *Ave Maria* 56, no. 4 [July 25, 1942]: 549).

16. "Women in Industry," National Council of Catholic Women, Resolutions of the Twenty-first Annual Convention, Hollywood, Florida, 1942; "Legislation for Workers, A Family Need," National Council of Catholic Women, Resolutions of the Twenty-second National Convention, 1944, Toledo, Ohio.

17. "Women in Factory Seen Imperilling Nation Birth Rates: Sociologists Told Only Religion Can Stop Bad Decline," *Catholic Transcript* (January 7, 1943): 1.

18. Joseph B. Schuyler, S.J., "Women at Work," *Catholic World* 157 (April 1943): 27, 30. See too Mother M. Berenice, O.S.U., "Training All-Out Mothers," *Catholic World* 158 (October 1943): 78–81.

19. "Women and War," *Commonweal* (March 27, 1942): 549.

20. "Catholics v. WAACs," *Time* (June 15, 1942): 39.

21. Degler, "Women," 994.

22. Note that some scholars have questioned whether the war actually changed women's economic roles or whether the rising numbers of women in the work force represented an expected, continued growth of women wage earners. Kessler-Harris, for example, argues that most of the women remaining in the labor force after the war ended would have been employed regardless, and that

the wartime advances amounted to few lasting gains. See Kessler-Harris, *Out to Work,* 277, 287.

23. AB, interview by author, tape recording, Brighton, Massachusetts, April 7, 2000.

24. "Goodbye Mammy, Hello Mom," *Ebony* 2 (March 1947): 36.

25. Ibid.

26. Ruth Grant, interview by Georgia Maheras, tape recording, Roxbury, Massachusetts, August 14, 2000.

27. Bruce Levine et al., *Who Built America?* (New York: Pantheon Books, 1989), 518.

28. Ibid., 520.

29. John T. McGreevy, *Parish Boundaries: The Catholic Encounter with Race in the Twentieth-Century Urban North* (Chicago: University of Chicago Press, 1996), 62.

30. AB, interview, April 7, 2000.

31. Cynthia Taeuber, *Statistical Handbook on Women in America* (Phoenix, Ariz.: Oryx Press, 1991), A2–1, p. 20.a.

32. *www.tvland.com/shows/litbeaver/character1.jhtml.*

33. Margaret Hickey, "Child-Care Centers," *Ladies' Home Journal* (September 1951): 25. Hickey did not place full blame on mothers, as she noted a lack of adequate childcare and argued that the "community, too, must face its share of responsibility if industrial mobilization of young mothers is encouraged."

34. Ibid., 26.

35. Benjamin Spock, M.D., "What's She Got That I Haven't?" *Ladies' Home Journal* (October 1952): 195.

36. Mariam K. Chamberlain, ed., *Women in Academe: Progress and Prospects* (New York: Russell Sage Foundation, 1988), 6.

37. Ryan, *Womanhood in America,* 281.

38. Anonymous "wife and mother," "Comments," *Integrity* 8, no. 12 (September 1954): 39–40.

39. Ibid., 40.

40. Levine et al., *Who Built America?* 521.

41. Janet Mary Riley, telephone interview with author, November 2, 2001.

42. Janet Mary Riley, "I Found It Very Difficult to Be Heard," in *Generations: A Century of Women Speak about Their Lives,* ed. Myriam Miedzian and Alisa Malinovich (New York: Atlantic Monthly Press, 1997), 403.

43. Riley, telephone interview with author, November 2, 2001.

44. Riley, written communication to author, March 3, 2002.

45. Riley, telephone interview with Sarah Dekoven, tape recording, April 24, 2002.

46. Riley, written communication to author, March 3, 2002.

47. Riley, telephone interview with Sarah Dekoven, tape recording, April 24, 2002.

48. Riley, "I Found It Very Difficult to Be Heard," 406.

49. This is Mary P. Ryan's term, from the title of chapter 6 of *Womanhood in America.*

50. In 1950, for example, Pius XII urged the leaders of religious communities to improve "theological education and professional credentials for those teaching and doing other professional work." See Marjorie Noterman Beane, *From Framework to Freedom: A History of the Sister Formation Conference* (Lanham, Md.: University Press of America, 1993), 2.

51. See masthead on *Sisters Formation Bulletin,* beginning with vol. 2, no. 1 (October, 1955).

52. Beane, *From Framework to Freedom,* 133.

53. See Jay P. Dolan, *The American Catholic Experience: A History from Colonial Times to the Present* (Notre Dame, Ind.: University of Notre Dame Press, 1992), 416.

54. Robert L. Reynolds, "Christ at Your Work Bench," *Voice of St. Jude* (April 1953): 12.

55. Speech by Janet Kalven, cited in Debra Campbell, "The Heyday of Catholic Action and the Lay Apostolate, 1929–1959," in *Transforming Parish Ministry: The Changing Roles of Catholic Clergy, Laity, and Women Religious,* ed. Jay Dolan et al. (New York: Crossroad, 1990), 242. See also Campbell, "*Both Sides Now:* Another Look at the Grail in the Postwar Era," in *U.S. Catholic Historian* 2, no. 4 (fall 1993): 23.

56. Quotes are from Janet Kalven, cited in Alden V. Brown, *The Grail Movement and American Catholicism, 1940–1975* (Notre Dame, Ind.: University of Notre Dame Press, 1989), 46, 54, 55. Thus, Grail scholar Patricia Mary DeFerrari rightly notes: "Grail programs developed in light of women's participation in the economy not only as industrial workers but also, and perhaps more significantly, as consumers and home producers." See Patricia Mary DeFerrari, "Theologies of Work in the U.S. Grail: The Founder's Vision," in *American Catholic Traditions: Resources for Renewal,* ed. Sandra Yocum Mize and William Portier (Maryknoll, N.Y.: Orbis, 1997), 105.

57. Flyer, Grail Council on Service Careers, Detroit, Michigan, summer 1957, cited in DeFerrari, "Theologies of Work in the U.S. Grail," 105.

58. See Jeffrey M. Burns, *Disturbing the Peace: A History of the Christian Family Movement, 1949–1974* (Notre Dame, Ind.: University of Notre Dame Press, 1999), 4, and Dolan, *The American Catholic Experience,* 395.

59. For a comprehensive history of the Christian Family Movement, including discussion of these women's roles, see Burns, *Disturbing the Peace.*

60. Burns, *Disturbing the Peace,* 97.

61. Sociologist Mirra Komarovsky studied working-class families in the late 1950s. In her book *Blue-Collar Marriage* (1962), she noted that one-third of the housewives she studied expressed a strong desire to take a job at least part-time,

"to get out of the house." See excerpt in Susan Ware, *Modern American Woman: A Documentary History* (Chicago: Dorsey Press, 1989), 301.

62. Ware, *Modern American Woman*, 283–84.

63. Dolan, *The American Catholic Experience*, 356.

64. Andrew Greeley, *The Church and the Suburbs* (New York: Sheed & Ward, 1959), 94.

65. Juliet Schor, *The Overworked American: The Unexpected Decline of Leisure* (New York: Basic Books, 1992), 8.

66. Crystal Kathleen Jackson, "Mothers, Go Home!" *Together* (September 1959): 18.

67. Ibid., 19.

68. Mary Mannix, "Toward a New Generation," *Integrity* 1, no. 8 (May 1947): 13–14.

69. "A Challenge to the Girls in YCW," undated, p. 20. Young Christian Workers archives, University of Notre Dame (Box 105, "Impact" folder).

70. Reverend George A. Kelly, *The Catholic Marriage Manual* (New York: Random House, 1958), 117, 115.

71. Campbell, "The Heyday of Catholic Action and the Lay Apostolate, 1929–1959," 247.

72. Welter, "The Cult of True Womanhood, 1820–1860," 151–74.

73. Paul L. Blakely, "Men and Women," *Catholic Mind* 41, no. 964 (April 1943): 16.

74. Levine et al., *Who Built America?* 522.

75. See Ronald W. Schatz, "Connecticut's Working Class in the 1950s: A Catholic Perspective," *Labor History* 25 (1984): 98.

76. Patricia Zavella, *Women's Work and Chicano Families: Cannery Workers of the Santa Clara Valley* (Ithaca, N.Y.: Cornell University Press, 1987), 88.

77. Ibid., 168–69. The author writes: "Particularly when their children were young, and with few child-care resources, women needed jobs, yet had limited options in securing employment. Women's family obligations and their commitments to a traditional family ideology made them prime participants in occupational segregation within the canning industry. Struggles with husbands also pressured women to seek temporary jobs.... Seasonal jobs — in which they anticipated remaining only temporarily — complemented women's home obligations."

78. Ibid., 169.

79. Jacqueline Jones, *Labor of Love, Labor of Sorrow: Black Women, Work, and the Family from Slavery to the Present* (New York: Basic Books, 1985), 305.

80. "The Women — God Bless Them," *Ebony* 8 (May 1953): 78.

81. "Lady Cops," *Ebony* 9 (August 1954): 26.

82. "Wright Girls Combine Careers and Marriage," *Ebony* 6 (January 1951): 74.

83. Ibid.

84. MK, interview with author, tape recording, Brighton, Massachusetts, April 7, 2000.

85. Ibid.

86. I am indebted to Robert Orsi's book *Thank You, St. Jude: Women's Devotion to the Patron Saint of Hopeless Causes* (New Haven: Yale University Press, 1996), which sparked my research into women, work, and devotion to St. Jude.

87. Mrs. C.C., letter in "St. Jude's Mail," *Voice of St. Jude* (June 1953): 33.

88. Dolan, *The American Catholic Experience*, 385.

89. Dolan describes the decline of the devotion after the early 1940s; see ibid.

90. Janet Ivancak, letter in "Favors Granted," *Novena Notes* (August 10, 1945): 8.

91. Miss Patricia Dikin, letter in "Favors Granted," *Novena Notes* (August 31, 1945): 10.

92. Julia C. Brown, letter in "Favors Granted," *Novena Notes* (July 22, 1955): 10.

93. Anne Mary Benak, letter in "Favors Granted," *Novena Notes* (January 21, 1955): 6.

94. Joseph Kelly and Timothy Kelly, "Our Lady of Perpetual Help, Gender Roles, and the Decline of Devotional Catholicism," *Journal of Social History* 32, no. 1 (fall 1998): 20.

95. Mrs. Mary L. Egan, letter in "Favors Granted," *Novena Notes* (August 23, 1963): 10. Thus, while older women increasingly were taking paid employment, letters also revealed the experiences of older women who had been in the work force for decades. A married woman who had been working at the same company since 1935 thanked Our Sorrowful Mother for helping her find a job at an older age: "I promised to thank Our Sorrowful Mother if she would help me secure a position. I had been working 25 years for one company, when they decided to close the business. It is difficult at my age to start with another company, but through her help I have a position." See Mrs. C. Corbett, letter in "Favors Granted," *Novena Notes* (September 9, 1960): 12.

96. Mrs. Ruby Lewis, letter in "Favors Granted," *Novena Notes* (September 9, 1960): 12.

97. William J. Whalen, "Financial Goals of the Christian Family," *Voice of St. Jude* (September 1960): 15–16.

Chapter 2: Debating Women's Place

1. Rosemary Santana Cooney, "Changing Labor Force Participation of Mexican American Wives: A Comparison with Anglos and Blacks," *Social Science Quarterly* 56, no. 2 (September 1975): 253. Cooney found that whereas 24.4 percent of married Mexican American women (aged fourteen to fifty-four) held paid employment in 1960, that figure rose to 34.6 percent by 1970. This represented a 41.8 percent relative increase, compared to a 26.6 percent relative increase among Anglo married women and a 25.2 percent relative increase among black

married women. However, Mexican American wives' rates of employment still fell below those of Anglo wives (43.7 percent) and well below that of black wives (58.1 percent).

2. Cynthia Taeuber, *Statistical Handbook on Women in America* (Phoenix, Ariz.: Oryx Press, 1991), A2–1, p. 20.

3. Robert McClory, *Turning Point* (New York: Crossroad, 1995), 137.

4. JM, interview with author, tape recording, Newton, Massachusetts, September 27, 2000.

5. Mercedes Espinoza, interview, in *Five Mexican-American Women in Transition: A Case Study of Migrants in the Midwest,* ed. Kristina Lindborg and Carlos J. Ovando (San Francisco: R&E Research Associates, 1977), 82.

6. Margaret Mead and Frances Bagley Kaplan, eds., *American Women: The Report of the President's Commission on the Status of Women and Other Publications of the Commission* (New York: Charles Scribner's Sons, 1965). On percentages of female workers who were married, see chart 11 on p. 47. On women's motives for working, see p. 45. On the advisability of an executive order, see p. 48.

7. *www.eeoc.gov/35th/1965-71/index.html.*

8. For U.S. Census Bureau reporting of male and female median wages from 1947 to 2000, see *www.census.gov/hhes/income/histinc/p53.html.*

9. Betty Friedan, *The Feminine Mystique* (New York: Dell Publishing, 1983), 67.

10. Ibid., 48.

11. Ibid., 49.

12. Ibid., 333.

13. Mary Freeman, "The Marginal Sex," *Commonweal* 75 (February 2, 1962): 485.

14. Mary Gordon, "Coming to Terms with Mary," *Commonweal* 109 (January 15, 1982): 11.

15. Cited in Cheryl Townsend Gilkes, " 'Liberated to Work Like Dogs!': Labeling Black Women and Their Work," in *The Experience and Meaning of Work in Women's Lives,* ed. Mildreth Y. Grossman and Nia Lane Chester (Hillsdale, N.J.: Lawrence Erlbaum Associates, 1990), 171.

16. Judith Coburn, "Dolores Huerta: La Pasionaria of the Farmworkers," *Ms.* 5, no. 5 (November 1976): 13.

17. Ibid.

18. Rosalyn Terborg-Penn, "Survival Strategies among African-American Women Workers: A Continuing Process," in *Women, Work, and Protest,* ed. Ruth Milkman (Boston: Routledge & Kegan Paul, 1985), 141.

19. Andrew Greeley, *The Church and the Suburbs* (New York: Sheed & Ward, 1959), 84.

20. James O'Gara, "Oh Dad, Poor Dad," *Commonweal* 77 (October 12, 1962): 64.

21. U.S. Department of Labor, "The Negro Family: The Case for National Action," in *The Moynihan Report and the Politics of Controversy: A Trans-Action Social Science and Public Policy Report,* ed. Lee Rainwater and William Yancey (Cambridge, Mass.: MIT Press, 1967), 78–79.

22. Ibid., 75.

23. See, for example, T. C. Bambara, ed., *The Black Woman: An Anthology* (New York: New American Library [1970]), and P. Murray, "The Liberation of Black Women," in *Women: A Feminist Perspective,* ed. Jo Freeman (Palo Alto, Calif.: Mayfield, 1975).

24. Willie Cors, letter to the editor, *Commonweal* 83 (December 24, 1965): 359.

25. "The Negro Woman," *Ebony* 15 (August 1960): 45.

26. "Ambassador of Goodwill for Police Department," *Ebony* 19 (March 1964): 44.

27. Jones, *Labor of Love,* 274.

28. Pope John XXIII, *Pacem in Terris,* no. 41, in *The Papal Encyclicals 1958–1981,* 111.

29. Ibid., no. 15, p. 109.

30. See Pope John XXIII, address of December 7, 1960, *The Pope Speaks* 7 (1961): 172–73. A year later, John XXIII lent support to the idea of the family wage and stated: "Anyone can understand that this prolonged absence from home and the attendant dispersion of energies creates a situation which prevents the wife from carrying out her duties of wife and mother, as she should." See Pope John XXIII, address of September 6, 1961, cited in Richard L. Camp, "From Passive Subordination to Complementary Partnership: The Papal Conception of a Woman's Place in Church and Society since 1978," *Catholic Historical Review* 76 (July 1990): 520.

31. Cardinal Leon Joseph Suenens, *The Nun in the World* (London: Burns & Oates, 1962), 13–14.

32. Ibid., 14.

33. Suenens writes: "The classical picture in which initiative lies with the man, and woman's part is submission, is no longer current.... There is nothing in this advancement as such that militates in Christian eyes against the subordination to her husband in the home demanded by St. Paul, but this subordination can no longer be realistically carried over to the whole of life" (14). Suenens maintains women's central role as the "heart of the family" and the guardian of moral values but unites this with a significant public vocation for women.

34. "Dogmatic Constitution on the Church" (*Lumen Gentium*), no. 11, in *Documents of Vatican II,* ed. Austin P. Flannery (Grand Rapids, Mich.: Eerdmans, 1975), 362.

35. "Decree on the Apostolate of Lay People" (*Apostolicam Actuositatem*), no. 9, in *Documents of Vatican II,* 777.

36. "Order of Nuns Here Plans to Modernize," *Los Angeles Times* (October 18, 1967): 1, 8, cited in Mark Massa, *Catholics and American Culture: Fulton Sheen, Dorothy Day, and the Notre Dame Football Team* (New York: Crossroad, 1999), 185.

37. "Coast Nuns Plan a Secular Order," *New York Times* (February 3, 1970): 1, 40.

38. Massa documents the disputes involving the IHM community. See *Catholics and American Culture,* 180–91.

39. Arlie Hochschild, *The Second Shift* (New York: Avon Books, 1989), 4.

40. Margaret Fortes, interview by author, tape recording, Roxbury, Massachusetts, June 13, 2000.

41. Ibid.

42. Ibid.

43. Ibid. Parents, educators, and suburban residents established METCO (Metropolitan Council for Educational Opportunity) in 1966. The nonprofit organization integrates children of minority ethnic backgrounds from Boston into suburban schools. Fortes recalled how parents fought for METCO, once humming "We Shall Overcome" and sitting at a meeting until midnight.

44. "Baker Interview," pp. 95, 111, in *Twentieth Century Trade Union Women: Vehicle for Change Oral History Collection,* Schlesinger Library, Radcliffe College, Cambridge, Massachusetts.

45. Irwin Garfinkel and Sara S. McLanahan, *Single Mothers and Their Children: A New American Dilemma* (Washington, D.C.: The Urban Institute Press, 1986), 16.

46. Paula Smith Avioli and Eileen Kaplan, "A Panel Study of Married Women's Work Patterns," *Sex Roles* 26, nos. 5/6 (1992): 229.

47. Phyllis Moen, "Continuities and Discontinuities in Women's Labor Force Activity," in *Life Course Dynamics: Trajectories and Transitions, 1968–1980,* ed. Glen H. Elder Jr. (Ithaca, N.Y.: Cornell University Press, 1985), 117.

48. For example, within the Catholic Church, this professionalization occurred as laity took on more active ecclesiastical roles following the Second Vatican Council, and large numbers of clergy and religious left their vocations. Paid positions such as the parish director of religious education and director of music ministry emerged.

49. Myriam Miedzian and Alisa Malinovich, eds., *Generations: A Century of Women Speak about Their Lives* (New York: Atlantic Monthly Press, 1997), 413.

50. Jean Holzhauer, "Doing Daddy In," *Commonweal* 79 (October 18, 1963): 102.

51. AC, personal communication to author, August 8, 2001.

52. Diana Pearce coined the term in her 1978 article "The Feminization of Poverty: Women, Work, and Welfare," *Urban and Social Change Review* (February 1978): 28–36.

53. Garfinkel and McLanahan, *Single Mothers and Their Children,* 49.

54. U.S. Bureau of the Census, "Household and Family Characteristics, March 1983," *Current Population Reports,* series P-20, no. 388 (Washington, D.C.: U.S. Government Printing Office, 1984).

55. Diana M. Pearce, "The Feminization of Poverty: A Second Look," paper presented at the American Sociological Association Meetings, San Francisco, August 1989.

56. Key social scientists in this research include Diana Pearce, Sara McLanahan, and Paula England. For a helpful article on feminization of poverty research, see Sara S. McLanahan and Erin L. Kelly, "The Feminization of Poverty: Past and Future," working paper, MacArthur Research Networks, *www.olin.wustl.edu/macarthur/working%20papers/wp-mclanahan3.htm.* A theological treatment of the subject can be found in Pamela Couture, *Blessed Are the Poor? Women's Poverty, Family Policy, and Practical Theology* (Nashville: Abingdon Press, 1991).

57. AB, interview by author, tape recording, Brighton, Massachusetts, April 7, 2000.

58. JM, interview, September 27, 2000.

59. Robert Wuthnow, *The Restructuring of American Religion: Society and Faith since World War II* (Princeton, N.J.: Princeton University Press, 1988), 228.

60. Pope John Paul II, *Familiaris Consortio,* no. 23, p. 40.

61. John Paul II, *Mulieris Dignitatem* ("On the Dignity and Vocation of Women"), no. 17 (Boston: Daughters of St. Paul, 1988), p. 61.

62. National Conference of Catholic Bishops, *Economic Justice for All* (Washington, D.C.: United States Catholic Conference, 1986), 101–2, 88, 98.

63. See, for example, James Davison Hunter, *Culture Wars: The Struggle to Define America* (New York: Basic Books, 1991). For an important study of religion, family, and the culture wars, see Don S. Browning et al., *From Culture Wars to Common Ground: Religion and the American Family Debate* (Louisville: Westminster John Knox Press, 1997).

64. Hunter, *Culture Wars,* 180.

65. John Paul II, *Mulieris Dignitatem,* no. 31, p. 104.

66. John Paul II, "Letter to Women," (June 29, 1995), no. 2, in *Pope John Paul II on the Genius of Women* (Washington, D.C.: United States Catholic Conference, 1997), 47.

67. Ibid., no. 12, pp. 57–58.

68. John Paul II, *Mulieris Dignitatem,* no. 30, p. 111.

69. National Conference of Catholic Bishops, Committee on Women in Society and in the Church, *From Words to Deeds: Continuing Reflections on the Role of Women in the Church* (Washington, D.C.: United States Catholic Conference, 1998), 13–14.

70. "Women in Diocesan Leadership Positions: A Progress Report," prepared by William Daly, National Association of Church Personnel Administrators, at the request of the Committee on Women in Society and in the Church, National

Conference of Catholic Bishops, June 1999. Results are based on responses from American dioceses surveyed by the National Association of Church Personnel Administrators. See particularly pp. 3 and 11. Women also held 60 percent of nonsupervisory professional positions (e.g., accountants) in dioceses surveyed. Dioceses in the South and the West hired the greatest percentages of women administrative and professional staff (50–52 percent), while the Northeast hired the smallest (about 38 percent).

71. Mary Parella, interview by Georgia Maheras, tape recording, Acton, Massachusetts, June 15, 2000.

72. Ibid.

73. JM, interview, September 27, 2000.

74. Monthly Labor Review Online, February 16, 1999, *http://stats.bls.gov/ opub/ted/1999/feb/wk3/art01.htm.*

75. U.S. Bureau of Labor Statistics, *Employment Status of the Civilian Population by Sex and Age,* Table A-1, *http://stats.bls.gov/news.release/empsit.t01.htm.*

Chapter 3: Friedan and the Fiat

1. Mary Gordon, "Women of God," *Atlantic Monthly* (January 2002): 65.

2. MK, interview with author, tape recording, Brighton, Massachusetts, April 7, 2000.

3. Eileen Farrell, interview by author, tape recording, Brighton, Massachusetts, June 2, 2000.

4. Marian Burkhart, "Prayer: When? How? Why?" *Commonweal* 116 (February 10, 1989): 74.

5. This reflection about vocational questions is informed by James W. Fowler, *Becoming Adult, Becoming Christian: Adult Development and Christian Faith* (San Francisco: Harper & Row, 1984).

6. Francis Schüssler Fiorenza, "Religious Beliefs and Praxis: Reflections on Catholic Theological Views of Work," in *Work and Religion,* ed. Gregory Baum, *Concilium* 131, no. 1/1980 (New York: Seabury Press, 1980), 93–95.

7. Betty Friedan, *The Feminine Mystique* (New York: Dell Publishing, 1983), 333.

8. Mrs. James Arnold, letter to the editor, *Commonweal* 79 (January 10, 1964): 428.

9. Ibid., 429.

10. Jean Holzhauer, letter to the editor, *Commonweal* 79 (January 10, 1964): 430.

11. Mary Freeman, "The Marginal Sex," *Commonweal* 75 (February 2, 1962): 484.

12. Ibid., 485.

13. I am indebted to my colleague Chris Schlauch for pointing out the "estrangement" theme present in this history of women, work, and Catholicism.

14. Friedan, *The Feminine Mystique,* 42, 351, 352.

15. Ibid., 351.

16. Ibid., 352.

17. Huerta as cited in Barbara L. Baer, "Stopping Traffic: One Woman's Cause," *The Progressive* (September 1975): 39.

18. Jean Holzhauer, "Doing Daddy In," *Commonweal* 79 (October 18, 1963): 102.

19. Friedan, *The Feminine Mystique,* 313.

20. John XXIII, *Mater et Magistra,* no. 256, in *The Papal Encyclicals 1958–1981,* ed. Claudia C. Carlen, 86.

21. John Paul II, *Laborem Exercens,* no. 23, in *The Papal Encyclicals 1958–1981,* 304.

22. The association of vocation with perfection has a long precedent in Catholic thought. Francis de Sales, for example, wrote: "The means of attaining perfection vary according to the diversity of callings: religious, widows, and married persons — all must seek this perfection, but not all by the same means." See Francis de Sales and Jane de Chantal, *Letters of Spiritual Direction* (New York: Paulist Press, 1988), 102. Thomas Aquinas too had asserted that Christians in different states of life could reach the state of perfection proper to that state of life. However, de Sales deemphasized the hierarchy of perfection assumed in Thomistic thought. For a helpful brief overview of different understandings of vocation, including the thought of Thomas Aquinas, see Paul D. Holland, "Vocation," in *The New Dictionary of Theology,* ed. Joseph A. Komonchak et al. (Wilmington, Del.: Michael Glazier, 1987), 1087–92.

23. National Conference of Catholic Bishops, *Economic Justice for All* (Washington, D.C.: United States Catholic Conference, 1986), no. 97, p. 50. The bishops continue: "Second, it is the ordinary way for human beings to fulfill their material needs. Finally, work enables people to contribute to the well-being of the larger community."

24. John Paul II, *Mulieris Dignitatem,* no. 18, p. 63. The letter reiterates the "superiority of virginity over marriage," deriving the longstanding church teaching from 1 Corinthians 7:38 and Matthew 19:10–12. See no. 22, pp. 76–77.

25. Ibid., no. 18, p. 66.

26. Friedan, *The Feminine Mystique,* see 310–11, 290.

27. Note, for example, that in the 1980s Friedan critiqued developments in the feminist movement that she did so much to create. See her book *The Second Stage* (New York: Summit Books, 1981).

28. Frances Ayvish, "Where Are You Going, My Pretty Wife?" *U.S. Catholic* 40, no. 10 (October 1975): 38–39.

29. Joyce Harvey, interview by Georgia Maheras, tape recording, Boston, July 27, 2000. Harvey holds a degree in sociology and worked as a social worker for the Massachusetts Department of Public Welfare from 1973 to 1993. She now works for the Division of Medical Assistance.

30. Ibid.

31. National Conference of Catholic Bishops, *Called and Gifted for the Third Millennium* (Washington, D.C.: United States Catholic Conference, 1995), 4.

32. Martin Luther, "The Estate of Marriage," in *Luther's Works,* vol. 45, ed. Walther I. Brandt (Philadelphia: Muhlenberg Press, 1962), 39–40.

33. Ibid., 40.

34. Luther sharply distinguished between the heavenly kingdom and the worldly kingdom. Law governs the kingdom of the world, while the gospel of Christ rules the spiritual kingdom. Each has a different purpose, and though they are not opposed, they must not be confused: "For this reason these two kingdoms must be sharply distinguished, and both be permitted to remain; the one to produce piety, the other to bring about external peace and prevent evil deeds; neither is sufficient in the world without the other. For no one can become pious before God by means of the secular government, without Christ's spiritual rule.... Without the Holy Spirit in the heart no one becomes really pious, he may do as fine works as he will." See Martin Luther, "Secular Authority: To What Extent It Should Be Obeyed," in *Martin Luther: Selections from His Writings,* ed. John Dillenberger (Garden City, N.Y.: Anchor Books, 1961), 371. See too Gustav Wingren's important book *Luther on Vocation* (Philadelphia: Muhlenberg Press, 1957).

35. Weber argued: "This ascetic conduct meant a rational planning of the whole of one's life in accordance with God's will. And this asceticism was no longer an *opus supererogationis,* but something which could be required of everyone who would be certain of salvation.... This rationalization of conduct within this world, but for the sake of the world beyond, was the consequence of the concept of calling of ascetic Protestantism." Ironically, Weber noted, while beliefs about vocation contributed to the development of capitalism, workers today follow the "Protestant work ethic" without any sense of a religious motivation. See Max Weber, *The Protestant Ethic and the Spirit of Capitalism* (New York: Charles Scribner's Sons, 1958), 153–54.

36. Francis de Sales, *Introduction to the Devout Life* (New York: Doubleday, 1966), 40–41.

37. Ibid., 43.

38. For a more developed discussion of lay spirituality in the twentieth century, see my book *American Catholics in the Twentieth Century: Spirituality, Lay Experience, and Public Life* (New York: Crossroad, 2001).

39. "Dogmatic Constitution on the Church" (*Lumen Gentium*), no. 40, in *Documents of Vatican II,* 397.

40. "Pastoral Constitution on the Church in the Modern World," (*Gaudium et Spes*), no. 43, in *Documents of Vatican II,* 943.

41. Ibid., nos. 48, 47, in *Documents of Vatican II,* 950, 949.

42. "Decree on the Apostolate of Lay People" (*Apostolicam Actuositatem*), no. 2, in *Documents of Vatican II,* 768.

43. John Paul II, *Letter of John Paul II to Women* (Washington, D.C.: United States Catholic Conference, 1995), no. 12.

44. Elizabeth May, comment in "Work of Human Hands: Fifteen People Talk about Faith on the Job," *U.S. Catholic* 57, no. 9 (September 1992): 7–8.

45. Kathy Petersen Cecala, "Meeting God in Others," *Commonweal* 116 (July 14, 1989): 400.

46. JG, interview with author, January 13, 2002.

47. For more on the Christian churches' discomfort with the subject of money and their subsequent difficulties with the middle class, see Robert Wuthnow, *The Crisis in the Churches: Spiritual Malaise, Fiscal Woe* (New York: Oxford University Press, 1997).

48. Cecala, "Meeting God in Others," 401.

49. Nancy M. Haegel, "Eureka Moments," *Commonweal* 119 (June 5, 1992): 15. Laura Wharton, another engineer, also described the moral and religious ambiguity of her job: "Are we supposed to be stewards of creation? Are we supposed to take it and use it? Or are we supposed to keep it as pristine as possible, as some environmentalists argue?" See "Work of Human Hands," 8.

50. Laura I., interview with author, tape recording, June 22, 2001, Woodburn, Oregon. All subsequent quotations by Laura I. come from this interview.

51. Joan M. Martin, *More Than Chains and Toil: A Christian Work Ethic of Enslaved Women* (Louisville: Westminster John Knox Press, 2000), 128.

52. Francis Schüssler Fiorenza, "Religious Beliefs and Praxis: Reflections on Catholic Theological Views of Work," in *Work and Religion,* ed. Gregory Baum, *Concilium* 131, no. (1/1980 (New York: Seabury Press, 1980), 98.

53. Note that theologians have described the "contrast experience" as a powerful force leading human beings to resist injustice. See, for example, Elizabeth A. Johnson, *She Who Is: The Mystery of God in Feminist Theological Discourse* (New York: Crossroad, 1992): "What transpires here is a negative contrast experience, giving rise through the violation of a good to a glimpse of its strong value in a new configuration. It is the kind of fruitful experience that transpires when persons bump up against the stubborn resistance of historical reality to what they sense to be true, good, and beautiful" (63).

54. Schüssler Fiorenza, "Religious Beliefs and Praxis," 98.

55. Robert Ellsberg, ed., *Dorothy Day: Selected Writings* (Maryknoll, N.Y.: Orbis Books, 1982), 241. Day continued: "When men are striking, they are following an impulse, often blind, often uninformed, but a good impulse — one could even say an inspiration of the Holy Spirit." Day also endorsed the idea that all have a vocation to be saints. She wrote in a 1942 letter: "In *The Catholic Worker* we will quote our Pope, our saints, our priests. We will go on printing the articles of Father Hugo, who reminds us today that we are all 'called to be saints,' that we are other Christs, reminding us of the priesthood of the laity." See Ellsberg, *Dorothy Day,* 262.

56. See "The Mill Girls," brochure published by the Lowell National Historical Park, Lowell, Massachusetts, *www.nps.gov/lowe/millgirls.htm*.

57. Friedan, *The Feminine Mystique*, 333.

58. John Paul II, *Laborem Exercens*, no. 26, p. 304.

59. Bruce Levine et al., *Who Built America?* (New York: Pantheon Books,
1989), 414.

60. George E. Ganss, S.J., ed., *Ignatius of Loyola: The Spiritual Exercises and
Selected Works* (New York: Paulist Press, 1991), 130.

61. Thomas Aquinas, *Summa Contra Gentiles,* chapter 19, in *Introduction to
St. Thomas Aquinas,* ed. Anton C. Pegis (New York: Random House, 1948), 418.

62. Frederick Buechner, *Wishful Thinking: A Theological ABC* (New York:
Harper & Row, 1973), 95.

63. Holzhauer, letter to the editor, *Commonweal* 79 (January 10, 1964): 430.

64. The Gospel of Luke relates that the angel Gabriel went to Mary in Nazareth and told her that she would bear Jesus, the Son of the Most High. Perplexed
and afraid, Mary was assured that with God nothing is impossible. Her "fiat"
was her faithful response: "Here I am, the servant of the Lord; let it be with me
according to your word" (Luke 1:38).

65. Mrs. James S. Arnold, letter to the editor, *Commonweal* 79 (January 10,
1964): 429.

66. Jean Holzhauer, letter to the editor, *Commonweal* 79 (January 10,
1964): 430.

67. I am indebted to M. Shawn Copeland's essay "Saying Yes and Saying No,"
in *Practicing Our Faith: A Way of Life for a Searching People,* ed. Dorothy C.
Bass (San Francisco: Jossey-Bass, 1997), 59–73.

68. JM, interview with author, tape recording, Newton, Massachusetts,
September 27, 2000.

69. Mary Catherine Bateson, *Composing a Life* (New York: Plume Book,
1990).

70. Kathleen Fischer, *Women at the Well: Feminist Perspectives on Spiritual
Direction* (New York: Paulist Press, 1988), 120.

71. John Paul II, *Laborem Exercens,* no. 23, p. 304.

Chapter 4: Sanctifying Time

1. U.S. Department of Labor, *The United Nations Decade for Women,
1976–1985: Employment in the United States* (Washington, D.C.: U.S. Department of Labor, Women's Bureau, 1985).

2. U.S. Bureau of Labor Statistics, *Employment Status of the Civilian Population by Sex and Age,* Table A-1, *http://stats.bls.gov/news.release/empsit.t01.htm*.

3. Phyllis Moen and Donna I. Dempster-McClain, "Employed Parents: Role
Strain, Work Time, and Preferences for Working Less," *Journal of Marriage and
the Family* 49 (August 1987): 588.

4. Ibid., 579, 580, 583.

5. Juliet Schor, *The Overworked American: The Unexpected Decline of Leisure* (New York: Basic Books, 1992), 8.

6. Ibid., 134.

7. "A Two-Job Family," *Together* (January 1965): 62.

8. Vicki L. Ruiz, *From Out of the Shadows: Mexican Women in Twentieth-Century America* (New York: Oxford University Press, 1998), 133.

9. Ruth Grant, interview by Georgia Maheras, tape recording, Roxbury, Massachusetts, August 14, 2000.

10. Barbara L. Baer and Glenna Matthews, "The Women of the Boycott," *The Nation* 218, no. 8 (February 23, 1974): 233.

11. Ibid., 234.

12. Dorothy C. Bass, *Receiving the Day: Christian Practices for Opening the Gift of Time* (San Francisco: Jossey-Bass, 2000), 11. On God as creator of time, see p. 4.

13. JM, interview with author, tape recording, Newton, Massachusetts, September 27, 2000.

14. James D. Whitehead, "An Asceticism of Time," *Review for Religious* 39 (1980): 9.

15. Diane E. Lewis, "Americans Putting in More Hours Than Most," *Boston Globe* (September 9, 2001): K2. Schor argues that Americans have been working more hours each year since the late 1940s, leaving a shrinking amount of leisure time (1–2). It should be noted, however, that social scientists disagree about whether Americans' work hours have increased, largely due to variances in how work hours are calculated.

16. The Qur'an states: "Guard strictly your (habit of) prayers, especially the Middle Prayer; and stand before Allah in a devout (frame of mind)" (Qur'an 2:238).

17. "The Constitution on the Sacred Liturgy" (*Sacrosanctum Concilium*), nos. 84, 88, in *Documents of Vatican II*, 24, 25.

18. Kathleen Norris, *The Quotidian Mysteries: Laundry, Liturgy, and "Women's Work"* (New York: Paulist Press, 1998), 82.

19. Kathleen Norris, poem entitled "Housecleaning," in *The Quotidian Mysteries*, 32.

20. "The Constitution on the Sacred Liturgy" (*Sacrosanctum Concilium*), no. 89, in *Documents of Vatican II*, 25–26. Revisions included suppressing the prime hour, inviting people to choose one out of the three midday times, and suggesting that the matins prayer (said by monks in the middle of the night) be prayed at a more convenient time.

21. Nancy M. Haegel, "Eureka Moments," *Commonweal* 119 (June 5, 1992): 15.

22. For a very basic example, see Dennis Linn, et al., *Sleeping with Bread: Holding What Gives You Life* (New York: Paulist Press, 1995).

23. Mary Parella, interview by Georgia Maheras, tape recording, Acton, Massachusetts, June 15, 2000.

24. Ibid.

25. However, few developmental psychologists have given specific attention to women and work. Daniel Levinson is one exception. His posthumously published book, *The Seasons of a Woman's Life* (New York: Alfred A. Knopf, 1996), compares homemakers, businesswomen, and women professors. More research needs to be done in this area.

26. See, for example, Joann Wolski Conn, "A Feminist View of Thérèse," in *Women's Spirituality: Resources for Christian Development,* ed. Joann Wolski Conn (New York: Paulist Press, 1996), 452–75. Conn follows Robert Kegan's developmental model. See too Conn, *Spirituality and Personal Maturity* (New York: Paulist Press, 1989).

27. James W. Fowler, *Becoming Adult, Becoming Christian: Adult Development and Christian Faith* (San Francisco: Harper & Row, 1984), 142.

28. Ibid., 95.

29. "Table 12. Estimated Life Expectancy at Birth in Years, by Race and Sex: Death-Registration States, 1900–28, and United States, 1929–97," *National Vital Statistics Report* 47, no. 28 (December 13, 1999): 32–33. It should be noted that black women consistently lagged behind white women in life expectancy in the twentieth century. In 1900, black women could expect only 33.5 years, compared with the 48.7 years white women enjoyed. In 1940, black women could expect to live for about 55 years but white women could expect about 66 years. In 1970, a seven-year gap existed between black and white women's life expectancies. By 1997, that gap had narrowed to five years, with black women living nearly 75 years and white women nearly 80. Also important is the fact that the gap between black women's life spans and black men's life spans increased noticeably in the twentieth century. In 1900, black women could expect only one year more life than could black men. By the end of the twentieth century, black women outlived black men by more years — eight — than white women outlive white men — six. Note too that the increase in divorce from the 1960s onward, spurred by the introduction of no-fault divorce, also meant that more women lived alone for some time in their lives, and they had to support themselves and dependents economically.

30. MK, interview with author, tape recording, Brighton, Massachusetts, April 7, 2000.

31. Harriet White, interview by Georgia Maheras, tape recording, Roxbury, Massachusetts, July 13, 2000.

32. Grant, interview, August 14, 2000.

33. Ibid.

34. Parella, interview, June 15, 2000.

35. *www.nccw.org/inquiries.htm.*

36. Annette Kane, interview by author, tape recording, Washington, D.C., June 22, 2000.

37. Arlie Hochschild, *The Second Shift* (New York: Avon Books, 1989), 8.

38. "Baker Interview," pp. 95, 111, in *Twentieth Century Trade Union Women: Vehicle for Social Change,* Oral History Collection, Schlesinger Library, Radcliffe College, Cambridge, Massachusetts.

39. The Book of Deuteronomy reads: "Observe the sabbath day and keep it holy, as the LORD your God commanded you.... Remember that you were a slave in the land of Egypt, and the LORD your God brought you out from there with a mighty hand and an outstretched hand; therefore the LORD your God commanded you to keep the sabbath day" (Deut 5:12–15).

40. Ignatius of Loyola, "The Spiritual Exercises," nos. 223 and 236, in *Ignatius of Loyola: Spiritual Exercises and Selected Works,* ed. George E. Ganss (New York: Paulist Press, 1991), 176–77.

41. Dorothy C. Bass, "Keeping Sabbath," in *Practicing Our Faith: A Way of Life for a Searching People,* ed. Dorothy C. Bass (San Francisco: Jossey-Bass, 1997), 79.

42. Max Weber, *The Protestant Ethic and the Spirit of Capitalism* (New York: Charles Scribner's Sons, 1958), 181–82.

43. Abraham Joshua Heschel, *The Sabbath* (New York: Farrar, Straus and Giroux, 1951), 28.

44. Ibid., 29.

45. The resistance that arose in the 1950s and 1960s to the "Blue Laws" in the United States revealed that Sabbath-keeping challenged an increasingly consumerist society. However, this resistance also raised important questions about the advisability of legislating Sabbath in a pluralistic society.

46. Evelyn Eaton Whitehead and James D. Whitehead, *Christian Life Patterns: The Psychological Challenges and Religious Invitations of Adult Life* (Garden City, N.Y.: Doubleday, 1979), 69–70.

47. Heschel, *The Sabbath,* 28.

48. Anne Morrow Lindbergh, *Gift from the Sea* (New York: Pantheon, 1955), 28.

49. Delia Halverson, "Home Management Leads to Future Careers," *Daughters of Sarah* 14, no. 2 (March–April 1988), 12.

50. Sandra H. Johnson, "I Wondered If I Would Pass the Test," *Commonweal* 116 (April 7, 1989): 208.

51. Kathy Petersen Cecala, "Meeting God in Others," *Commonweal* 116 (July 14, 1989): 401.

52. Sandra Schneiders, "Theology and Spirituality: Strangers, Rivals, or Partners?" *Horizons* 13, no. 2 (1986): 266.

53. Anne Carr, *Transforming Grace: Christian Tradition and Women's Experience* (San Francisco: Harper & Row, 1988), 203.

54. Bradley Holt, *Thirsty for God: A Brief History of Christian Spirituality* (Minneapolis: Augsburg Fortress, 1993), 3.

55. Philip Sheldrake, *Spirituality and History: Questions of Interpretation and Method* (Maryknoll, N.Y.: Orbis Books, 1995), 50.

56. Judi Neal, "Begin Again," *Spirit at Work* (February 1999).

57. "The International Alliance for Spirit at Work," undated pamphlet.

58. "What Do We Mean by 'Spirituality'?" *Guide to the Symposium,* 38. Third International Symposium on Spirituality and Business, Babson College, Wellesley, Massachusetts, March 24, 2000.

59. Deborah Smith Douglas, "Broken Pieces," *Commonweal* 118 (May 3, 1991): 292.

60. Ibid., 292–93.

61. Several authors have used this term. See, for example, the discussion in Mary Catherine Hilkert, *Naming Grace: Preaching and the Sacramental Imagination* (New York: Continuum, 1997). See too the influential book by David Tracy, *The Analogical Imagination: Christian Theology and the Culture of Pluralism* (New York: Crossroad, 1981).

62. Katherine Dale Makus, "Who Baked the Bread?" in *Daughters of Sarah* 14, no. 2 (March–April 1988): 15.

63. Dietrich Bonhoeffer, *Letters and Papers from Prison,* ed. Eberhard Bethge (New York: Macmillan, 1953), 215. Bonhoeffer writes here about a fragmentation that prevents the development of a full, balanced life. This is not a fragmentation caused by too many spheres of action, but rather too few. Bonhoeffer writes to his parents from prison in 1944: "Our generation cannot now lay claim to such a life as was possible in yours — a life that can find its full scope in professional and personal activities, and achieve balance and fulfillment....Even if the pressure of outward events may split our lives into fragments, like bombs falling on houses, we must do our best to keep in view how the whole was planned and thought out" (215).

64. Latin Missal, see also *Catechism of the Catholic Church* (Collegeville, Minn.: Liturgical Press, 1994), no. 1353, p. 341.

65. Pierre Teilhard de Chardin, "The Mass on the World," in Pierre Teilhard de Chardin, *Hymn of the Universe* (New York: Harper & Row, 1961), 19–20.

66. Ibid., 20.

67. "Liturgy of the Eucharist," Mass of the 1970 Missal.

Chapter 5: Models of Holiness for Women Workers

1. Elisabeth Schüssler Fiorenza, *Discipleship of Equals: A Critical Feminist Ekklesia-logy of Liberation* (New York: Crossroad, 1993), 40.

2. Bonnie J. Miller-McLemore, *Also a Mother: Work and Family as Theological Dilemma* (Nashville: Abingdon Press, 1994), 39.

3. "Baker Interview," p. 142, in *Twentieth Century Trade Union Women: Vehicle for Change Oral History Collection,* Schlesinger Library, Radcliffe College, Cambridge, Massachusetts.

4. "The Queenship of Mary," Resolutions of the Twenty-Seventh National Convention (1954), National Council of Catholic Women, Archives at Catholic University of America, Washington, D.C.

5. See the discussion in, for example, William M. Brinner, "Prophet and Saint: The Two Examplars of Islam"; Tu Wei-Ming, "The Confucian Sage: Exemplar of Personal Knowledge"; and John Stratton Hawley, "Morality beyond Morality in the Lives of Three Hindu Saints," all in *Saints and Virtues,* ed. John Stratton Hawley (Berkeley: University of California Press, 1987).

6. Laurie Beth Jones, *Jesus, CEO: Using Ancient Wisdom for Visionary Leadership* (New York: Hyperion, 1995), xiv–xv.

7. Ibid., xiii, xv.

8. Ibid., see 15–18, 21–24, 62–64, and 76–78.

9. Ibid., 166–68, 160–61.

10. Donald Weinstein and Rudolf Bell, *Saints and Society* (Chicago: University of Chicago Press, 1982), 161.

11. See Congregation of the Causes of Saints, *Index ac Status Causarum* (1999), also see *www.ca-catholics.net/saints/notes.htm.*

12. John A. Coleman, "Conclusion: After Sainthood?" in *Saints and Virtues,* 207. Coleman refers to Lawrence Cunningham's book *The Meaning of Saints* (San Francisco: Harper & Row, 1980).

13. Ann W. Astell, "Introduction," in *Lay Sanctity, Medieval and Modern: A Search for Models,* ed. Ann W. Astell (Notre Dame, Ind.: University of Notre Dame, 2000), 1–26.

14. André Vauchez, *The Laity in the Middle Ages* (Notre Dame, Ind.: University of Notre Dame Press, 1993), 72.

15. Elizabeth A. Johnson, *Friends of God and Prophets: A Feminist Theological Reading of the Communion of Saints* (New York: Continuum, 1999), 229.

16. "Prayer to Saint Joseph for the Spirit of Work," *www.catholic-forum.com/saints/pray0142.htm.*

17. John Paul II, *The Role of the Christian Family in the Modern World (Familiaris Consortio),* no. 16, pp. 29–30. For an earlier rendition of this teaching, note that the Council of Trent (1545–63) stated: "If anyone saith that the marriage state is to be placed above the state of virginity or celibacy, and that it is not better and more blessed to remain in virginity or in celibacy than to be in matrimony; let him be anathema." See "Doctrine on the Sacrament of Marriage," in *Dogmatic Canons and Decrees* (Rockford, Ill.: Tan Books and Publishers, 1977), 164.

18. Johnson, *Friends of God,* 28.

19. Christian Duquoc, "Editorial," in *Models of Holiness,* ed. Christian Duquoc and Casiano Floristán, *Concilium* 129 (New York: Seabury Press, 1979), x.

20. Marina Warner, *Alone of All Her Sex: The Myth and Cult of the Virgin Mary* (New York: Macmillan, 1976; Vintage Books, 1983), cited in Ann W. Astell, "Feminism, Deconstructing Hierarchies, and Marian Coronation," in *Divine Representations: Postmodernism and Spirituality,* ed. Ann W. Astell (New York: Paulist Press, 1994), 164–66.

21. Johnson, *Friends of God,* 28.

22. Ibid.

23. Ruth Grant, interview by Georgia Maheras, tape recording, Roxbury, Massachusetts, August 14, 2000.

24. Mary Gordon, "Coming to Terms with Mary," *Commonweal* 109 (January 15, 1982): 11.

25. AC, personal communication to author, August 8, 2001.

26. "A Challenge to the Girls in YCW," undated, 6–7, Young Christian Workers archives, University of Notre Dame (Box 105, "Impact" folder).

27. "The Queenship of Mary," Resolutions of the Twenty-Seventh National Convention (1954), National Council of Catholic Women, Archives at Catholic University of America, Washington, D.C.

28. Rev. Richard M. McKeon, S.J., "Mary of Nazareth: Management Consultant," *Our Lady's Digest* 20, no. 5 (January–February 1966). See especially 264–67.

29. Astell, "Feminism, Deconstructing Hierarchies, and Marian Coronation," 164.

30. Ibid., 168.

31. Mary Gordon, "Coming to Terms with Mary," *Commonweal* 109 (January 15, 1982): 11.

32. AC, personal communication to author, August 8, 2001.

33. Ibid.

34. Ibid.

35. Duquoc, "Editorial," xii.

36. Margaret Fortes, interview by author, tape recording, Roxbury, Massachusetts, June 13, 2000.

37. Pope Paul VI, *Evangelii Nuntiandi* ("On Evangelization in the Modern World"), no. 63 (Washington, D.C.: United States Catholic Conference, 1975), 46.

38. Miller-McLemore, *Also a Mother,* 38.

39. Mrs. James S. Arnold, letter to the editor, *Commonweal* 79 (January 10, 1964): 429.

40. Duquoc, "Editorial," x.

41. Sister Esperanza Jasso Beltran, interview by author, tape recording, June 23, 2001, Woodburn, Oregon.

42. Laura I., interview by author, tape recording, June 23, 2001, Woodburn, Oregon.

43. Virgilio Elizondo, "Our Lady of Guadalupe as a Cultural Symbol: 'The Power of the Powerless,'" in *Liturgy and Cultural Religious Traditions,* ed. Herman Schmidt and David Power, *Concilium* 102 (New York: Seabury Press, 1977), 32.

44. See, for example, *Francis de Sales, Jane de Chantal: Letters of Spiritual Direction,* ed. Wendy M. Wright and Joseph F. Power, trans. Péronne Marie Thibert (New York: Paulist Press, 1988).

45. Richard Strier, "Sanctifying the Aristocracy: 'Devout Humanism,'" in François de Sales, John Donne, and George Herbert," in *Journal of Religion* 69 (January 1989): 36–58.

46. See, for example, James T. Fisher, *The Catholic Counterculture in America, 1930–1962* (Chapel Hill: University of North Carolina Press, 1989), and Mel Piehl, *Breaking Bread: The Catholic Worker and the Origin of Catholic Radicalism in America* (Philadelphia: Temple University Press, 1982).

47. Jay Dolan, *The American Catholic Experience: A History from Colonial Times to the Present* (Notre Dame, Ind.: University of Notre Dame Press, 1992), 411.

48. *Catholic Worker* 3 (February 1936): 4, cited in Fisher, *The Catholic Counterculture in America,* 39.

49. She wrote this prayer at age seventy-six while in a Fresno, California, jail, having been arrested with other supporters of grape workers: "Dear Pope John — please, yourself a *campesino,* watch over the United Farm Workers. Raise up more and more leader-servants throughout the country to stand with Cesar Chavez in this nonviolent struggle with Mammon." See Robert Ellsberg, ed., *Dorothy Day: Selected Writings* (Maryknoll, N.Y.: Orbis Books, 1982), 257.

50. Ellsberg, *Dorothy Day,* 339.

51. Dorothy Day, *The Long Loneliness* (New York: Harper & Brothers: 1952), 286.

52. Ibid., 149.

53. Ellsberg, *Dorothy Day,* 183.

54. Day, *The Long Loneliness,* 135.

55. As June O'Connor wrote: "Day did not belabor any opposition or dichotomy between 'public' and 'private,' 'historical' and 'personal,' nor did she struggle to combine or integrate two aspects of life which were somehow preconceived or experienced as opposed or conflictual. As a communitarian radical by inclination and choice, Day operated out of a fundamental sense of connection between the public and the private." See June O'Connor, *The Moral Vision of Dorothy Day: A Feminist Perspective* (New York: Crossroad, 1991), 31.

56. Ibid.

57. AC, personal communication to author, August 8, 2001.

58. Mary Parella, interview by Georgia Maheras, tape recording, Acton, Massachusetts, June 15, 2000.

59. Eileen Farrell, interview by author, tape recording, Brighton, Massachusetts, June 2, 2000.

60. Grant, interview, August 14, 2000.

61. Johnson, *Friends of God,* 27, 29.

62. Parella, interview, June 15, 2000.

63. "Dogmatic Constitution on the Church" (*Lumen Gentium*), no. 50, in *Documents of Vatican II,* 411.

Chapter 6: Pastoral Ways Forward

1. Jim Sessions, Sue Thrasher, and Bill Troy, "To Be Prophetic: Black Ministers Speak Out on the Black Church," *Southern Exposure* 4, no. 3 (winter 1977): 42.

2. For a more in-depth treatment of *lectio divina,* see Guigo II, *The Ladder of Monks: A Letter on the Contemplative Life and Twelve Meditations* (Garden City, N.Y.: Image Books, 1978), and Michael Casey, *Sacred Reading: The Ancient Art of Lectio Divina* (Liguori, Mo.: Liguori, 1995).

3. See *Working: Making a Difference in God's World* (Chicago: Evangelical Lutheran Church in America, 1995).

4. See Kathleen Norris's essay *The Quotidian Mysteries: Laundry, Liturgy, and "Women's Work"* (New York: Paulist Press, 1998).

5. "Labor Sunday Prayers," in *The Book of Worship for Church and Home* (Nashville: Methodist Publishing House, 1965), 155–56.

6. Ruth Needleman, "The Feminization of Unions," *The Witness* (February 1989): 23.

7. Barbara L. Baer and Glenna Matthews, "The Women of the Boycott," *The Nation* 218, no. 8 (February 23, 1974): 234.

8. Annette Kane, interview by author, tape recording, Washington, D.C., June 22, 2000.

9. Mary Parella, interview by Georgia Maheras, tape recording, Acton, Massachusetts, June 15, 2000.

10. Jane DuBose, "Working Man: Virginia Chaplain Takes His Ministry to the Workplace," *Interpreter* (February–March 2000): 25.

11. "Qualifications to Serve as a Marketplace Ministries Inc. Chaplain," *www.marketplaceministries.com/feedback.htm.*

12. Data taken from the organization's Web site: *www.nibic.com.*

13. Michelle Conlin, "Religion in the Workplace: The Growing Presence of Spirituality in Corporate America," *Business Week* (November 1, 1999): 154.

14. Whitney Roberson, *Spirituality at Work: A Handbook for Conversation Convenors and Facilitators* (1999).

15. "Introduction to the Woodstock Business Conference." Undated Pamphlet.

16. Woodstock Business Conference, "Formation Book: Affirming the Relevance of Religious Faith to Business Practice" (1998), 5.

17. Ibid., 21.

18. "The Soul of the Executive: Supplementary Information" (2000–2002 program), 1.

19. For wage gap statistics from 1970 to 1999, broken down by gender and race, see the chart compiled by the National Committee on Pay Equity, *www.infoplease.com/ipa/A0882775.html*.

20. Lester C. Thurow, "Deterioration in Men's Pay Family Income Stagnates," *Boston Globe* (June 15, 1999): C4.

21. Diane E. Lewis, "Amid Boom, Widening Gender Wage Gap Seen," *Boston Globe* (January 27, 2002): Business, E1, E8.

22. See Sara S. McLanahan and Erin L. Kelly, "The Feminization of Poverty: Past and Future," working paper, MacArthur Research Networks.

23. See Antoinette Iadarola, "The American Catholic Bishops and Woman: From the Nineteenth Amendment to ERA," in *Women, Religion, and Social Change,* ed. Yvonne Yazbeck Haddad and Ellison Banks Findly (Albany: State University of New York Press, 1985), 457–76.

24. "All the Livelong Day," Reports to the 200th General Assembly of the Presbyterian Church USA (1988): 42.080, 42.083.

25. Ibid., 42.127, 42.141, 42.230, and 42.141.

26. "The Status of Women," *Book of Resolutions of the United Methodist Church* (Nashville: United Methodist Publishing House, 1996), 403.

27. "Pay Equity in the U.S.A.," *Book of Resolutions of the United Methodist Church* (Nashville: United Methodist Publishing House, 1996), 469.

28. "The Status of Women," *Book of Resolutions,* 403.

29. "Emphasis of Concern for Workers," *Book of Resolutions of the United Methodist Church* (Nashville: United Methodist Publishing House, 1996), 441.

30. "On Economic Justice for Women," Central Conference of American Rabbis, 1984, *www.ccarnet.org/cgi-bin/resodisp.pl?file=women&year=1984*.

31. "Women in the Jewish Workplace," Central Conference of American Rabbis, 1993, *www.ccarnet.org/cgi-bin/resodisp.pl?file=women&year=1993*.

32. National Conference of Catholic Bishops, *Economic Justice for All* (Washington, D.C.: United States Catholic Conference, 1986), nos. 207, 179, 147, and 208, pp. 102, 88, 74, 102.

33. Ibid., no. 337, p. 169.

34. See discussion on the USCC Web site, under the Department of Social Development and World Peace: *www.nccbuscc.orgdwp/national/childcare.htm*.

Selected Bibliography

Akst, Daniel. "When Business Gets Religion." *New York Times* (October 4, 1998): 5.

"All the Livelong Day: Women and Work." Joint Report of the Council on Women and the Church and the Committee on Women's Concerns. Reports to the 200th General Assembly of the Presbyterian Church USA 42.040–42.252a, 1988.

Ammerman, Nancy Tatom, and Wade Clark Roof, eds. *Work, Family, and Religion in Contemporary Society*. New York: Routledge, 1995.

Astell, Ann W., ed. *Divine Representations: Postmodernism and Spirituality*. New York: Paulist Press, 1994.

———. *Lay Sanctity, Medieval and Modern: A Search for Models*. Notre Dame, Ind.: University of Notre Dame Press, 2000.

Baer, Barbara L., and Glenna Matthews. "The Women of the Boycott." *The Nation* 218, no. 8 (February 23, 1974): 232–38.

"Baker Interview." In *Twentieth Century Trade Union Women: Vehicle for Social Change*. Oral History Collection, Schlesinger Library, Radcliffe College, 1978.

Bass, Dorothy C. *Receiving the Day: Christian Practices for Opening the Gift of Time*. San Francisco: Jossey-Bass, 2000.

Beane, Marjorie Noterman. *From Framework to Freedom: A History of the Sister Formation Conference*. Lanham, Md.: University Press of America, 1993.

Berger, Peter L. "Four Faces of Global Culture." *The National Interest* 49 (fall 1997): 23–29.

———. "Protestantism and the Quest for Certainty." *Christian Century* (August 26–September 2, 1998): 782–96.

Bonhoeffer, Dietrich. *Letters and Papers from Prison*, edited by Eberhard Bethge. New York: Macmillan, 1953.

Brown, Alden V. *The Grail Movement and American Catholicism, 1940–1975*. Notre Dame, Ind.: University of Notre Dame Press, 1989.

Browning, Don S., et al. *From Culture Wars to Common Ground: Religion and the American Family Debate*. Louisville: Westminster/John Knox Press, 1997.

Bruce, Steve, ed. *Religion and Modernization: Sociologists and Historians Debate the Secularization Thesis*. Oxford: Clarendon Press, 1992.

Buechner, Frederick. *Wishful Thinking: A Theological ABC.* New York: Harper & Row, 1973.

Burns, Jeffrey M. *Disturbing the Peace: A History of the Christian Family Movement, 1949–1974.* Notre Dame, Ind.: University of Notre Dame Press, 1999.

Camp, Richard L. "From Passive Subordination to Complementary Partnership: The Papal Conception of a Woman's Place in Church and Society Since 1978." *Catholic Historical Review* 76 (July 1990): 506–25.

Campbell, Debra. "The Heyday of Catholic Action and the Lay Apostolate, 1929–1959." In *Transforming Parish Ministry: The Changing Roles of Catholic Clergy, Laity, and Women Religious,* edited by Jay Dolan et al., 222–52. New York: Crossroad, 1990.

———. "*Both Sides Now:* Another look at the Grail in the Postwar Era." *U.S. Catholic Historian* 2, no. 4 (fall 1993): 13–27.

Carr, Anne. *Transforming Grace: Christian Tradition and Women's Experience.* San Francisco: Harper & Row, 1988.

Chamberlain, Mariam K., ed. *Women in Academe: Progress and Prospects.* New York: Russell Sage Foundation, 1988.

Conlin, Michelle. "Religion in the Workplace: The Growing Presence of Spirituality in Corporate America." *Business Week* (November 1, 1999): 150–58.

Conn, Joann Wolski, ed. *Women's Spirituality: Resources for Christian Development.* New York: Paulist Press, 1996.

Cooney, Rosemary Santana. "Changing Labor Force Participation of Mexican American Wives: A Comparison with Anglos and Blacks." *Social Science Quarterly* 56, no. 2 (September 1975): 252–61.

Copeland, M. Shawn. "Saying Yes and Saying No." In *Practicing Our Faith: A Way of Life for a Searching People,* edited by Dorothy C. Bass, 59–73. San Francisco: Jossey-Bass, 1997.

"Decree on the Apostolate of Lay People" (*Apostolicam Actuositatem*). In *Vatican Council II: Constitutions, Decrees, Declarations,* edited by Austin Flannery, O.P., 766–98. Northport, N.Y.: Costello Publishing Company, 1984.

Degler, Carl N. "Women." In *Encyclopedia of American Economic History: Studies of the Principal Movements and Ideas,* vol. 3, edited by Glenn Porter, 988–1000. New York: Charles Scribner's Sons, 1980.

Dillenberger, John, ed. *Martin Luther: Selections from His Writings.* Garden City, N.Y.: Anchor Books, 1961.

"Dogmatic Constitution on the Church" (*Lumen Gentium*). In *Vatican Council II: Constitutions, Decrees, Declarations,* edited by Austin Flannery, O.P., 350–427. Northport, N.Y.: Costello Publishing Company, 1984.

Dolan, Jay. *The American Catholic Experience: A History from Colonial Times to the Present.* Notre Dame, Ind.: University of Notre Dame Press, 1992.

Dorsey, David. "The New Spirit of Work." *Fast Company* (August 1998): 125–34.

Douglas, Deborah Smith. "Broken Pieces." *Commonweal* 118 (May 3, 1991): 292–93.

Duquoc, Christian, and Casiano Floristán, eds. *Models of Holiness.* New York: Seabury Press, 1979.

Elizondo, Virgilio. "Our Lady of Guadalupe as a Cultural Symbol: 'The Power of the Powerless.'" In *Liturgy and Cultural Religious Traditions,* edited by Herman Schmidt and David Power. *Concilium* 102. New York: Seabury Press, 1977.

Ellsberg, Robert, ed. *Dorothy Day: Selected Writings.* Maryknoll, N.Y.: Orbis Books, 1982.

"Emphasis of Concern for Workers." *Book of Resolutions of the United Methodist Church,* 440–42. Nashville: United Methodist Publishing House, 1996.

Finke, Roger. "An Unsecular America." In *Religion and Modernization: Sociologists and Historians Debate the Secularization Thesis,* edited by Steve Bruce, 145–69. Oxford: Clarendon Press, 1992.

Fischer, Kathleen. *Women at the Well: Feminist Perspectives on Spiritual Direction.* New York: Paulist Press, 1988.

Flannery, Austin P. *Documents of Vatican II.* Grand Rapids, Mich.: Eerdmans, 1975.

Foner, Philip S. *Women and the American Labor Movement: From the First Trade Unions to the Present.* New York: The Free Press, 1982.

Fowler, James W. *Becoming Adult, Becoming Christian: Adult Development and Christian Faith.* San Francisco: Harper & Row, 1984.

Francis de Sales. *Introduction to the Devout Life.* New York: Doubleday, 1966.

Francis de Sales and Jane de Chantal. *Letters of Spiritual Direction.* Edited by Wendy M. Wright and Joseph F. Power. Translated by Péronne Marie Thibert. New York: Paulist Press, 1988.

Friedan, Betty. *The Feminine Mystique.* New York: Dell Publishing, 1983.

Ganss, George E., ed. *Ignatius of Loyola: The Spiritual Exercises and Selected Works.* New York: Paulist Press, 1991.

Gilkes, Cheryl Townsend. "'Liberated to Work Like Dogs!': Labeling Black Women and Their Work," In *The Experience and Meaning of Work in Women's Lives,* edited by Hildreth Y. Grossman and Nia Lane Chester, 165–88. Hillsdale, N.J.: Lawrence Erlbaum Associates, 1990.

———. "The Storm and the Light: Church, Family, Work, and Social Crisis in the African-American Experience." In *Work, Family, and Religion in Contemporary Society,* edited by Nancy Tatom Ammerman and Wade Clark Roof, 177–98. New York: Routledge, 1995.

Gluck, Shema Berger. *Rosie the Riveter Revisited: Women, the War, and Social Change.* Boston: Twayne Publishers, 1987.

Gordon, Mary. "Coming to Terms with Mary." *Commonweal* 109 (January 15, 1982): 11.

Greeley, Andrew. *The Church and the Suburbs.* New York: Sheed & Ward, 1959.

Haddad, Yvonne Yazbeck, and Ellison Banks Findly, eds. *Women, Religion, and Social Change.* Albany: State University of New York Press, 1985.

Haughey, John F. *Converting 9 to 5: Bringing Spirituality to Your Daily Work.* New York: Crossroad, 1994.

Hertel, Bradley R. "Work, Family, and Faith: Recent Trends." In *Work, Family, and Religion in Contemporary Society,* edited by Nancy Tatom Ammerman and Wade Clark Roof, 81–121. New York: Routledge, 1995.

Heschel, Abraham Joshua. *The Sabbath.* New York: Farrar, Straus and Giroux, 1951.

Hochschild, Arlie. *The Second Shift.* New York: Avon Books, 1989.

Huber, Raphael, ed. *Our Bishops Speak: National Pastorals and Annual Statements of the Hierarchy of the United States, 1919–1951.* Milwaukee: Bruce, 1952.

Hunter, James Davison. *Culture Wars: The Struggle to Define America.* New York: Basic Books, 1991.

Irish Catholic Bishops' Conference, *Prosperity with a Purpose: Christian Faith and Values in a Time of Rapid Economic Growth.* Dublin: Veritas, 1999.

John XXIII. *Mater et Magistra.* In *The Papal Encyclicals 1958–1981,* edited by Claudia Carlin, 59–90. Raleigh, North Carolina: Purian Press, 1990.

———. *Pacem in Terris.* In *The Papal Encyclicals 1958–1981,* edited by Claudia Carlin, 107–29. Raleigh, North Carolina: Purian Press, 1990.

John Paul II. *On the Dignity and Vocation of Women on the Occasion of the Marian Year: Apostolic Letter Mulieris Dignitatem.* Boston: Daughters of St. Paul, 1988.

———. *On Human Work: Laborem Exercens.* Boston: St. Paul Editions, 1981.

———. *The Role of the Christian Family in the Modern World: Familiaris Consortio.* Boston: St. Paul Editions, 1982.

Johnson, Elizabeth A. *Friends of God and Prophets.* New York: Continuum, 1998.

———. *She Who Is: The Mystery of God in Feminist Theological Discourse.* New York: Crossroad, 1992.

Jones, Jacqueline. *Labor of Love, Labor of Sorrow: Black Women, Work, and the Family from Slavery to the Present.* New York: Basic Books, 1985.

Jones, Laurie Beth. *Jesus, CEO: Using Ancient Wisdom for Visionary Leadership.* New York: Hyperion, 1995.

Kelly, Rev. George A. *The Catholic Marriage Manual.* New York: Random House, 1958.

Kelly, Joseph, and Timothy Kelly. "Our Lady of Perpetual Help, Gender Roles, and the Decline of Devotional Catholicism." *Journal of Social History* 32, no. 1 (1998): 5–26.

Kennelly, Karen, C.S.J., ed. *American Catholic Women: A Historical Exploration.* New York: Macmillan, 1989.

Kessler-Harris, Alice. *Out to Work: A History of Wage-Earning Women in the United States.* New York: Oxford University Press, 1982.

Lehrer, Evelyn. "The Effects of Religion on the Labor Supply of Married Women." *Social Science Research* 24, no. 3 (September 1995): 281–301.

Leo XIII. *Rerum Novarum.* In *The Papal Encyclicals, 1878–1903,* edited by Claudia Carlin, 241–62. Wilmington, N.C.: McGrath Publishing Co, 1981.

Levine, Bruce, et al. *Who Built America?* New York: Pantheon Books, 1989.

Lindbergh, Anne Morrow. *Gift from the Sea.* New York: Pantheon, 1955.

Lindey, Susan Hill. *You Have Stept Out of Your Place: A History of Women and Religion in America.* Louisville: Westminster John Knox Press, 1996.

Luther, Martin. "The Estate of Marriage." In *Luther's Works,* vol. 45, edited by Walter I. Brandt, 39–40. Philadelphia: Muhlenberg Press, 1962.

———. "Secular Authority: To What Extent It Should Be Obeyed." In *Martin Luther: Selections from His Writings,* edited by John Dillenberger, 363–402. Garden City, N.Y.: Anchor Books, 1961.

Martin, David. *A General Theory of Secularization.* Oxford: Basil Blackwell, 1978.

———. *Tongues of Fire: The Explosion of Protestantism in Latin America.* Oxford: Blackwell, 1990.

Martin, Joan. *More Than Chains and Toil: A Christian Work Ethic of Enslaved Women.* Louisville: Westminster John Knox Press, 2000.

Massa, Mark S. *Catholics and American Culture: Fulton Sheen, Dorothy Day, and the Notre Dame Football Team.* New York: Crossroad, 1999.

McDannell, Colleen. "Catholic Domesticity, 1860–1960." In *American Catholic Women: A Historical Exploration,* edited by Karen Kennelly, C.S.J., 48–80. New York: Macmillan, 1989.

McGinn, Bernard. "The Letter and the Spirit: Spirituality as an Academic Discipline." *Christian Spirituality Bulletin* 1, no. 2 (fall 1993): 1–10.

McGreevy, John T. *Parish Boundaries: The Catholic Encounter with Race in the Twentieth-Century Urban North.* Chicago: University of Chicago Press, 1996.

McLeod, Hugh. *Religion and the People of Western Europe 1789–1970.* Oxford: Oxford University Press, 1981.

Miedzian, Myriam, and Alisa Malinovich. *Generations: A Century of Women Speak about Their Lives.* New York: Atlantic Monthly Press, 1997.

———. "Women Workers, Feminism, and the Labor Movement Since the 1960s." In *Women, Work, and Protest,* edited by Ruth Milkman, 300–22. Boston: Routledge & Kegan Paul, 1985.

Miller-McLemore, Bonnie J. *Also a Mother: Work and Family as Theological Dilemma.* Nashville: Abingdon Press, 1994.

Moen, Phyllis. "Continuities and Discontinuities in Women's Labor Force Activity." In *Life Course Dynamics: Trajectories and Transitions, 1968–1980,* edited by Glen H. Elder Jr., 113–56. Ithaca, N.Y.: Cornell University Press, 1985.

Morgan, Mary Y., and John Scanzoni. "Religious Orientations and Women's Expected Continuity in the Labor Force." *Journal of Marriage and the Family* 49 (May 1987): 367–79.

National Conference of Catholic Bishops, *Called and Gifted for the Third Millennium.* Washington, D.C.: United States Catholic Conference, 1995.

———. *Economic Justice for All.* Washington D.C.: United States Catholic Conference, 1986.

———. *From Words to Deeds: Continuing Reflections on the Role of Women in the Church.* Washington, D.C.: United States Catholic Conference, 1998.

Norris, Kathleen. *The Quotidian Mysteries: Laundry, Liturgy, and "Women's Work."* New York: Paulist Press, 1998.

Oates, Mary J. "Catholic Laywomen in the Labor Force, 1850–1950." In *American Catholic Women: A Historical Exploration,* edited by Karen Kennelly, C.S.J., 81–124. New York: Macmillan, 1989.

O'Connor, June. *The Moral Vision of Dorothy Day: A Feminist Perspective.* New York: Crossroad, 1991.

O'Farrell, Brigid, and Joyce L. Kornbluh. *Rocking the Boat: Union Women's Voices, 1915–1975.* New Brunswick, N.J.: Rutgers University Press, 1996.

Orsi, Robert. *Thank You, St. Jude: Women's Devotion to the Patron Saint of Hopeless Causes.* New Haven: Yale University Press, 1996.

"Pastoral Constitution on the Church in the Modern World" (*Gaudium et Spes*). In *Vatican Council II: Constitutions, Decrees, Declarations,* edited by Austin Flannery, O.P., 903–1001. Northport, N.Y.: Costello Publishing Company, 1996.

Paul VI. *On Evangelization in the Modern World* (*Evangelii Nuntiandi*). Washington, D.C.: United States Catholic Conference, 1976.

"Pay Equity in the U.S.A." *Book of Resolutions of the United Methodist Church,* 468–72. Nashville: United Methodist Publishing House, 1996.

Pius XI. *Casti Connubi.* In *The Papal Encyclicals 1903–1939,* edited by Claudia Carlen, 391–414. Raleigh, N.C.: Pierian Press, 1990.

———. *Quadragesimo Anno.* In *The Papal Encyclicals 1903–1939,* edited by Claudia Carlen, 415–43. Raleigh, N.C.: Pierian Press, 1990.

Rahner, Karl. *The Practice of Faith: A Handbook of Contemporary Spirituality.* New York: Crossroad, 1992.

Rainwater, Lee, and William L. Yancey. *The Moynihan Report and the Politics of Controversy: A Trans-Action Social Science and Public Policy Report.* Cambridge, Mass.: MIT Press, 1967.

Roberson, Whitney. *Spirituality at Work: A Handbook for Conversation Convenors and Facilitators.* 1999.

Ryan, Mary P. *Womanhood in America: From Colonial Times to the Present.* New York: Franklin Watts, 1983.

Ruiz, Vicki L. *Cannery Women, Cannery Lives: Mexican Women, Unionization, and the California Food Processing Industry, 1930–1950.* Albuquerque: University of New Mexico Press, 1987.

———. *From Out of the Shadows: Mexican Women in Twentieth-Century America.* New York: Oxford University Press, 1998.

Schneiders, Sandra. "Theology and Spirituality: Strangers, Rivals, or Partners?" *Horizons* 13, no. 2 (1986): 253–74.

Schor, Juliet. *The Overworked American: The Unexpected Decline of Leisure.* New York: Basic Books, 1992.

Schüssler Fiorenza, Elisabeth. *Discipleship of Equals: A Critical Feminist Ekklesialogy of Liberation.* New York: Crossroad, 1993.

Schüssler Fiorenza, Francis. "Religious Beliefs and Praxis: Reflections on Catholic Theological Views of Work." In *Work and Religion,* edited by Gregory Baum, 92–102. New York: Seabury Press, 1980.

Sheldrake, Philip. *Spirituality and History: Questions of Interpretation and Method.* New York: Crossroad, 1992.

Sölle, Dorothee, with Shirley A. Cloyes. *To Work and To Love: A Theology of Creation.* Philadelphia: Fortress Press, 1984.

Spock, Benjamin. "What's She Got That I Haven't?" *Ladies' Home Journal* (October 1952): 56–57, 194–95.

"Status of Women, The." *Book of Resolutions of the United Methodist Church,* 402–05. Nashville: United Methodist Publishing House, 1996.

Suenens, Cardinal Leon Joseph. *The Nun in the World.* London: Burns & Oates, 1962.

Teilhard de Chardin, Pierre. *Hymn of the Universe.* New York: Harper & Row, 1961.

Tentler, Leslie Woodcock. *Wage-Earning Women: Industrial Work and Family Life in the United States, 1900–1930.* New York: Oxford University Press, 1979.

Terborg-Penn, Rosalyn. "Survival Strategies among African-American Women Workers: A Continuing Process." In *Women, Work, and Protest,* edited by Ruth Milkman, 139–55. Boston: Routledge & Kegan Paul, 1985.

U.S. Bureau of Labor Statistics. *Figure 1: Employment Status of the Civilian Population by Sex and Age.* Table A-1. *http://stats.bls.gov/news.release/empsit.t01.htm.*

———. *Employment Status of the Civilian Population by Sex and Age.* Table A-1. *http://stats.bls.gov/news.release/empsit.t01.htm.*

———. "Monthly Labor Review Online." February 16, 1999. *http://stats.bls.gov/opub/ted/1999/feb/wk3/art01.htm.*

U.S. Department of Labor. "The Negro Family: The Case for National Action." In *The Moynihan Report and the Politics of Controversy: A Trans-Action*

Social Science and Public Policy Report, edited by Lee Rainwater and William L. Yancey, 47–124. Cambridge, Mass.: MIT Press, 1967.

Van Leeuwen, Mary Stewart. *Gender and Grace: Love, Work, and Parenting in a Changing World.* Downers Grove, Ill.: InterVarsity Press, 1990.

Vauchez, André. *The Laity in the Middle Ages.* Notre Dame, Ind.: University of Notre Dame Press, 1993.

Ware, Susan. *Modern American Woman: A Documentary History.* Chicago: Dorsey Press, 1989.

Weber, Max. *The Protestant Ethic and the Spirit of Capitalism.* New York: Charles Scribner's Sons, 1958.

Welter, Barbara. "The Cult of True Womanhood, 1820–1860." *American Quarterly* 18 (summer 1966): 151–74.

Westbrook, Robert B. "Fighting for the American Family: Private Interests and Political Obligations in World War II." In *The Power of Culture: Critical Essays in American History,* edited by Richard Wightman Fox and T. J. Jackson Lears, 195–222. Chicago: University of Chicago Press, 1993.

Whitehead, Evelyn Eaton, and James D. *Christian Life Patterns: The Psychological Challenges and Religious Invitations of Adult Life.* Garden City, N.Y.: Doubleday, 1979.

Whitehead, James D. "An Asceticism of Time." *Review for Religions* 39 (1980): 3–17.

Wilcox, Clyde, and Ted G. Jelen. "The Effects of Employment and Religion on Women's Feminist Attitudes." *International Journal for the Psychology of Religion* 1, no. 3 (1991): 161–71.

Wingren, Gustav. *Luther on Vocation.* Philadelphia: Muhlenberg Press, 1957.

Wolfteich, Claire. *American Catholics Through the Twentieth Century: Spirituality, Lay Experience, and Public Life.* New York: Crossroad, 2001.

Woodstock Business Conference. *Formation Book: Affirming the Relevance of Religious Faith to Business Practice.* 1998.

Working: Making a Difference in God's World. Chicago: Evangelical Lutheran Church in America, 1995.

Wuthnow, Robert. *The Crisis in the Churches: Spiritual Malaise, Fiscal Woe.* New York: Oxford University Press, 1997.

———. *The Restructuring of American Religion: Society and Faith since World War II.* Princeton, N.J.: Princeton University Press, 1988.

Zavella, Patricia. *Women's Work and Chicano Families: Cannery Workers of the Santa Clara Valley.* Ithaca, N.Y.: Cornell University Press, 1987.

Index